The Art of Cricket

Sir Donald Bradman

THE ART
OF CRICKET

HODDER AND STOUGHTON
LONDON SYDNEY AUCKLAND TORONTO

NOTE
*All references in this book (except where otherwise stated)
are to be taken as applying to right-hand bowlers
and right-hand batsmen. The necessary adjustments
must naturally be made where left-handers are concerned.*

British Library Cataloguing in Publication Data
Bradman, *Sir*, Donald 1908–
    The art of cricket.—New Ed.
    1. Cricket
    I. Title
    796.358

    ISBN 0-340-52910-5

Originally published 1958 by Hodder and Stoughton, London

Fifth impression, revised, 1969

Revised edition, reset, published 1984 by
Hodder and Stoughton (Australia) Pty Ltd

This redesigned, reset edition published 1990 by
Hodder and Stoughton, London

Published by Hodder and Stoughton,
a division of Hodder and Stoughton Ltd,
Mill Road, Dunton Green, Sevenoaks, Kent TN13 2YA.
Editorial Office: 47 Bedford Square, London WC1B 3DP.

Photoset by Rowland Phototypesetting Ltd,
Bury St Edmunds, Suffolk
Book Design by Trevor and Jacqui Vincent

Printed in Great Britain by
Butler and Tanner Ltd, Frome and London.

Foreword

In 1934 I wrote a short instructional book on 'How to play cricket'. At that time I was somewhere along the road of my international playing career which ended in 1948.

With certain interruptions brought about by illness, World War II, etc., I had by then been on the stage for twenty years, and in my judgment that was long enough. Whilst my mental powers may still have been adequate for the task, my muscles certainly were not.

The final act of renunciation of an active playing career is never easy, and the irrevocable decision to retire is so often delayed in the search for some final gesture of pleasurable farewell. Or perhaps it is postponed because the player himself realises he loves to be in the fray and knows that as a non-player he can never again occupy the stage as he did when a performer.

And no matter how much one may genuinely dislike publicity and the fierce spotlight on your everyday doings, there is inevitably a thrill in the achievement of some fleeting glory.

For my part I can truthfully say I had no regrets about retirement. I knew my best days were over and believed I could thereafter render my best service to cricket outside the playing arena.

For some time I found it a relief to be spared the strain and the anxious moments associated with playing international sport.

At first I resisted a natural impulse to put on paper my theories about how the game should be played but eventually thought perhaps it was my duty so to do – not briefly, as in 1934, but at some length, and drawing upon the many subsequent years of experience.

I have tried faithfully to portray the many aspects of cricket as they appear to me.

During my playing career I thought I had learnt a great deal about the game, but humbly admit I have learnt a great deal more since retiring. And I am still learning.

Indeed, I sometimes feel like the old English professional bowler who retired and took up umpiring. When asked what he had found out he replied, 'Just that a lot of the wickets I took LBW when I was bowling were not out.'

When Sir Jack Hobbs made his hundredth century, Prince Ranjitsinhji, the Jam Sahib of Nawanagar, marvellous batsman though he was, sent the Surrey idol a souvenir inscribed 'From a humble student of the game'. He knew one man could never hope to absorb all there was to know about cricket.

One of cricket's greatest administrators was the late Sir Frederick Toone. He was Secretary of the Leicester County Cricket Club (1897–1902), Secretary of the Yorkshire County Cricket Club (1903–1930) and managed three MCC touring teams to Australia. One of his most notable utterances included the phrase 'Cricket is a science – the study of a lifetime – in which you may exhaust yourself but never your subject.'

During one of my visits to England I had the great pleasure of meeting and dining at the Savage Club with that distinguished author, orator and cricket lover, A. A. Thomson.

He made a memorable contribution to cricket literature through such delightful books as *Cricket my Happiness, Cricket my Pleasure*, etc. – books full of human interest and understanding of the characters of his day (and earlier).

Mr Thomson did not profess to understand all the technical aspects of the game. But he loved it as few men could, and I think his description of England's gift to the world of sport seems to portray its meaning to the watching public better than anything I know.

He says, 'There are several ways of looking at

5

the game of cricket; first, and probably best, it is a game played for enjoyment. It is an art, rich in the expression of subtle technical skills, where grace and strength may be magically blended. It is a long picaresque romance, as rich in comedy and character as *Don Quixote* or *Pickwick Papers*. It is also a fascinating form of controversy. It is a spectacle, it is drama, it is good fun. It is undoubtedly an art; an art that can give pleasure to those who practise it and to those who watch.'

Since joining the ranks of watchers I have obtained a great deal of pleasure – albeit somewhat less exhilarating and intimate than in playing days – and find it has the virtue of being less demanding on one's concentration and responsibility.

From the Test cricketer may I request tolerance for the space taken in describing simple things (such as a yorker). He may feel my descriptions are superfluous, but this book is designed to help all classes of cricketers, including children.

Then to the youngster who may find the technical portions somewhat advanced may I just say – pass them by for the time being. Concentrate on the more elementary matters and come back to the Test match stage refinements when you are older.

May I express my grateful thanks to all those who assisted in its preparation. Particularly do I thank Dr Lyttleton for his contribution on the science of swing and Arthur Mailey for his humorous sketches. To Advertiser Newspapers Limited and News Limited of Adelaide and their staffs for their help in tracking down suitable illustrations. To my willing assistants in our efforts to produce suitable movie film strips. All have played a valuable part.

The illustrations are not perfect but nevertheless they have been carefully selected to portray what was required, and action, rather than photographic excellence, has dictated my choice.

If this book can be the means of kindling enthusiasm in the breasts of some youngsters or of assisting older players to overcome the game's complexities, I shall be rewarded for the time spent in compiling it.

Contents

Equipment

The Bat

I am a great believer in taking very special care to obtain the best equipment. It can play a tremendous part in building up confidence, and from personal experience I know how much easier it is to compile a score with the right equipment than with unsuitable components.

This applies more forcibly to the highest grade of cricket but is applicable right through one's career.

A legend has been built up around certain players, particularly Victor Trumper, who, so it is said, would take out any old bat and play equally well with it. If that is true I admire his skill all the more, because frankly I could not do so.

For the young lad it is important to get a bat of the right size. When Mother and Father show their generosity by producing a lovely bat for Christmas or birthday, the tendency is for them to get one which is too big. The cost of bats is high and they say the boy is growing.

One can fully sympathise with their point of view. Nevertheless, it is a grave handicap for any youngster to try to learn the rudiments of the game with a bat which is substantially wrong in size.

A full-size man's bat is some 90 cm (35 inches) long, and a good serviceable weight is about 1 kg or 2 lb. 4 oz.

What is known as a Short Handle bat has a blade of normal size but the handle is a little shorter.

The Harrow size is usually about the same as a Short Handle but slightly lighter.

Then we come to size six bats, which are about 84 cm (33 inches) long and sizes five and four, which are correspondingly smaller.

Purely as a guide it is generally taught that a boy 165 cm (5 feet 5 inches) tall is big enough to use a Harrow size or Short Handle bat.

However, many grown men use Short Handle bats.

I started my Test career with a full size but changed later on to a Short Handle which I used for the greater part of my career. My height is about 173 cm (5 feet 8 inches) and I found the full-length handle slightly cumbersome for my build and stroke play.

But many taller men have used Short Handle bats. There is no infallible rule. The player concerned must decide which type suits him best.

There is a great thrill about having one's very own bat. I can still remember the excitement of my first possession. A teammate gave me one of his old bats which had split at the bottom. My father sawed off the damaged end and partially reshaped the blade. Despite the need for repairs and the obvious defects, no other bat ever quite took the place of that one in my affections.

By a remarkable coincidence this bat was located in 1983 and presented to the New South Wales Cricket Association which is using it for display purposes.

I have checked that it is indeed authentic but who possessed it and where it had been for over fifty years after I stopped using it remain a mystery.

I believe it is a good thing to encourage pride of ownership at an early age. It is good for one's play and also one's morale.

In choosing a bat, I am satisfied one should be guided by the feel or balance and not by the appearance. The most beautiful-looking piece of timber in the world may turn out to be dead, whilst the unattractive blade will become a treasure. So no. 1 priority is the way the bat feels in your own hands.

It is wise to oil the blade before using it, especially in the drier climates. A light coating of raw linseed oil (or one of the proprietary lines of bat oil) once a day for a week should do, and for those who want to extract the maximum durability from the blade, some preliminary hitting with an old ball in a sock or rubbing the blade with the shin-bone of an ox, may help.

And is there a lovelier aroma to the true cricket enthusiast than that which ensues from raw linseed oil on a new piece of willow?

Don't oil the bat too frequently. A very light sandpapering, followed by a thin coat of oil after a day's play, is ample. And be careful not to oil over the splice.

The Sykes Don Bradman bat with which I made the then world record score in first-class cricket of 452 not out (Sydney–N.S.W. v Queensland, 1930.)
(Slazengers Ltd)

If possible, prevent the blade getting wet, as this will cause the willow to swell and lift. But should it occur, the prompt use of sandpaper followed by an oiling is recommended.

If the face of the bat becomes clogged by the oil, scrape it off at once and start again.

Minor bruises or cracks may be repaired with adhesive tape, which is light and moderately effective. Major damage may require dowelling and binding. This will often prove a good investment and will prolong the bat's life, especially where the implements are community property and endure hard usage.

The foregoing remarks relate of course to natural willow bats.

In today's world we find that many manufacturers produce bats with plastic coatings which protect the wood and also make oiling or any other form of preparation superfluous.

These protective coatings appear to have a special value for clubs whose members don't take much care of communal property and the treatment accorded bats may be described as 'rugged'.

Economics are becoming increasingly important at club level.

When I was very young it was not uncommon to find bats with various kinds of grips, even leather ones, on the handles. Today, I think the rubber grip is universally used, but one still finds occasionally the 'patterned' type of grip. One could almost liken it to the tread in a motor tyre.

I always found the plain rubber grips far superior to any other type.

A brief wash in cold water followed by a wipe down with a towel will leave the plain rubber grip slightly tacky and with that velvety feel which is so desirable.

And make sure the grip is securely glued down. Many a wicket has been lost because the rubber grip twisted on the bat handle as a stroke was being played.

Your bat is a trusty friend and well deserves all the care and attention you can bestow upon it, even to the extent of providing it with a waterproof cover and a coat of oil before putting it away for the winter.

Pads

There are many well-known makes of batting pads available on the market. Most of them offer splendid protection against injury and they vary mainly because of the differences which are required to satisfy a manufacturer's registered design.

The most essential quality is comfort. Bulky, clumsy pads which give more protection against injury but which retard speed of movement are not a good investment.

One of my international contemporaries always wore pads which I feel sure restricted his freedom. Naturally, it was his business, but I always thought he would have been a greater player if he had worn lighter and more flexible pads.

One gets hit on the leg mainly by accident, and there isn't much satisfaction in taking special pains to guard against a mishap which may never occur and losing your wicket in the process. Remember that speed of movement in getting the feet into position is one of the keys to successful batting.

There are special pads made for wicket-keepers which give added protection. Even for this position I don't entirely trust them. Again, speed of movement is vital and some of the greatest wicket-keepers I have seen wore the conventional batting pads.

After many years wearing conventional pads Rod Marsh turned to a new style in which the portion above the knee was eliminated, whilst another Sheffield Shield wicket-keeper dispensed with pads altogether and merely wore shin guards under his trousers.

In both cases I imagine the theory was to gain more mobility but from my observation I doubt whether the changes achieved anything worthwhile.

When the leg-guards are new they have straps which are much too long for the average player. These should be cut off to suit the individual so that only about 2 cm of the strap protrudes through the buckle.

This cannot be done, of course, in a club where the pads are community property, but in

DONT LEAVE YOUR LEGGING STRAPS DANGLING

AM

that case the overhanging strap should be tucked in underneath so that there is no chance of the ball flicking it.

A top-grade cricketer should discard his pads and get new ones if the portion above the knee becomes floppy. This is a common fault with club pads which are neglected. They become limp, and lose their shape. Apart from the untidy appearance, there is the danger of being given out caught behind when the ball hits this loose portion.

It happened to me once. I was in the eighties and thought I was comfortably placed for a century when the bowler brought one back sharply from the off. It got through inside my bat and just touched the top of the pad which had flopped away from the leg. On appeal I was given out.

The umpire could scarcely be blamed, for there was the sharp click, similar to the sound of ball touching bat, and my bat and pad were so close together the decision must have been extremely difficult.

They were old pads which I had used overlong and I paid the penalty. Naturally they soon were changed.

This question of wearing comfortable, snug-fitting pads is important. It is just another of those little refinements which no top-grade player can afford to neglect.

Batting Gloves

Instinctively, a young boy is inclined to dislike wearing batting gloves. They feel clumsy and prevent his skin making contact with the bat handle as he would desire.

But it is essential that he should get over this feeling quickly, for no batsman can afford the risk of batting without gloves. Moreover, they tremendously increase one's confidence, especially when the ball is inclined to fly.

And don't think a glove on the bottom hand is enough. Both hands must be protected.

There are various types of gloves. The most common are gauntlet types in which the hand fits right into the glove and there is no contact whatever between the skin and the bat handle. These are mainly used by players who perspire freely, because the material helps absorb the moisture.

Left-hand open-palm glove which gives the maximum feel of the bat handle. I liked to use this type, but it is not favoured by batsmen who perspire freely.

Gauntlet-type glove with cotton palm and tubular back. Probably the most widely used.

Right-hand open-palm glove with kid finger stalls and tubular back. A most comfortable glove.

Occasionally, I have seen a batsman take his gloves off and place them on the grass, palm upwards, when coming off for lunch or tea so that they would dry out during the interval.

I personally preferred the type of glove made with open palms because I did not perspire much and always felt I had better control of the bat when my bare hand was in contact with the rubber handle. It seemed to provide more delicacy of touch.

The difference in the two types of gloves is clearly shown by the illustrations. It is purely a matter of personal choice.

That great English batsman Walter Hammond sometimes wore the open-palmed glove with a thin pair of ordinary white cotton gloves underneath. They could be changed when wet, and if a hole wore in the finger he did not have to scrap his whole batting glove but merely bought a new cotton inner. A good idea for those preferring this type.

Some of the open-palm gloves are held in place by a strip of elastic which winds criss-cross round the wrist and is attached to the thumb. This elastic is frequently too long. If it is, have a tuck put in the back to adjust it.

Regarding the protective covering on the back, I always preferred the tubular leather filled with rubber. A common protection is the porcupine rubber, but I never felt it took the blow as well as the more solid tubular types which could be of strip rubber, leather filled

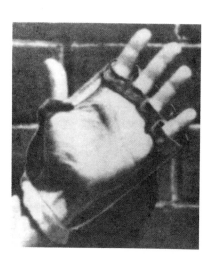
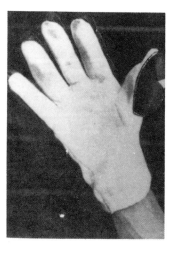
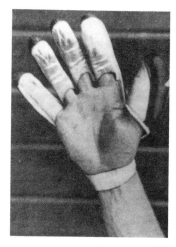

with padding, or leather filled with granulated rubber.

The last-named were my choice both for protection and comfort.

Protector

No batsman should run the risk of playing without one of these confidence producers.

They are made of aluminium or plastic and will stand a very hard blow without damage.

Some types are worn attached to a strap around the waist, but this is clumsy and outmoded. The best method is to wear an elastic belt or jock strap with a pouch into which the protector snugly fits. It can be slipped in at the last moment before one goes in to bat or taken out in a second at intervals and it cannot get out of place.

Never bat without one. If you do, I'll defy you not to flinch when a fastish ball rises a shade and comes back sharply from the off. The protector gives confidence as well as protection.

Thigh Pads and Arm Guards

In the higher realms of cricket it is common for batsmen, especially the openers, to wear a thigh pad. It consists of an oblong piece of sponge rubber (fitted into a material bag) which is worn to protect the outer portion of the front leg between the top of the pad and the hip. It is very useful against a fastish bowler who is getting a bit of lift bowling inswingers.

Without a thigh pad there is a tendency to get the body right inside the line of flight and so run the risk of being caught behind from a very fine glance.

With the pad, a batsman may be willing to stay more on the line so that the very fine glance hits the leg and falls safely to the ground.

The pad is not very thick, usually about 1 cm. It is light and held in place by thin tapes tied around the waist at the top and round the leg at the bottom.

I had the bottom tape removed and replaced it with elastic, sewn on to the pad both sides. With this method the pad is put on by slipping it over the foot and up the leg but it doesn't shift or stray around the leg in running.

The thigh pad is not essential and, in fact, I only wore one if facing certain types of bowlers such as the left-handed Bill Voce, whose pacey in-dippers could give you a nasty rap on the thigh. The less bulk one has to wear the better.

In more recent years the predominance of fast bowling has meant that the thigh pad has become virtually standard equipment.

During the 1932/33 season we Australians even resorted to large, kidney-shaped rubber chest protectors, which covered the ribs and heart on the left side, but I hope this piece of my equipment may be referred to purely as an heirloom.

Some players who were prone to injury to the forearm had specially made arm guards moulded to suit themselves, the material being foam rubber, fibreglass or some such. Frankly I think such guards are a handicap to one's movements and rather than turn towards protection, the players concerned would have been better advised to change the techniques which had rendered them liable to be hit on the arm.

Helmets

In my playing days the risk of getting hit in the face or on the head was regarded as an inevitable accidental hazard associated with the sport.

I cannot recall any serious discussion about wearing protective headgear until the 1932/33 bodyline season when the risk of injury became greater due to the tactics employed. But manufacturers did not mass produce helmets in those days as they do now.

In the early 1930s that mercurial and lovable England and Middlesex batsman Patsy Hendren had a type of helmet made and caused a bit of a sensation by wearing it in a match at Lord's.

It was particularly interesting because Hendren was one of the best hookers in the game. But he was short of stature and getting old and probably reasoned that it would help him to continue essaying his aggressive hook and pull shots if he could eliminate the risk of a serious head injury.

The young player with keen eyesight and quick reflexes should have no difficulty in avoiding the short-pitched bouncer. It becomes a different matter if the player decides to stand his ground and make shots, or if a ball flies off a reasonable length.

Throughout my career I was never once hit on the head by a 'bouncer', nor did I ever feel in any real danger of being hit. Nevertheless I am sure that if I were playing today in an era when, regrettably, the use of short-pitched bowling seems in general terms to be more prevalent than fifty years ago (bodyline excepted), I would wear a helmet batting against fast bowlers.

It surely must give added confidence and protection.

The use of helmets for close-to-the-wicket fieldsmen is now common practice. This has caused men such as the 'short-leg' fieldsmen to stand closer to the striker than was normally the case 'pre-helmets', and to that extent has given fieldsmen an advantage.

The legislators obviously recognised this by decreeing that a striker may not be caught if a ball has touched a protective helmet worn by a fieldsman, but it still gives the fieldsman an intimidatory advantage.

I don't think the wearing of helmets by fieldsmen can be banned (my understanding is that such a ban would raise legal complications) but frankly I would prefer the laws to force 'front-of-the-wicket' fieldsmen to stand further away from the striker. An arbitrary distance of, say, 3 metres (10 feet) appeals to me much more than the present law which allows a man to stand where he pleases as long as no part of his person extends over the pitch.

Boots and Socks

I have yet to see anything better than the good old-fashioned buckskin boots with properly studded leather soles. Manufacturers have improved the styling, and the modern boot can be made as light and comfortable as a walking shoe.

Several tips may be worth remembering.

If the boots have no inner sole for cushioning, it will probably pay you to invest in a pair of rubber insoles or at least sponge rubbers for the heels.

During a long and tiring hot day, when the ground is hard, the heel can get very sore, especially in the case of fast bowlers, who should see to it that their boots have no toe-caps, or if they do, that the stiffening is removed. Many a bowler has saved himself a bruised and bleeding big toe, with the resultant loss of his toe nail, by this simple precaution.

Some players like to wear long soccer laces which they pass under the instep, thereby tying the boot on with great firmness. A good idea.

As for the spikes, there are several varieties. Perhaps the most common are those which are screwed in with a thumb screw or which are just nailed in. An ordinary screw threaded into the

This shows the position and the number of sprigs in one of my boots. They proved quite satisfactory.

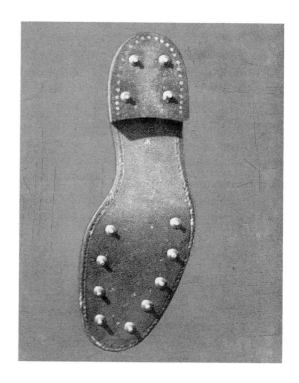

sole and with the head cut off by a hacksaw is quite effective.

I preferred running spikes built into the soles. They were cut down in length and had the great advantage that they could not come out. However, they had the disadvantage that when they wore down, the whole sole had to be removed to replace them.

There is an alternative idea which has advantages. Boots can be procured which have a threaded metal slot built into the sole, and into which the sprig is screwed. If it wears (or comes out) another one can be wound into the cavity and by this method the sprigs can always be kept perfect without resoling the boot.

Fast bowlers should have metal toe protectors fitted, otherwise they will quickly go through the leather.

Up to this point I have been writing about the type of footwear which stood the test of time for roughly the first hundred years of international cricket, and I include in the word 'type', rubber-soled boots which were occasionally used some fifty years ago.

But time marches on – with footwear as with other things.

The modern craving for lightness, speed and comfort – not to mention the entrepreneurial flair of manufacturers – has now brought a flood of shoes with rubber soles of various designs which are very popular with the players. They are beautiful to wear and undoubtedly ease the pain of a long day in the field. Nevertheless observers of modern cricket can't help noticing how many fieldsmen now slip and find themselves prone on the earth. The big beneficiaries are the dry cleaners.

Apart from fielding, the rubber sole, even when studded, does not enable the batsmen to prop and turn with the speed and surety of the sprigged leather.

It is an individual choice. But anyone who aspires to the highest level should not expect sympathy if, through wearing ineffective footwear which places comfort before utility, he slips and is run out.

And it is wise to keep the boots in a small linen bag. In this way dirt off the soles will not soil your clothes.

A good thick pair of socks is desirable and if procurable, hand-knitted. Some players even wear two pairs to get the extra cushioning, but this is a matter for individual choice.

Ian Johnson often played without socks at all, but how he could do so I never understood.

It is also wise to use foot powder or talc powder for comfort.

One old trainer with a wonderful reputation for his ability to handle injuries, advised me to use a small amount of sulphur inside the socks. He claimed it helped prevent cramp. Another trainer suggested mustard. Whether either has any effect I can't say, but cramp is not uncommon on a hot day and I frequently used the sulphur as a precaution.

Once again, the primary requisite is comfort.

Trousers and Sweaters

It is wise to have a spare pair of trousers for batting, preferably with a fraction more room than normal around the seat and the thighs. One is constantly bending when at the crease and if a thigh pad is worn it will show up clearly should the trousers fit too snugly. You need plenty of room around the buttocks.

Apart from the normal type, it is useful to have a sleeveless sweater. It provides the warmth for the body without the bulkiness and discomfort of covering the arms, and can be especially useful to a fast bowler who wishes to take added precautions against catching a chill between overs.

Cap

Unless the weather is dull, I think it advisable to wear a cap. I have seen more than one player affected by the sun in hot climates, and I have also seen many catches missed by capless players who would certainly have had a better chance of seeing the ball with a cap on.

Some players prefer to remain capless on the hottest day, but that is rather foolish and courting trouble.

Long after my playing days were over I was considerably troubled by skin cancers on the face, needing, in some cases, surgery.

My medico was emphatic that the cause had been so many days in the sun in my youth. It was noticeable that the area worst affected was the left side of my face at eye level, the area which would be facing the bowler when batting.

As I was normally a cap wearer, the risk for one remaining capless must be increased.

It is the sort of experience a boy of twenty would not be contemplating but as one who has been through the mill I cannot too strongly advise wearing a cap or washing hat to guard against the sun, and cream or other protection for the skin.

General

I know it is rather hackneyed to say one should always look like a cricketer even if you aren't one, but the adage will always hold good.

The sum of greatness is made up of small things. The player who is interested enough and takes care of minute details is the one who is likely to triumph at a critical moment.

If I were asked to go and watch a bowler who allegedly had great potential and I found a man who had his sleeves hanging loose, dirty boots and a cap protruding from his hip pocket, I could scarcely take away a good impression. These things would indicate a careless approach and lack of concentration.

Cut off sleeves never look as dressy as long sleeves rolled up. White trousers or shirt somehow do not seem as appropriate as creams.

Your dress is important. The player who takes pride in his appearance and deportment sets a fine example and is all the better for it.

Attention to detail denotes enthusiasm, without which there can be no good or really enjoyable cricket.

ROLL
UP
YOUR
SLEEVES

A.M

Tossing for Innings

I have heard so many arguments over so many years about this topic that I feel it warrants a brief discussion.

The laws provide that the team winning the toss shall have the choice of batting first.

Straightaway the winner is presented with a problem.

It may be so simple that he automatically says 'We'll bat'. The laws cover all classes of cricket, including hard-wicket games, and on concrete one need have no fears of a deterioration in the quality of the pitch as the match proceeds.

But don't for one moment imagine that winning the toss always confers an advantage on the winner.

In England in the 1948 Tests I won the toss once only. That was at Lord's in the second Test. The pitch was grassy and green and to be honest I didn't know whether it was wise to bat or not. I would have preferred the opposing captain to face the problem.

Where the argument gets really heated is when one team wins several tosses in succession in a Test series and obviously gains a winning advantage from so doing. Straightaway there are people who advocate a change in the laws.

The commonest suggestion is that the team losing the toss in the first match shall have the option of batting first in the second and fourth Tests so that the score of tosses will then be even and a further toss shall be made in the fifth and final Test.

That may sound fine in theory. But it may happen that the team winning the toss in the first Test loses the match. Would it then be fair that this team must contemplate beforehand that it has already lost the toss for the second Test, thereby possibly giving its opponents the right to bat first on a lovely pitch?

Rules have to be made in advance. They can't be produced out of a hat as you go along.

One of the great moments of every Test is when the captains walk out to toss. Think of the discussion beforehand by Press, public and players. They are all curious. So much may hinge on the unpredictable. It would be a crime to take away this intriguing element.

And who would have missed that great moment at Leeds when an English captain threw his coin to the crowd in apparent disgust when he lost, hoping, so we are led to believe, that he would thereby influence the other captain in his decision.

But over and above all these things is one paramount consideration. When nobody knows in advance which side will have the right to bat first no charges can ever be substantiated about preparing a pitch to suit one side or the other.

I still remember Melbourne 1932/33 when there were irresponsible charges that the pitch had been prepared to tame England's four fast bowlers. If that were so, why did Douglas Jardine, hailed for his masterly judgment and knowledge by the same people, elect to play his four fast bowlers after seeing the pitch and forming his judgment thereof?

The same sort of cries went forth when at Manchester in 1956 the wicket crumbled very early to favour England's spinners. I heard the charge seriously made that the groundsman had been instructed to prepare such a pitch.

What an absurdity. If there was to be a pitch which would play well for a day and a half and then suddenly crack up, surely the team winning the toss, if it could play at all, would gain an overwhelming advantage.

Why gamble everything on the toss when you have a team with at least a fifty-fifty chance on any pitch?

There is also the question of team selection. If one side were two up with two matches to go and the right to bat first in the penultimate match, what a temptation for the batting team's selectors to pack the side with batsmen so that an unbeatable score could be made to ensure a draw.

The way would be paved for undesirable practices.

So I cast my vote without any hesitation in favour of a continuation of the present system of tossing for innings. At times it may appear to cause unfairness but I have no doubt any alteration would bring far greater dissatis-faction.

My comments apply with equal force to one-day games where the decision of the captain winning the toss can so easily affect the whole tactical approach.

From the painting 'Tossing for Innings'
by R. James.
(Sport & General Press Agency Ltd)

The Art of Batting

General Qualifications

Before attempting to describe in detail the various strokes, I think some general comments are advisable.

Batsmanship is an art which consists in some measure of relatively indefinable things – such as timing and judgment.

When I see an artist like Denis Compton play a cover drive with that sweet sound which denotes perfect timing, and I see the ball travel with great speed after an effortless shot, I know what timing means and I know I am watching a great batsman.

The dictionary definition of timing as applied to sport says – 'the control of the speed of an action in order that it may reach its maximum at the proper moment'.

Some people are born with this natural aptitude – this ball sense – this physical coordination; others can never achieve it.

The greatest of players can improve by means of concentration and practice but the natural athlete must start with a great advantage.

One hallmark of good batting is that the player appears to have plenty of time in which to play his shots.

Bill (W. A.) Brown was an outstanding case of one who, from the pavilion, never seemed to be in a hurry for any stroke.

It was said of me, too. In fact, at one time the story was strongly circulated that my ability to make runs was because of exceptional eyesight which enabled me to see the ball earlier than others and react more speedily.

The professor of physics at the Adelaide University, hearing of this, requested that I submit myself to tests to check up on the theory.

I willingly did so. The result was that he discovered my reaction was minutely slower than that of the average university student.

So that theory was exploded and again I find myself in difficulties trying to explain how some people appear to have more time than others, and yet it seems undeniably true to the onlooker.

One cause may be the relative moments at which different batsmen start to move their feet and lift their bats.

In theory one could make out a case for standing still and not moving the bat until you see the ball in the air and know where it is pitching.

In practice this doesn't happen, and I am all in favour of the batsman starting to lift his bat and making a preliminary movement with his feet before the ball is actually delivered.

It saves a precious fraction of a second and appears to serve the same purpose as the preliminary waggle before starting your swing at golf. It is not part of the swing but it gets you started.

Let me emphasise that this is not an endorsement of the attitude of some batsmen who actually stand with their bat in the air, some 15 to 30 centimetres above the ground, as the bowler is running up. Not only does it look ungainly, it hinders rather than helps a player start co-ordinating the movements of his bat and feet.

I firmly believe the bat should rest on the ground (subject perhaps to a couple of waggles or taps as the bowler is running up) but the final lifting of the bat should not occur until just before the bowler actually delivers the ball.

Footwork and balance and their coordination will always remain the cornerstones of batting.

The 'bat in the air' technique was probably devised by a tall player or one with an exaggerated back lift in the hope that it would save precious time. It is negative and defensive and I'm sure it inhibits versatility and mobility in attack and therefore should not be embraced by anyone aspiring to the highest grade.

I have heard it said that Tony Greig, being very tall, was vulnerable to a yorker on the leg stump and adopted this technique to combat the weakness. I can't vouch for the accuracy of that statement. But true or false I am an opponent of the method.

My movements at the crease prior to the bowler delivering the ball depended to some extent on the type of bowler who was operating. I was never conscious of a precise and pre-determined movement, but slow-motion pictures of me batting, both in matches and in demonstration films, prove conclusively that I always began lifting the bat just prior to the ball being delivered. At the instant of delivery, the bottom of my bat was usually almost level with the bails and against fast bowlers, my rear foot was already in the process of shifting back and across.

I feel sure that films would disclose a foot and bat movement before delivery by all leading batsmen, though not necessarily similar to mine.

Success with the bat does not, according to

Here we see Peter May playing forward defensively. Notice how the left hand, wrist and forearm control the movement. No power is required.

history, depend on any particular type of physique. The Test match records are shared by men of all shapes and sizes, from the rotund Warwick Armstrong to the diminutive Lindsay Hassett, the tall and graceful Frank Woolley and the gloriously athletic Walter Hammond.

Then who shall define temperament? The dictionary gives the word a meaning though from a cricket sense I find it unsatisfactory.

More important still, nobody can tell you how to acquire a good temperament if it is lacking in your basic nature.

Some players are marvellous at the nets but cannot reproduce their form in matches. Others are poor net players but succeed because they possess the so-called 'big-match temperament'.

A tremendous premium must be placed on this peculiar characteristic, which is probably more essential for a batsman in cricket than any form of sport I can think of.

The golfer may fluff his drive, the tennis player miss his smash and so on, there is still time to recover, but one mistake by a batsman and there is no second chance.

Hand in hand with temperament must go concentration, which can and must be cultivated by anyone who wishes to rise to international standard. It is one of the essentials.

Moreover, the concentration needs to be harnessed for long periods. Many batsmen can survive a short period, say half an hour, and score double figures, but they are unable to keep going. Test cricket demands the utmost concentration for hours on end.

The two most important pieces of advice I pass on to young batsmen are to (a) concentrate and (b) watch the ball.

They could well be the last words before anyone goes in to bat.

Watching the ball means that the batsman must first carefully observe the bowler's hand as he is in the act of delivering the ball. The movement of hand and arm gives the first clue as to the bowler's intentions – whether he is trying to impart off spin, leg spin or something else. Once the ball leaves the hand, the ball must be the sole object of your attention.

Undoubtedly some people have keener eyesight than others. The wizard Ranjitsinhji was supposed to see the ball very clearly. Indeed, there is a story that a certain prominent batsman on being questioned as to his own ability to see the ball said, 'Yes, I had good eyesight – I could see the seams, but Ranji could see the stitches.'

In his early years a batsman should be able to see the ball turning in the air as it comes down the pitch towards him when the bowler is a slow spinner.

This is necessary against a class googly bowler like Arthur Mailey. Even if he disguises his googly you still have the added insurance of watching the spin of the ball to make sure which way it will turn on pitching. Try to glue the eyes on the ball until the very moment it hits the bat. This cannot always be achieved in practice but try.

Blessed is the boy who finds himself possessed of these attributes as a natural gift.

But like the boy prodigy who at, say, five years of age, finds himself able to play the piano, practice and more practice is needed to perfect his talent.

The fellow who sees the ball leave the bowler's hand, sees it land and then plays 'at the pitch', is always in trouble when the ball moves in the air or after hitting the ground.

I would counsel every boy who is interested in batting to play with a ball at every opportunity. Whether it be a golf ball, tennis ball, baseball or any other kind doesn't matter. It will help train the eye and co-ordinate brain, eye and muscle.

When it comes to detailed execution of the art, batting at the nets is the first method of improving one's efficiency. So many things can be tried out there.

You can experiment with your grip, your stance, stroke execution, etc., until satisfied you have the right method.

Throughout his career a batsman, even though he may have achieved fame, must continue assiduously at net practice.

That notable left-handed opening batsman Warren Bardsley once made a century in a Test match and, so we are told, went straight out to the practice nets because he was dissatisfied with his form.

How different from another Test match example I saw. A player who was to bat that day, and upon whom a heavy responsibility lay, was observed in civilian clothes on the balcony outside the players' dressing-room five minutes before play was due to commence. He was in full view of the public and the opposing team. He failed miserably – a just reward.

Confidence in one's own ability is admirable in moderation but it does not absolve anyone from the need for practice.

The early formative years of a boy's career can have a tremendous bearing on his technique.

I learnt my cricket on hard wickets and undoubtedly this was responsible for the development of certain shots in preference to others. But it does not in any sense alter the cardinal virtues, such as 'watching the ball', which are common under all conditions.

Take advantage of your natural assets, improve them and adapt them to changing circumstances.

It is a good idea to try to obtain net practice against the type of bowler who worries you most, or against whom you expect to play in forthcoming matches.

An outstanding example of this need was the 1956 tour of England by Australia. To the most casual observer it was obvious the Australians were having more trouble with off-spinner Laker than any other type. It was a clear case where net practice against off-spinners was a very special need.

Whilst it is true that some players are born, or achieve greatness without coaching, and equally true that some players are overcoached, I still believe in the desirability of sound coaching.

The trouble is that coaches vary just the same as players. They should always build upon and improve existing talent, and seldom is it wise completely to alter anybody's style.

One's physical movements are decided by muscular and bodily structure. It would be useless trying to coach the dynamic Learie Constantine to emulate the slow, easy rhythm and grace of Frank Woolley. But it would be correct for a coach to make sure each man played his drives with the bat reasonably close to the front leg.

The value of coaching is to pick out departures from fundamental soundness and build on nature, not to try to mould every player into precisely the same type.

The coach who insists on every batsman having complete control with his top hand is wrong, because it does not suit everyone. I'm sure Denis Compton's genius would never have blossomed if he had been compelled, as a youth, to allow his top hand to become the master.

Conversely Sir Leonard Hutton was a marvellous example of top-hand control. It suited him.

Denis Compton making a full-blooded pull shot to the square-leg boundary. In this case the right hand has supplied the power and the direction, whilst the left hand has acted as a balancing agent.
(Advertiser Newspapers Ltd)

The coach must have sufficient intelligence not to be dogmatic but to discern what method is best for his pupil.

For any player the top hand is of supreme importance when playing a forward defensive shot. But when it comes to a full-blooded pull, the story is very different. There cannot be sufficient power without the bottom hand, nor adequate control without the other. Co-ordination is the thing.

I think it much more important that coaches should devote their time to things where there should be basic soundness irrespective of grip, stroke production, etc. – for instance, footwork, which I think is one of the keys to great batsmanship. Good footwork is a characteristic common to all great batsmen, irrespective of physique or other peculiarities.

Get into the correct position for your shots and it is marvellous how much easier they become.

Footwork should, generally speaking, be constantly taking the batsman towards the off.

Young batsmen have a natural tendency to draw away from a ball directed at the body. This impulse must be overcome. Don't let that rear

foot retreat to the leg side. Almost invariably one should move towards the off, whether it is forward with your left foot or back with your right.

By going back with your right foot I mean back and towards the stumps – not back towards the umpire.

I am a great believer in back play providing the player will look upon it as an offensive as well as a defensive medium.

History shows that the outstanding batsmen were mostly strong off the back foot. They could drive, of course, but their initial protective movement was back rather than forward.

Ranji expressed himself very much in favour of back play, and went on to say, 'No forward stroke is absolutely safe unless the ball is smothered.' By that I assume he meant it had to be played as a genuine half-volley.

No batsman can fail to get into difficulties if he persists in driving well away from his body, in driving against a turning leg-break and so on.

To some extent footwork is based on judgment, and straightaway we revert to the need for practice to acquire judgment. You see how inextricably all these things are interwoven.

Eventually a batsman should reach the stage where his judgment of whether to play forward or back becomes instinctive rather than deliberate.

The sight of the ball seems to trigger off a corresponding reaction so that movement becomes almost a habit.

Despite the essential feet and body movements, I don't like to see a player allowing his head to bob about. Keep the head and eyes as still as you can, even though the arms and the body are moving.

I am a firm believer in attacking batsmanship. It is a batsman's duty to take the initiative and play shots.

His training in the cultivation of a sound defence should not mean that he becomes defence-minded.

All bowlers deteriorate under a well-planned, intelligent attack and much of the enjoyment of batting comes from the battle of wits and the thwarting of a bowler's plans.

Any batsman who has achieved international status should be able to visualise the position of every fieldsman just as though he were looking at them on a radar screen. He should be able to shut his eyes and know precisely the location of fine-leg, third-man and so on.

In no other way can he concentrate on the ball and still give free rein to the art of placing the ball to the maximum advantage.

It is so simple to pull a short ball to square-leg. But if there is a man on the fence square, how much more satisfaction can be gained by deliberately pulling it finer to try and pick up four.

Cricket is like chess – the move and counter-move. I would often deliberately play a ball to a certain position just to try and keep a fieldsman there. Why? Because I didn't want him shifted to a position which would have saved four instead of one.

There are dozens of shots played in any long innings which can scarcely be described as drives, pulls, cuts, or by any authentic name. They may range from a deflection down the gully with a perpendicular bat to a pat towards cover for a single or a push towards mid-on.

I have, in the following pages, only described those strokes which are clearly and easily definable.

Batting is a fascinating art and worth all the study you can give it.

The Grip

Having dealt with certain generalities, I now turn to the important details of the actual playing side of cricket.

The first requisite of any batsman is to get his grip right, and I recently saw an interesting method of attaining it.

A splendid coach was asked by a lad what the correct grip was. The coach told the boy to lay his bat face down on the ground with the handle pointing towards him and then stoop down and pick it up with two hands as though proposing to use it.

The boy did and was immediately told that this was the proper grip.

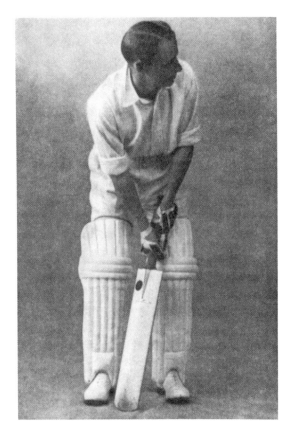

Try it and see what result you get.

For my part I refuse to be dogmatic about one's grip, because I believe various holds can be satisfactory. So much depends on the batsman's methods.

My normal grip is clearly depicted in this book, showing both the front view and the side view.

Notice that the inverted V formed by the thumb and first finger of the right hand is straight in line with the insertion of the handle down the back of the blade. The bottom hand will be 3 to 5 cm from the shoulder of the blade.

For the position of my left hand, look at the illustration. This is what might be termed, in golfing parlance, a slightly shut face. I think it helps to keep the ball on the ground, especially when playing on-side strokes.

However, I unhesitatingly admit that the left wrist could be more towards the front than mine and be perfectly correct. W. G. Grace and Sir Jack Hobbs both favoured this latter method. The photograph of Sir Jack opposite illustrates my point splendidly.

Denis Compton was rather half-way between what I might term the 'Hobbs grip' and mine. He is shown here, without batting gloves.

The Hobbs grip is very common amongst Englishmen, whereas one would seldom find a player with his left wrist more behind the blade than mine.

The two hands should be very close to one another – in fact just about touching with the batting gloves on.

I refuse to condemn an unorthodox grip just because it is different. The use of wrists and

Above, left. Side-on view of my grip showing the position of the right hand relative to the blade.
(Sport & General Press Agency Ltd)

Left. As the bowler sees the batsman my own grip is outlined. About 3 cm of the bat handle is visible below the right hand and perhaps 2 cm above the left hand. Gloves are touching.
(Sport & General Press Agency Ltd)

Although I did not see Victor Trumper bat, the fact that he held the bat very high is clearly shown by the photograph on page 26.

There is much to be said in favour of keeping the two hands in the happy medium position for maximum power and control.

The left-hand position must remain firm irrespective of the attempted stroke, but the right hand may be allowed to move down the blade for greater control in defensive strokes.

As evidence of the difference of the left-hand position of great players in playing defensively, I cannot do better than refer you to the photographs of May and Compton.

Denis Compton (below) with a normal but extremely firm right hand and a left which is roughly half-way between that used by Sir Jack Hobbs and Peter May (page 27). (P.A. Reuter Photos Ltd)

Sir Jack Hobbs (above) had a natural, easy, relatively high grip with normal right-hand position but left wrist facing towards the bowler. A model of orthodoxy.

arms and the method of stroke production cannot be stereotyped.

One fine Sheffield Shield cricketer had his right hand so far down the handle that his index finger actually went along the back of the blade. As you might expect, he had good defensive control and played strokes behind the wicket splendidly but his driving was incompetent.

Then I remember a Test match batsman whose two hands were very high up on the handle. This position gave rise to a high back lift and a flourish. He was a good driver but was always prone to snick the ball into slips. I distrust that position against a lifting or swinging ball.

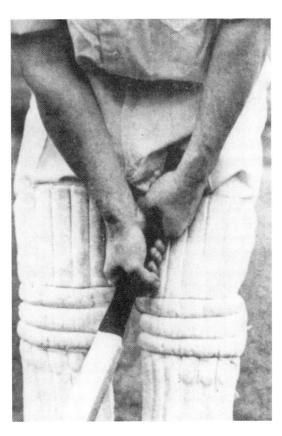

Peter May's method suited me, but Denis Compton's wonderful record dares us to question the efficiency of his.

As further evidence that leading players very often follow the habit of dropping the right hand down the blade when playing defensively, look at the photograph (opposite) of the Grand Old Man, W. G. Grace.

Sometimes I dropped the hand down when square cutting or in pulling the ball, but the movement must be so natural that the player is scarcely conscious of it, for one has little time to think where his hands are when moving into a shot.

Whatever you do be comfortable and natural and make control your guiding star.

Victor Trumper (above) jumping out to drive. A glorious body and shoulder position but hands very high up the handle. (Mrs G. W. Beldam)

Peter May (opposite, top left) plays forward defensively and gets the left wrist behind the handle. (P.A. Reuter Photos Ltd)

Denis Compton (opposite, left) plays forward defensively and keeps the left wrist well in front of the bat handle. (P.A. Reuter Photos Ltd)

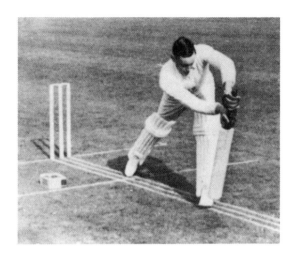

The Grand Old Man himself – W. G. Grace – let his bottom hand go right down to the blade in his back movement to give him better control over his defensive stroke.

The Stance

Once again I refuse to lay down any hard and fast unalterable rules, because Test players have been successful with quite different stances. However, there are certain principles which can be enunciated.

The main purpose of this initial position when awaiting delivery of the ball is to be in such a comfortably relaxed and well-balanced position that you are able to go forward or back, attack or defend, with equal speed. (See over.)

Weight evenly balanced, feet apart, right toe about 8 cm behind the crease, bat on the crease line.

As the bowler sees the batsman. Bottom of the bat between middle and leg stumps, left shoulder.

Below. I have adopted for demonstration purposes the orthodox stance of bat behind the toe, left wrist well forward but otherwise my normal position remains unchanged.

Notice how the bat takes on a straighter appearance from the bowler's end. Also the legs and body are drawn more towards the off side.

The knees should be slightly relaxed. It is a mistake to crouch right over or to stand completely erect.

My stance is shown by the photographs.

Notice that the feet are about 15 cm apart and that the weight is equally distributed.

Quite a large number of players stand with their feet together. I don't like it because I am certain it militates against balance and speed of movement and, in fact, necessitates a preliminary change of foot position to obtain proper balance before one can move into a stroke.

The rear foot should be at least a couple of centimetres behind the batting crease. This is to allow for a slight drag when playing forward. Remember the foot must be behind the crease to avoid a stumping. On the line is out.

The front foot should be parallel to the batting crease and some 8 cm in front of it. Should the front toe be turned slightly towards cover that would not be wrong.

Looking down the pitch from the bowler's end, the batsman's toes should be just about in line with the leg stump.

I allowed my bat to rest on the ground between my feet simply because it was a comfortable and natural position.

It is regarded as more orthodox to teach a pupil to rest his bat just behind the right toe as illustrated by the two photographs at the bottom of page 28.

This position encourages a straighter back lift, is perhaps sounder for defensive play, but I feel has greater limitations in versatile stroke making.

It will be seen from the photographs that the batting gloves rest lightly against the left pad. There is a possibility that the batting glove may get caught in the top of the pad. For this reason I always lifted my wrists and patted the pitch at least once in taking up my stance to ensure the hands were completely free.

As mentioned earlier this might be likened to what is termed a preliminary 'waggle' in golf.

Cricket, too, possesses its 'waggles' or mannerisms.

There are many photographs of Sir Jack Hobbs, waiting for the ball to be delivered, with his front heel on the ground but his toe in the air. I remember seeing him do this repeatedly in the days when I played against him.

But before the ball was delivered he would pat the ground with his bat and return to an evenly balanced position.

The wrong position at the crease, showing the toe on the line. The batsman could be stumped when his toe was on the line, as he would not be within his crease.

The correct position at the crease, with the toe well behind the line.

*A wonderful study (above) of how to keep
your toe behind the line when playing
forward and missing. The batsman is Bill
Edrich playing against South Australia in
1946.
(Advertiser Newspapers Ltd)*

*W. G. Grace, even late in his career, when
the athleticism of youth had passed, was
obviously comfortable and relaxed in his
stance.
(British Film Institute)*

W. G. Grace had a similar mannerism. In fact Sir Jack may have copied him. I sense in it a means of reducing tension – which is a good thing.

Dear old Phil Mead touched his cap to the square-leg umpire, then patted the ground four times and took four tiny shuffling steps to his position before every ball. It was just part of his method of becoming relaxed and comfortable.

The left shoulder should be pointing down the pitch or very nearly so, with the head turned so that both eyes are clearly focused on the bowler.

One often hears about the two-eyed stance. This is a misnomer. What people really mean is a stance where the shoulders are turned so that the chest is facing the bowler. A chesty stance is wrong because it prevents the batsman getting into the correct driving position. But obviously nobody would be silly enough to try to watch the bowler with one eye only.

I think it extremely important to keep the head as still as possible during the bowler's run up and even during one's movement into a shot.

That may sound absurd, for obviously the head must move if the body does. But I mean to convey the impression that there should be no bobbing or weaving about and that any jerky movement which might cause a batsman to take his eye off the flight of the ball is dangerous.

Perhaps I should exclude the case where one has to duck quickly to avoid a bumper, but I'll deal with that later.

Concentrate the eyes on the ball and it is surprising how natural the body movement becomes.

Once again comfort and relaxation are the key words.

Taking Guard or Block

Every batsman, upon arriving at the crease, must take block.

There are three common positions: middle stump, leg stump, and two legs (meaning halfway between the middle stump and the leg stump).

I did once hear a batsman ask for middle and

Taking guard or block.

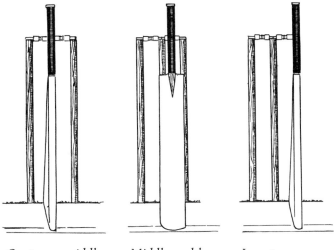

Centre or middle.   *Middle and leg or two-legs.*   *Leg stump or one-leg.*

leg inclined to leg, but I thought he was stretching things a bit too far.

The sole purpose of taking guard is to enable the batsman to judge the direction of the ball relative to his wicket.

The striker will, upon getting the required position, mark it on the ground back from the popping crease.

Spectators sometimes wonder why batsmen may ask for guard several times during an innings. The answer is that a mark on the ground may become obliterated or damaged.

Occasionally the two batsmen at the wickets take a different block or one may be a left-hander. Obviously the one is inclined to make rather a mess of the other fellow's mark, especially if he is the nervous type who is constantly patting the ground whilst awaiting delivery of the ball. The sprigs can also tear across one's mark when making certain foot movements.

I do not think it is normally of great importance which guard is taken, though from my own experience I found middle and leg to be the most serviceable.

It means your legs are stationed originally some 5 cm more towards the leg side than they would be if you took middle stump.

In this way it is easier to be sure that a ball travelling towards your pads is outside the leg stump, and precise judgment of the direction of a ball is a 'must' in developing the batting art.

When an off-break bowler is operating to a strong leg field, many batsmen take guard on the leg stump or even, in extreme cases, just outside. By so doing they endeavour to counter his wiles. They feel it gives them greater freedom to hit at any ball directed at their pads, and a better chance of steering away from the clutching hands of leg slips any ball directed at the stumps. There is much to be said for the theory.

On the other hand a batsman whose great weakness is that he fails to cover the ball outside the off stump, especially against a fast or medium-pace attack, would be wise to consider taking middle stump for his guard. It would take him those extra few centimetres towards the line of flight before the ball is delivered.

So take your choice. You will have to stand or fall by your judgment.

My back lift was usually in the direction of second slip, as depicted here. This still was taken from the movie strip of the straight drive.

The Back Lift

Reams of matter have been written about the necessity of taking one's bat back perfectly straight. Some coaching books even advocate taking the bat back towards the stumps.

Well now, this is the sort of illustration which proves the need for intelligent coaching as distinct from strict rule of thumb.

Don't let me be misunderstood. I am all in favour of a straight bat at the right time and place, but technique must be the servant not the master.

Too many players fail because their thoughts are concentrated on where their left elbow is or where something else is, instead of on hitting the ball.

I was never conscious of my back lift and I did not take any particular notice where the bat went until I saw movie shots of me in action. Then it was clear my initial bat movement almost invariably was towards the slips.

This was accentuated by my grip and stance and perhaps it should have been straighter, but to me, anyway, the important thing was where the bat went on the down swing. My movie strips in this book illustrate the position very clearly.

For defensive shots the bat should naturally be as straight as possible, but for a pull shot, for instance, a perfectly straight back lift would make it far harder to execute the stroke.

I believe in a sensible back lift and agree that it should not be that of the muscular man who strikes the gong in the J. Arthur Rank films, but there must be some degree of latitude and it must not become an obsession clogging up stroke production.

By going to extremes the player who uses the crease area and takes the bat back absolutely straight would find himself out hit wicket.

So long as the batsman is in the correct position at the top of the back lift, I don't think he can go far wrong.

If we could take moving pictures of all leading batsmen in action, particularly when they were not conscious that a camera was focused on them, I think we would find the majority of

them take the blade back rather more towards first or second slip. That initial movement probably allows a flexibility which the strictly orthodox does not.

Even that arch disciple of a straight bat, Trevor Bailey, offends the text book as much as I do in making some strokes. The strip photographs in this book illustrating various shots clearly show the back lift is not always straight. His bat, like mine, is sometimes taken back towards the slip fieldsmen, but of course it comes down straight.

And even W. G. Grace, with his famous 'left-wrist in front of the handle' grip, lifted his bat up towards slips, as you will see from the precious photograph (left). I say precious because the movie film from which this photograph was reproduced was taken around the year 1900 and is believed to be the only film ever made of W.G.

Again I emphasise that one must not be a slave to technique and one should not have to be conscious of such movements. They should be natural and involuntary.

Whether the bat is taken back straight towards the stumps or towards first slip, be careful it is not too high. Remember that the higher the back lift the longer it will take to bring the bat down. There is always a happy medium, but the back lift should be no higher than is necessary for a proper balance between control in defence and power in attack.

Some coaches teach players to take the bat back with the left hand. Again I fear the mental result. A defensive complex starts to build up.

I was never conscious that either hand was playing any special part in the initial movement. It was just a natural process.

In the picture at the top of this page the father of cricket, whose grip was ideal for a straight-bat style, is seen taking his bat back — not over the stumps, but towards the slips. But notice, in the bottom picture, that when he brought it down the blade was absolutely perpendicular — left elbow well up.
(British Film Institute)

When I stop to analyse it I'm inclined to think my right hand predominated sometimes – in the pull shot for instance – and the left hand sometimes – especially in defence. But the whole purpose of the movement is to enable one to hit the ball as accurately as possible and I am more inclined to teach boys what to do than how to do it – so long as there is no fundamental or glaring error.

Better to hit the ball with an apparently unorthodox style than to miss it with a correct one.

I have spent some time dealing with these preliminaries but things must be kept in the right perspective.

Everything in batting leads up to stroke play which may be divided into (a) defensive shots and (b) attacking shots.

Again each may be classified into two sections, (a) strokes played with the weight predominantly on the front foot, (b) strokes played with the weight predominantly on the back foot.

I shall deal with these individually.

Footwork

How often have we heard the saying 'Jones is a great batsman – his footwork is superb'. What is meant by this term footwork?

It is not a question which can be answered simply, even though instinctively a cricketer knows what is meant.

I imagine most people would say good footwork implies correct footwork. Perhaps it does. But what is the use of a man going back on to his stumps in the approved fashion if he moves so slowly that he is late in completing his shot and is trapped LBW? This surely means one requires speed as well.

But too much speed may bring disaster. If one jumps out to drive, gets there too soon and lofts a catch, that could be fatal.

Conversely I have seen a player jump out to drive only to find himself too short, yet by speedy footwork regain his crease in time to prevent a stumping. Therefore, speed can at times overcome faulty judgment.

These reflections cause me to say that basically, to be good, footwork should be correct, it should be of the required speed and it must be co-ordinated with perfect judgment. Certainly it should never be too slow.

As I mentioned earlier, one of the outstanding characteristics of great players is the apparent ease with which they play their shots. They always seem to be in the right position with plenty of time to spare.

I am reminded of a man's commentary on Walter Lindrum's billiards. He said, 'Lindrum never appears to play a difficult shot'. The reason, of course, was that he controlled the balls so that they came to rest in a relatively easy position for the next shot.

So it is with footwork in batting. The right position is half the battle in playing any stroke.

I cannot remember having seen a truly great player whose footwork was clumsy or slow. There may have been some who were nearly great – men who relied upon forward play and whose scores were mainly compiled by driving – but I am thinking in terms of batsmen who were able to command every shot in the book and were at home to all classes of bowling.

I doubt if one could truthfully say there is any single key to batsmanship, but footwork is certainly one of the keys to unlock the innermost secrets. It is to batting what a foundation is to a house. Without it, there can be no structure.

Back Defence

When playing back defensively I believe the back lift should be as straight as conveniently possible, and that in its downward path the bat should pass just outside the right pad as it comes forward to meet the ball.

In this shot I always used more right hand, both in the back lift and the downward movement, than in the forward defence. There is an important reason.

Suppose you are playing back to an off-break pitched several centimetres outside the off stump, and the ball, after pitching, turns across on to the middle and leg stumps. It would no longer be any use playing dead straight towards the pitch of the ball. It would be necessary to

The opening movements of a back defensive shot.

follow the direction of the ball, and to do this some power or impetus must come from the right hand which can't therefore be entirely relaxed. That change of direction to follow the ball cannot satisfactorily be controlled by the left hand.

Also it is possible to move into position for a back defensive stroke but later convert it into an attacking shot if you see fit to do so.

The back defensive shot.

foot is automatically brought across so that the stumps are completely protected.

In case you think the position of the left leg is unimportant, just have a glance at the photograph (left) of Freddie Brown being bowled. The ball has obviously come back from the off side and, without a protective left leg, has got through. Incidentally, Freddie's expression is lovely. What do you think he is saying?

Advantage should be taken of the area between the batting crease and the stumps, a distance of 122 cm (4 feet). Obviously one cannot go back the full distance, but even 60 cm (2 feet) extra in which to sight the ball, helps.

Ron Archer playing back to Tyson. The rear foot has been taken back but not across, and the head is not over the line of flight. As a result the stumps are left wide open and the batsman finds himself in a position whereby a catch to the wicket-keeper is the most likely result.
(The News, Adelaide)

Freddie Brown (above) plays back to Lindwall but pays the penalty of neglecting to cover the stump with his left leg, thereby enabling the ball to get through between the pads.
(The Herald, Melbourne)

But when purely on the defensive there should be little or no follow-through. At least the left hand must be powerful enough to restrict any tendency to follow through too soon, whereby off a rising ball there might be a catch to a close-in fieldsman.

Coinciding with the initial movement of taking the bat back, the right foot must be moved back and across in front of the stumps. The left

Peter May playing back defensively. Clearly the right foot has been taken back well outside the off stump and the bat has been brought down with a slightly turning motion so that the blade is closing on the ball at contact and directing it towards mid-on. In that way he has guarded against giving a catch to slips.
(The Sydney Sun)

Far too many cricketers play back too directly. In other words they go back but not across, making the shot harder in every way. An illustration of how this can occur is shown in the photograph of Archer opposite on page 36.

When in form I liked to feel in playing back defensively that I was hitting the ball either towards the bowler or mid-on rather than towards cover. It gave me a feeling of security that I was, if anything, coming from outside the line of flight and therefore guarding against a possible slip catch from the ball which went away to the off. It is so much easier to follow the ball which goes towards the leg side. The photograph of Peter May, above, demonstrates what I mean very clearly.

Some coaches advocate that the toes shall remain parallel with the popping crease – others that they should point partially towards the bowler. I favour the latter with the front one falling into place alongside.

Back defensive play is vital. Master it at all costs if you have ambitions.

W. G. Grace is reputed to have said, 'I don't like defensive strokes – you only get three off 'em.'

I admire his aggressive tone, but one can't attack every ball.

To be correct the full weight should be taken on the right foot, leaving the movement of the left as more of a balancing medium.

The right hand slides down to the bottom of the handle to give added control though, as I said earlier, the grip should be firm.

Study the movie strips and the co-ordinated movement is easily followed.

Keep the head well over the line of flight and down. Lifting the head is fatal and generally results in cocking the ball up or hitting it on the edge.

It is not a bad idea to practise back and forward defence in front of a mirror to see precisely where your feet are placed and to follow the movement of your bat. So often the player thinks his bat is in the right place but to the onlooker it is wrong.

Archie Jackson and Alan Fairfax were renowned for practising in front of a mirror. I have seen them do it for an hour at a time. Whilst there are limitations in other directions, I certainly favour the idea for practising back and forward defensive shots, because your eyes remain looking straight ahead.

Forward Defence

This type of defensive stroke should be used when the ball is pitched farther up than a good length and is on, or very close to, a direct line between the two sets of stumps. Its purpose is to smother any spin or swing which may be on the ball.

Supposing the ball was spinning so much that it changed course from leg to off five degrees on

The forward defensive shot.

hitting the ground. If allowed to travel a mere 15 cm after pitching before hitting the blade, this deviation would not matter. But if allowed to travel a metre, it might touch the edge of the bat for a catch in the slips. Obviously, therefore,

to play forward to a short-pitched ball is bad theory.

It is desirable in forward play to keep the bat absolutely perpendicular throughout, therefore a reasonably straight back lift is required. The handle of the bat should be kept forward of the blade in order that the ball will be kept down. Always play close to the front leg so that the ball cannot get between bat and pad.

Remembering these things, take a look at the photograph (left) of Dewes being bowled by Miller in the fifth Test at The Oval in 1948. The caption will tell you where he has gone wrong.

The left shoulder and elbow should lean forward towards the pitch of the ball and really drag the front foot and the body forward. Bend the left knee slightly to hold the weight of the body in balance and point the left toe towards mid-off or cover, varying it slightly according to the direction of the ball.

Dewes bowled by Miller, fifth Test, The Oval, 1948. He has played perfectly straight but his front foot is still almost on the crease, therefore his bat has gone forward but not his body. Also there is a gap between pad and bat so that the in-swinger got through. Obviously it is not sufficient just to have the bat perpendicular.
(Fox Photos Ltd)

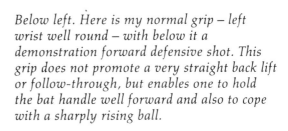

Below left. Here is my normal grip – left wrist well round – with below it a demonstration forward defensive shot. This grip does not promote a very straight back lift or follow-through, but enables one to hold the bat handle well forward and also to cope with a sharply rising ball.

Below right. This is a demonstration of an altered grip, left wrist in front of handle, and a forward defensive shot. It is easier to play perfectly straight but more difficult to stop the bat going through the perpendicular. Also it presents difficulties should the ball get up high.

If the ball is pitched on the leg stump, for instance, the left toe will point more towards the bowler than it would be for a ball pitched, say, just outside the off stump.

Keep the head well forward and down.

At the end of the stroke the right toe will be the balancing agent at the rear (right heel off the ground) and it must be kept firmly behind the batting crease. This precaution is necessary in case the ball misses the bat and the question of a stumping arises.

One of cricket's simplest errors is for a batsman to misjudge the length of a ball, play forward and be beaten by spin or swing. The tendency then is to overbalance forward – hence the need for keeping that right toe firmly down.

In forward defence the left hand is in control.

Note how the right-hand grip has changed until it has become almost a thumb and first two fingers only at the bottom of the handle. The right hand acts really as a guide. No power is required.

I like the feel of the left hand at the back of the handle in this forward shot because it curbs any tendency to follow through.

A splendid demonstration of this left-hand control is shown in the photograph of Peter May on page 20.

And yet look at the photograph of Sir Jack Hobbs below. A completely different left-hand position.

Sir Jack Hobbs playing forward. An extreme left-hand position – quite the reverse of that used by Peter May.
(P.A. Reuter Photos Ltd)

Back Cut or Late Cut

Modern players tend to eschew the late cut altogether and their expressed reason is 'too dangerous'. Providing proper judgment is used the rewards to be gained from the shot are well worth the risk.

It should only be attempted when the ball is reasonably short of length and not bouncing very high but is pitched well outside the off stump – it is cut rather in the direction of third or even second slip – and instead of hitting at right angles to the flight as with a square cut, the bat runs in an extreme case almost parallel with the line of flight at contact.

The ball is actually hit down on to the ground. It is normally on the rise when struck and therefore a snick is almost certain to result in a catch to the wicket-keeper. That is why extreme care and precision are required.

It is usually unsafe to try the stroke against fast bowlers. The safety margin is too small and, anyway, fast bowlers usually have slip fieldsmen who would be in the way.

Third Test, Leeds, 1930. As I slipped in trying to regain my crease, I managed to back-cut the ball away from the clutching hands of wicket-keeper Duckworth. A single to third-man resulted. (Central Press Photos Ltd)

Likewise it is very dangerous against off-spinners, but against medium-pace or leg-break bowlers there is a good chance of reward.

Power comes mainly from the wrists, but the ball's own momentum is the chief source of its speed. The stroke is a short, snappy one and not a long swing.

After contact with the ball, the end of the bat should go straight down and almost hit the ground. In fact some players actually do hit the ground. This is a good indication of playing the shot correctly.

Whether to risk the stroke or not will be governed by the type of pitch and bowler and the position of the fieldsmen. It may not be worthwhile for a chancy single, but it may well be if a certain four is in the offing.

The author playing a back cut.

Having watched such delightful cutters as Kippax, Macartney and Archie Jackson play this late cut to perfection, I deeply regret that it seems to be disappearing more and more from the play.

But I suppose you cannot be expected to late-cut when most of the balls are pitched around the leg stump (especially by the off-spinners) – a modern tendency which I deplore. Well played, the late cut is full of grace and artistry and can be most rewarding.

One contemporary Test batsman of mine played it with only moderate success because he invariably started to transfer his weight to his front foot (as though anxious to start running) as he was hitting the ball.

This action militates against watching the ball and very often drags the batsman out of his correct position, so that as often as not he cuts the ball too straight into the ground or gets it on the inside edge, sometimes pulling it on to the stumps.

It is vital that the weight shall be transferred to the rear foot and held there as the ball is struck.

Completely by accident the best shot I ever played was a late cut.

In the Leeds Test of 1930 I jumped down the pitch to drive but found I had misjudged the flight of the ball. When trying to get back I slipped and fell. However, by retaining my

balance and control, I managed to back cut the ball to third-man for a single. This incident is shown on page 41.

That, at least, was one occasion where a back cut saved my wicket rather than lost it.

Down the Gully

Sometimes opportunities provide themselves of picking up singles down the gully to third-man.

When a fast or medium-pace bowler drops the ball a little short outside the off stump, it is quite simple to make a position similar to that for the square cut off the right foot, only this time, instead of cutting with power, get more on top of and closer to the ball, hit slightly later, and glide it wide of third slip. The pace of the ball itself will produce the desired result without any real assistance from the batsman.

It is not dangerous providing the striker is well over the ball and makes sure of hitting it down on to the ground. This is particularly necessary if a fieldsman is stationed at third slip or at backward point.

The main danger lies in a ball which unexpectedly lifts off the pitch. That is why it is so necessary to be well across and on top of the line of flight.

The ball delivered for the demonstration shot shown here was bowled rather wide. It would be much more correct if the body were closer to the ball than the picture shows.

The Square Cut

There are two square cuts – the one played off the front foot, the other off the back foot. Let me deal first with the cut off the front foot, shown above, which is the more beautiful and powerful but unfortunately seldom seen.

With the modern emphasis on the perpendicular bat and what I might term the forward defensive lunge, few batsmen are prepared for the square cut off the front foot. It requires a very bad length ball for one to have the time to judge the shot and really go into it with full power.

However, assuming the ball is sufficiently short in length, and wide of the off stump, this is one of the most thrilling shots to play.

Obviously it must be made with a more or less horizontal blade and therefore the margin of error is small.

Before the ball lands, no striker can be sure how high it will bounce, but his aim should be to hit the ball near the apex of its flight after bouncing, and that will (to the right ball) be just in front of the batting crease.

The left leg should be advanced forward and across the wicket so that it finishes with the toes directed between point and cover and the left leg carrying the full weight.

The left shoulder at the start of the swing should be pointing towards mid-off so that the maximum power can be put into the swing.

The shoulders turn only with the impetus of the hit, which is made with the full force of right hand, forearm and shoulder.

If anything, the ball should be hit slightly down and the wrists rolled over, shutting the blade of the bat as contact is made. In this way the ball will be kept on the ground and not cut into the air. Its direction should normally be in front of point and just backward of cover.

Cut really hard – don't toy with it. Make the shot a full swing and not a jerk, otherwise it may tend to shift your head position and divert the eyes from the ball.

As I suggested previously the square cut off the back foot is much more prevalent than the forward square cut. Understandably so, because

Off the front foot.

first it can be played off a ball which is not so deficient in length, and secondly because the natural tendency of batsmen is to take the easy road and give themselves the maximum amount of time in which to see the ball and make the stroke.

The direction of the ball is the same in both cases. So long as it is short enough and well clear of the off stump, the batsman can position himself to make a cut either just behind point or even past the gully position.

Off the back foot.

This time, of course, it is the right foot which is thrown across and the left shoulder is not responsible for so much power, although photographs reveal it is kept surprisingly far round towards the off until well after contact.

The same essentials must be applied as off the front foot. Hit slightly down on the ball as the

Neil Harvey always showed a tendency to get caught in the slips when cutting. This photo shows why. He is attempting to square-cut a ball off Trevor Bailey but, instead of leaning into the shot and going over on top of the ball, he has pulled both the front shoulder and the front foot away to the leg side. The inevitable result of such a body movement must be to pull the bat away from the line of flight with the resultant danger of a slip catch.
(The News, Adelaide)

weight is transferred to the right leg. Flex the knee slightly to assist balance. Hit firmly and freely but not jerkily.

This stroke does not command the same power as the other one. More care should be taken to see that no mistake is made and that it is carefully placed.

Somehow or other I always felt more likely to mis-hit when I attempted to cut off the back foot. It seemed more difficult to maintain balance because this time there is no left side to hit against and hold your position.

The most common fault when cutting is for the batsman to pull the front shoulder away towards the on side too soon. If that is done, the tendency is immediately to drop the front shoulder and hit under the ball rather than on top of it. Result – a catch in the slips.

One must lean into the shot. And better a fraction too close to the ball than too far away. The latter will cause loss of balance and control.

A word of warning. It is extremely dangerous to try to cut off-spinners if the ball is turning to any extent. Some of the Australian Test team of 1956 found this out against Jim Laker. A player should not have to be taught such an elementary lesson in a Test match.

Because square cuts are played with an almost horizontal bat, there is a reasonable chance of getting away with a mis-hit. One on the top edge will often fly over slips and one on the bottom edge seldom causes any harm.

The ideal height for cutting is a ball slightly over stump high, but naturally one has to hit the ball wherever it is. Bounce cannot be regulated by the batsman.

With the end of the blade slightly lower than the handle as the ball is struck, and the turn of the wrists, it is not difficult to cut the ball downwards, thereby eliminating the risk of a catch to point.

May I repeat: Don't toy with it – cut hard.

Against Essex in 1948 Australia made the record score of 721 in a single day. The sequence (opposite) was taken during the play and shows me square-cutting off the back foot a leg-break from Peter Smith.

The Forward Drives

Broadly speaking these may be classified as:

a] Cover Drive
b] Off Drive
c] Straight Drive
d] On Drive

Basically, each shot has the same characteristics.

To be on the safe side a batsman would normally only attempt to drive a ball which we can term over-pitched, so that he can make the stroke without fear that the break or swing will evade his bat in the execution thereof.

The front shoulder must lean forward in all drives though it is pulled away quicker in the case of the on drive than the others, in order to assist the direction of the shot. The left hip, too, must go well forward as the weight is transferred on to the front foot.

The distance a batsman needs to advance his front foot down the pitch depends on the length of the ball. A full toss, say 15 cm off the ground, could be driven by just transferring the weight as the ball was struck, whereas a ball pitching, say, 150 cm in front of the popping crease would demand a full stretch forward.

For a cover drive the front foot would point towards cover, and then it would progressively point a little more directly towards the bowler for the other drives, round to mid-on.

The front leg must carry the weight of the body at the moment of contact but it should be comfortably bent at the knees to maintain balance. In all cases the rear heel is lifted and the rear leg is balanced on the toe, which is kept clearly behind the popping crease.

A most glorious study of W. R. Hammond making a cover drive. It is a perfect study in grace, power and balance and gives a true picture of the full splendour of this great batsman's stroke production.
(Sport & General Press Agency Ltd)

The back lift should be higher than it is for the forward defensive stroke and there should be a complete follow-through. The ball must be struck just before the bat reaches the perpendicular in order to keep it on the ground.

With the cover drive, the blade is a fraction open at contact, with off and straight drives it is practically square, but with the on drive (or when driving say between mid-on and square-leg) the face of the bat will be closing slightly on the ball. This will help to keep the ball on the ground and will also give added control over the direction. It will at the same time help counteract any tendency to hit across the flight, especially in the case of a drive wide of mid-on.

The direction of the ball for the on-side drive should be roughly towards the leg stump, straight drive middle to off stump, off drive from off stump to just outside, whilst cover drives should be played from balls pitched well clear of the off stump.

There must naturally be a considerable degree of flexibility in the direction because this is

A splendid action photo (right) of Sir Leonard Hutton playing a cover drive. Everything is in the right position but noticeably, with his Yorkshire caution, Sir Len is not allowing himself the luxury of a complete follow-through. Rather is the accent on control. (The Herald, Melbourne)

The cover drive.

The off drive.

The straight drive.

The on drive.

under the batsman's control and he will vary his shots according to the field placing.

There should not be much danger in any of the strokes, but with the cover drive one is using less than the full width of the blade and any deviation from an accurate blow can result in a slip catch off the outside edge, and there is the risk of pulling the ball on to the stumps from the inside edge.

With all drives play as close to the front leg as possible compatible with freedom.

Against fast or medium-pace bowlers one expects to play the various drives from the crease.

Against a slow bowler, however, a batsman may, by fast footwork and good judgment, essay out of his crease down the wicket to make a half-volley out of a ball which otherwise would have been of good length. In this way he can make punishing drives and upset the bowler's control. Indeed, it is one of the most potent weapons a batsman possesses and is used all too infrequently.

Particularly to an off-spinner there is often much less risk involved in jumping out to drive than in staying at home. You overcome the dangerous length ball, smother the break, cover with your pads any danger of stumping and confuse the bowler who will probably start to vary his length and thus provide you with other scoring opportunities.

I would like to stress the importance of the initial forward position of the front shoulder in driving. It aids power and is a tremendous factor in causing the bat to travel 'through the ball', just as one has the feeling of a hammer head going 'through the nail' as you drive it into the wood.

No reference to forward driving would be complete without mentioning the lofted drive.

From history one may deduce that this stroke was far more prevalent seventy or eighty years ago than it is now. There is always some element of risk when lofting the ball. One has not the margin of safety for a mis-hit in the air that one has for a shot along the ground.

However, the batsman may find there are occasions when the shot is called for by the state

of the game demanding aggression beyond that normally attempted. Or perhaps a very close attacking field may cause him to use it as a method of dispersing the fieldsmen.

Whilst I do not encourage batsmen to hit the ball in the air, I am all in favour of it when circumstances decree its wisdom, and every batsman should have the stroke in his repertoire.

But remember, it must be used with discretion. When a bowler has a man on the boundary behind mid-on, it is just suicide to try to loft a drive over mid-on, hoping it will fall safely in between, or go for six. That sort of indiscretion merely reflects on the batsman's mentality, unless, of course, runs are the only objective and wickets of no concern.

But I have seen a player in Test cricket, when his side was struggling to avoid defeat, try to swing the first ball he received over the fence at long-on even though there was a man stationed there to thankfully hold the catch which he duly received. Such players usually attribute their poor batting averages to bad luck instead of bad judgment.

A tall, powerful batsman who is a good driver is a joy to watch.

A splendid action study of Gary Sobers (below) whose glorious driving has seldom been equalled. Determination, concentration and real power fairly ooze from this photograph. (Sun Herald, Sydney)

My idea of the proper way to follow-through after making a full-blooded drive. A photo taken while making the world record score of 452 not out.
(Daily Telegraph Pictorial, Sydney)

With some of the modern new-ball fields, where there is an arc of seven men behind the stumps and only one fieldsman in front on each side, I have seen many golden opportunities of driving go begging because of timidity.

Some batsmen are so intent on defence that they are never ready for the initial movement to drive. In this way they find themselves at the mercy of an intelligent bowler who can keep the ball well up and give it the maximum chance to swing, knowing he is safe from the vicious forward drive.

Just because a ball swings doesn't mean it can't be driven. There is nothing better than a mildly curving, out-swinging half-volley to drive through the covers. The swing helps it like a charm.

Of course, a measure of skill is involved and fine judgment has to be exercised, but batsmen of international repute should possess these things abundantly.

Common faults in driving are (a) front foot not close enough to the line of flight and (b) not sufficient follow-through.

May I issue a warning not to drive against the swing. An out-swinger should only be driven to the off – an in-swinger to the on.

And make sure the blade of the bat does not get in front of the handle before contact with the ball except for the deliberately lofted drive. The hands must lead.

Jumping Out to Drive

When a slow spin bowler is operating, and is giving the ball a reasonable amount of air by tossing it up, he is naturally doing this to try to get more turn on the ball.

A batsman's job is to counter this idea, and one of the best ways is to use his feet by going down the wicket to attack the bowling, either hitting it on the half-volley or full-toss, to prevent the spin taking effect.

I maintain that far more batsmen who miss the ball are stumped by centimetres because they reach forward tentatively from the crease and overbalance, than are stumped by metres when going well down the pitch to drive.

If you decide to jump out there is no sense in going out only half-way. Such indecision very often proves fatal. It is much better either to change your mind and retreat back to the safety of your crease before you make the shot, or, alternatively, to go right on with it and risk the penalty of missing the ball.

I never mind a chap being stumped by two metres, but when he is stumped by two centimetres you can be almost certain he has played a bad or tentative shot, being dubious in his mind about the length of the delivery and groping forward, when he either should have gone well out of his ground to smother the spin or played back.

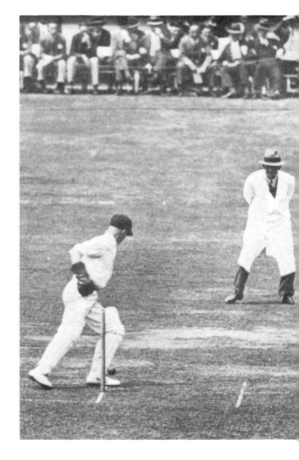

Jumping out to drive.

R. W. V. Robins (left) was never one to do things by halves and he certainly believed in my theory of 'better be stumped by two metres than by two centimetres'. Here he is shown stranded metres down the wicket playing for Gentlemen of England v Australia, but fortune favours the brave. Ben Barnett, Australia's keeper, has failed to gather the ball.
(Sport & General Press Agency Ltd)

The Pull Shot

When I was very young and just beginning to learn the rudiments of the game, I was compelled by circumstances to play most of my cricket on concrete pitches covered with coir matting.

As anyone with experience on them knows, these pitches produce a more uniform but much higher bounce than turf.

I was very short and consequently found great difficulty in playing with a straight bat the ball pitched short of a length on the stumps. It came too high for comfort. Remember, I was a schoolboy and often faced the bowling of grown men.

The pull shot (i) right foot back and across.

To overcome this predicament, I developed the pull shot to a marked degree.

It simply consisted of going back and across with the right foot and pulling the ball with a horizontal bat somewhere between mid-on and square-leg.

Because of my grip I was able to roll the wrists over as the stroke was played and keep the ball on the ground. Keen eyesight was needed, and one had to be careful the ball did not keep low, but this seldom happened on coir mats.

After arriving in Sydney and commencing my career on turf, I began exploiting the same shot.

Now turf is much more uncertain than concrete and I began to lose my wicket occasionally because the greater speed and lower bounce of the ball off turf sometimes caused me to hit over the ball and be bowled or LBW. When that happened the shot looked a real haymaker and I am sure this, above everything else, gave rise to the story that I played with a cross bat.

Actually, there is no other way to play the pull shot than with a cross bat, but on turf greater judgment is required and the stroke must be used more sparingly.

I was counselled by many older players to

Here I am playing a pull shot to a ball which would have gone over the stumps. The body is kept on the leg side so there is no danger of being hit should the ball fly. There has obviously been a conscious effort to hit the ball downwards by a combination of body movement and wrist action.
(The Herald, Melbourne)

give it up. They said it was too risky. But I was loath to do so because I felt sure it would bring me lots of runs, providing it was used with discretion.

A medium-pace bowler quite often operates without a fieldsman between mid-on and square-leg, and this huge unprotected area is most inviting. Even if a man is stationed there, one has plenty of room on either side.

Below is the result of trying to pull a ball which is too far up. It will get through underneath the horizontal bat and instead of the length of the blade being available to keep the ball out, you only have the width. Graeme Hole is the culprit in this photo, but as he had made a century and was trying to force the pace, he was excused.
(Associated Press Ltd)

Slow bowlers usually have a man or two on the fence, but a pull shot can be played with very great power and it can be placed with precision so that there may still be a reasonable hope of getting four runs.

No batsman should attempt to pull a ball which is over-pitched or of good length. This is courting disaster.

Look at the photograph below, right, and you will see what may happen.

However, assuming the ball to be the right sort, the method is very similar to the hook shot.

___

In this picture we see Gavin Stevens of South Australia pulling the ball without any body pivot. I don't like this position because, from experience, I have found you are in dire trouble if the ball either keeps low or bounces higher than you expect. In either case the batsman will find himself tangled up, out of balance and out of control.
(The News, Adelaide)

Go back and across with the right foot so that the toes are pointing almost straight down the pitch towards the bowler. Then as the ball comes along (normally knee to stomach high) pull it hard to mid-wicket – at the same time pivoting the body and rolling the wrists over to keep the ball on the ground. In many respects the movement is similar to a square cut, but instead of cutting against the line of flight, you pull with it.

In order to control the shot and to have the best chance of combating any uneven bounce, it is essential to pivot the body and to get the legs fairly well apart.

The general execution of the stroke is clearly discernible in the movie strip, (pages 56–7), but I have included four still pictures to make my meaning clearer.

___

This is proof of the possible consequences of getting into the position I dislike. Here the ball has obviously kept low and left the batsman between wind and water.

Three important aspects of the pull shot are balance, control and power. They are all visible in this photograph. The pivot has taken my left foot behind the level of the stumps, thereby giving more room to make the length of the ball suitable for the shot. (Sport & General Press Agency Ltd)

If my batting was known for any one particular shot, this was it, mainly because of (*a*) the frequency with which I employed it, and (*b*) because I was able to keep the ball on the ground.

The great majority of players who attempt the stroke hit the ball in the air because they hit up and under it, and in their grip they keep the left wrist more in front of the handle than I did.

When pulling with the left wrist in this position, the blade of the bat is slightly open.

The ball can be struck satisfactorily but it will automatically go in the air and the slightest mis-hit will cause it to fly off the top edge of the bat.

That is one reason why so few first-class players (especially Englishmen) try the shot at all. For them it isn't worth the risk. But they are missing a grand scoring medium.

The stroke is particularly effective against a slow leg-break bowler should he stray in his length. It then becomes a natural, even though it means hitting against the break and thereby flaunting one of cricket's so-called sacred principles.

Also it is tremendously valuable against the off-spinner with a close leg field. There is nothing like a full-blooded pull shot right into the teeth of the short-leg fieldsmen to disturb their confidence and shift them back a metre or two. That in itself is a big contribution in minimising their danger.

The pull shot (ii) right foot straight back.

If there is no outfield at all the ball can deliberately be lofted over the men close in, but the shot is such a powerful one and it is so seldom used, except with full power, that I found it satisfactory to hit the ball mainly on to the ground and be content with trying to place it between the fieldsmen.

At the finish of the shot the batsman will find himself facing square-leg, providing he has pivoted correctly and has swung right through the ball.

In addition to rolling his wrists the striker should, if possible, always keep the blade of the bat almost horizontal and pointing slightly downwards. This is of further assistance in keeping the ball on the ground.

A batsman need not hesitate to pull a ball from outside the off stump. The risk of pulling it on to the stumps from the underside of the bat is negligible, and in any case the legs are positioned so that they would stand a good chance of intercepting such a mis-hit.

I advocate concentrated net practice to perfect the technique, and repeat my warning not to try to pull the ball unless it is pitched well short of a length. Even then the great danger is the irregularity of the height of bounce after it pitches.

In addition to pulling the ball by the method outlined, I frequently employed a slightly dif-ferent technique. The difference between the two pull shots is this.

Instead of putting the right foot back and across to the off side, just put the right foot straight back. Then, as the ball is hit between mid-on and square-leg, pull your body away from the line of flight as the left foot is swung round to the leg side whilst you pivot on the right foot.

In this way tremendous power can be generated, even more than with the other method, because there seems to be scope for greater leverage. The whole mechanism of the wrists, arms and body can be harnessed to give the ball a tremendous crack.

Should the ball be missed, it will pass on the off side of the body (and if it keeps low often with fatal results), because the ideal ball to pull in this way is one delivered on the stumps.

With the orthodox pull one has to finish within the crease area and must be careful, in swinging the body round, not to hit the stumps. But this way there is virtually no limit to the pivotal action which ends with the weight on the left leg.

Sometimes I found myself behind the leg stump with my left leg, and in case this sounds like an exaggeration, you will find on page 59 an actual photograph taken during a Test match depicting such a position.

If a fast bowler is trying to engineer a catch on the leg side off a hook shot, this alternative type

of pull shot offers a counter because it holds better prospects of pulling a ball which is bouncing quite high and still keeping it down. In fact, it is the easiest of the lot to keep down with those rolling wrists.

But it has its risks, especially when the ball is coming in towards the body.

I tried it against Bill Bowes at Bramall Lane and had my cap tilted sideways when the ball hit the peak, but then who wants to play cricket at all if not prepared to take a chance occasionally?

Just one caution. Don't try the pull shot on a

greasy pitch after a shower of rain. Or if you do, have a spare set of teeth ready.

When the right foot is taken back and across, the left leg should be allowed to swing round as the body turns. From this position it seems to help balance and enables the batsman more easily to play the shot with a horizontal blade. The picture shows me batting against England at the Adelaide Oval.
(Advertiser Newspapers Ltd)

The Hook Shot

There is a good deal of argument as to the difference between a hook shot and a pull shot. I don't propose to try to settle the argument, which is not really important anyway.

However, my description of a hook applies to a ball delivered with some speed, pitched short either on the stumps or on the leg side thereof, where the batsman steps inside the line of flight and hooks the ball behind square-leg.

The pull shot to me is where the ball is literally pulled off direction from the stumps or even from the off side of the stumps with a horizontal bat, mainly in front of square-leg.

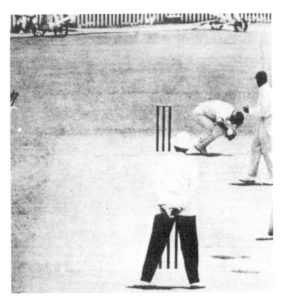

In this photograph, Colin McDonald has not been able to avoid a bouncer from Wes Hall and collapses on the pitch.

The penalty of not getting one's body in the correct position can be very severe and great courage is required to stand up to a real express bowler.
(Brisbane Courier Mail)

Richie Benaud caught in a disastrous position. Not only has he taken his eyes off the ball, but he has ducked in its direction of flight. The ball only has to keep low enough and a crack on the side of the head is inevitable. (The Sydney Sun)

It is usually executed against slow or medium-pace bowlers, whereas the hook is mostly played against the faster bowlers.

Assuming a fast bowler to be dropping the ball half-way up the pitch on or about the leg stump, it will normally rise somewhere about shoulder height and, in fact, will very often come up straight towards the batsman's left shoulder. By maintaining his original position, or by going back on to his stumps defensively, the batsman may find it hard to keep the ball down or steer it clear of those close-in fieldsmen on the leg side. Moreover, he is in danger of being struck by the ball.

The safest method, physically and cricket-wise, is for the striker to move inside the line of flight so that the ball will pass on the leg side of his body.

It is well known by experienced batsmen that this type of delivery (assuming right-handed batsman and bowler) will nearly always tend to come in towards the body after pitching. That is an additional reason why it is safer and more correct to move your body towards the off. Even if the ball bounces head high it will sail harmlessly by.

In addition to the movie film strip (pages 64–5) showing the consecutive movements, I managed to get some still photographs which very clearly show my points.

On these pages there are shown three disastrous positions. Firstly Richie Benaud (page 62, left) appears to have been caught unawares by a short one and is in trouble ducking to a ball perilously close to his head. Then Len Maddocks (below, left) is shown for some unaccountable reason ducking back into the line of flight of a short one from Tyson after first of all correctly moving into a safe position. Then Tyson himself (below, right), having done the same as Maddocks, pays the penalty of taking his eye off the ball.

To play the hook, move back and across with the right foot and, as the ball rises towards your chest or shoulder, swing it away somewhere between square-leg and the wicket-keeper. The right foot becomes a pivot so that, as the swing is made, the body naturally moves round in a

Len Maddocks has moved outside the off stump but evidently the ball pitched there, so, instead of going on in the same direction, he has ducked back rather dangerously and taken his eyes off the ball. A very awkward position to get into.
(The News, Adelaide)

Tyson ducks to a ball from Lindwall and turns his back on it. A terrific crack on the back of the head was his reward.
(The Sydney Sun)

Cyril Washbrook (above) has moved beautifully inside a Lindwall bumper and hooked it off his left shoulder. This shot was taken just after the ball was struck and before the body had completed its pivot.
(The Herald, Melbourne)

half circle, swinging clear of the ball, and finally the batsman finishes up facing almost round to the wicket-keeper – certainly well towards the leg side.

Two more still photographs, one of Cyril Washbrook (left) and one of myself (right), reveal clearly the foot movement which is necessary to play the shot safely and correctly.

Should the ball rise shoulder high or more it will be virtually impossible to keep the ball on the ground. By the nature of the stroke the tendency is to hit the ball upwards anyway. Therefore, the batsman must exercise care and judgment to try to steer it clear of any leg-side fielders.

The fast bowler will usually have a man on the long-leg boundary and possibly one or two close up. The latter are of no consequence with a hook shot – the man on the boundary is the danger.

It is quite possible so to control the hook that a degree of certainty in placing the ball can be achieved, and also one can go a long way towards avoiding a catch by keeping the power of the swing within bounds so that the ball will not carry on the full to the fieldsman.

It is a satisfying shot which many great players such as Sobers and Herbert Sutcliffe regularly employed.

I am sure that quite a number of batsmen

The hook shot.

would be more successful if they used it against the modern leg-side fields instead of trying to play every bumper defensively down at their feet, or ducking.

I should perhaps add that if the ball should bounce, say, head high, it is often best to go through with the body movement without making a shot at the ball. The difficulty of controlling the shot increases with its height, but keeping the body inside the line of flight is by far the safest way to avoid being struck.

Batting against Clark at The Oval in 1934 to a packed leg field, I am here seen at the completion of a hook shot where the body pivot is complete and I am well outside the off stump. It can be seen that I have hit under the ball and made no attempt to keep it down. That was because it was a no-ball – see the umpire's arm. Clark was bowling left arm round the wicket.
(Central Press Photos Ltd)

Forcing Shot off the Back Foot

Just because a ball is short of what we may term a good length and the striker has to play back, it does not follow that he must be on the defensive.

If the ball is pitched outside the stumps he may have several alternative shots to attempt. But if it is pitched on the middle stump, not short enough to pull, he is restricted on the grounds of safety to a forcing shot off the back foot past the bowler.

It is a safe shot but demands great power from wrists and forearms, and very good timing.

The author playing a forcing shot off the back foot.

Denis Compton (below), by drawing away to the leg side, has given himself room to force a ball away into the covers off his back foot.

The method is dangerous because it leaves the stumps completely unprotected and also the backward movement is against all sound principles of cutting.
(The Telegraph, Brisbane)

The initial movement should be similar to that for a back defensive stroke except that the right foot should be taken back rather straighter. This is in order to give the striker more freedom to swing the bat and put power into his shot, for now we are thinking in terms of a very solid hit and follow-through.

The left hand really becomes a guide. Power is generated from the right hand in co-ordination with wrists, forearms, etc. Nothing can teach the shot so well as a study of the moving-picture sequence above.

The shot depicted is that used when playing the ball back past the bowler between his position of delivery and mid-on.

Bowlers find it very hard to recover their balance and get across to stop a shot in that direction.

If mid-on is fielding wide, a couple of such drives will probably cause the bowler to put him straighter, and immediately a wider area of country becomes available for scoring shots between mid-on and square-leg.

A forcing shot off the back foot, similar in its general execution to that described, may be played whereby the batsman, by hitting slightly across the ball or by turning his blade on contact, will be able to drive firmly wide of mid-on.

Then, too, it may be used to force the ball through the covers when the direction of the ball is well clear of the off stump.

This latter stroke, however, demands great precision because the striker has committed himself to the shot by the time the ball lands and, therefore, it is well nigh impossible to change it should the ball do something unex-

A very good example of playing a forcing shot off the back foot through the covers. Note particularly how the batsman has gone well across. He has used his height splendidly and the body, shoulders and arms have obviously been co-ordinated to put punch into the stroke.
(The Sydney Sun)

pected off the pitch. One which cuts away, for instance, could easily cause a slip catch.

It is important to stand well up over the ball and lean into the shot. Any tendency to pull away will accentuate the chance of a slip catch.

That unpredictable genius, Denis Compton, would sometimes offend every text book by backing away to the leg side and playing the ball into the covers, especially against a slow leg-break bowler.

If you can do it and get away with it, well and good, but I don't recommend you to try unless your place in the team is already secure.

For interest a photograph is included showing how Compton did it (page 66, below left).

Leg Glances

There are two leg glances. One, termed the back leg glance, is played with the weight on the back foot and from behind the crease. The other, termed the forward leg glance, is played forward of the crease with the weight on the front foot.

In each case the purpose of the stroke is to glance the ball somewhere between the wicket-keeper and square-leg.

The direction which the ball follows after being struck will vary according to the fullness of the blade on impact. Being a glance, the full face of the bat is not employed.

When glancing very fine, only half (or even a quarter) of the blade may be visible to the bowler as ball strikes bat. When the ball is glanced more firmly, and therefore squarer, perhaps three-quarters of the blade may be visible. The blade is turning as the ball is struck and there is little margin for error.

I am a great believer in playing shots with the full face of the bat whenever possible, and a firm shot to mid-wicket may often be a better proposition than a glance. It depends largely on the field placing.

If there is a leg slip and a man on the fence at fine-leg, a leg glance may present no attraction. But assuming no leg slip and a man stationed at mid-wicket, then the glance would be the obvious choice when the right ball came along.

Whether played forward or back the glance is a delightful shot to watch and it is another reason why I deplore so much the frequent use of leg slips. On so many occasions they force the batsmen in their own interests to abolish all attempts at glancing.

However, opportunities do arise and the strokes should be in the repertoire of any complete batsman.

Back Leg Glance

One should only attempt this shot if satisfied that the ball would pass clear of the leg stump if not struck. Otherwise, there would obviously be too great a risk of LBW.

The ideal ball is one pitched just outside the leg stump. The right foot should be moved back and across in front of the stumps, with the right toe pointing down the pitch. As the body swivels round in the execution of the shot, the right foot acts as a pivot.

Contact should be made with the ball just several centimetres in front of the left leg, and it is a sound theory to suggest that the left leg shall be in such a position that the ball will hit it if not struck with the bat.

First, this means the ball is being played from

The back leg glance.

the correct position, and secondly it is a useful safeguard against being caught by the wicket-keeper should the ball be glanced too finely.

The left hand makes sure the bat is perpendicular (except that the handle should be slightly forward of the blade) at contact, at which stage the right hand dictates the turning movement to get the required deflection.

Dropping the right hand down the handle will aid control in glancing and can be safely done because no power is required. The ball generates its own.

The ideal ball to glance is one just short of a length from a fast or medium-pace bowler but, as with most shots, the batsman by his own prowess may extend the range. Bill Brown, for instance, was an adept at glancing even the slow leg-spinner simply because he possessed a delicacy of touch and a penchant for the stroke beyond that of most players.

Sir Leonard Hutton was the greatest master I ever saw at keeping the ball down on the leg side. This picture (right) shows why. He has moved back and inside the ball and then decided to let it pass. But see how, with head and shoulders forward and down, he has forced the bat handle ahead of the blade and if he was compelled to play the ball there would be no chance of it flying upwards. (The Herald, Melbourne)

Forward Leg Glance

The basic features of the two glances are similar but one naturally must select a different ball for each one.

A forward leg glance demands that the ball should be pitched a half-volley or at least farther up than a good length. Its direction would be the same as that for a back leg glance.

The initial foot movement by the batsman would be similar to that outlined for an on drive, with one exception. When playing an on drive, the ball is struck with power, and I liked to have the ball coming inside the front leg to give maximum freedom to the swing of the bat. But with the forward leg glance, accuracy is required, not power, and the front foot should be placed slightly more towards the off so that the ball would, if missed altogether by the bat, strike the outside edge of the pad.

The head and shoulders should be kept forward and down, the bat inclined forward, hands ahead of the blade at contact to try to make sure the ball is glanced downwards and not up in the air. If desired, the right hand may go down the handle to assist control.

One final word of advice. Don't try these glances against a new ball which is swinging towards slips. That would be courting trouble.

The forward leg glance.

The Sweep Shot

If you were batting against a slow spinner who frequently sent down slightly overpitched balls on or just outside the leg stump, how would you play them? That should be a fair question to a class of cricket students.

From those rabid disciples of a perpendicular bat I should expect answers varying between an intended on drive, a leg glance and a purely defensive shot. Each would carry some element of risk.

An attempted on drive against a leg-break needs care because the striker, by advancing his front foot down the pitch, could leave the way open to being bowled providing the ball turned enough from leg. He has deprived himself of a second line of defence for the stumps. There is also the possibility of a catch from the outside edge of the bat.

The purely defensive play against an off-spinner immediately brings into play the short-

Opposite. Keith Miller swings one of Laker's off-breaks straight at short-leg fieldsman Colin Cowdrey, who immediately protects his face. Actually Miller missed the ball but no fieldsman can wait to see what happens to the ball. Tony Lock, realising the swing is square, stands his ground. The Oval, 1956, fifth Test. (Associated Press Ltd)

The sweep shot.

leg fieldsmen, especially the leg-slips, who are there mainly to pick up a catch off the inside edge of the bat.

To try to avoid these possibilities, and at the same time attack the bowler in a reasonably safe manner, the sweep stroke can well be cultivated against this type of ball.

It is played simply by advancing the front leg down the pitch and swinging at the ball with almost a horizontal bat, so that the ball will in effect be swept behind square-leg.

There are two important points to remember. The first is that the ball must be hit on to the ground, and this is achieved by rolling the wrists over in the execution of the sweep and by keeping the bat slightly on top of the line of flight.

Sweeping against a leg-break without closing the face of the blade would mean a very great risk of skying a catch in the region of the square-leg umpire, because the ball only has to hit the top edge of the bat and it must fly up.

The second point is to make sure the front foot is correctly positioned. It must be placed so that it is in a direct line between the ball and the stumps.

This precaution is to make sure the ball cannot break round the leg and bowl the striker, and is vital against the leg-spinner. The bat sweeps across the line of flight so that the amount of turn on the ball doesn't really matter. The horizontal blade acts as a protection against the break in much the same way as a

Denis Compton demonstrates his sweep shot. I cannot fault his action. Feet, body, arms and hands are all in the right position, and he has rolled the bat over as it should be done. (Daily Express)

perpendicular blade protects against variations in height from a straight ball on the stumps.

Sir Jack Hobbs and Bob Wyatt were two batsmen who frequently indulged in the sweep stroke against Clarrie Grimmett. It brought them many runs but now and again they misjudged the position of the front foot and were bowled round their legs.

Here we see Bob Wyatt bowled round his legs by Grimmett, fifth Test, The Oval, 1934. It is quite evident from the photo that Wyatt's left leg position is a fraction too straight down the pitch.

Incidentally, that wicket gave Grimmett his 100th Test victim. Oldfield is the wicket-keeper, Chipperfield at slip.

The photograph of Bob Wyatt (page 73) is a perfect example of the leg being placed too straight down the pitch. The ball has curled round the legs and hit the leg stump. Had the left leg been 10 cm more to the on side, this could not have happened.

Denis Compton played the sweep shot more frequently and to greater effect than anyone I can remember. On page 72 is a photograph of Denis showing exactly how he did it.

Against a leg-spinner the stroke should only be attempted providing the ball is pitched outside the leg stump.

Greater latitude may prevail against an off-spinner providing he is consistently turning the ball and bowling over the wicket. In such circumstances the batsman may risk the shot even when the ball is pitching on the leg stump, because he knows that the angle of delivery plus the break would cause the ball to miss the leg stump if allowed to go through unimpeded.

Don't be quite so free when the off-spinner is going round the wicket. The angle is quite different.

Played correctly the sweep shot can bring many runs. There is seldom more than one deep fieldsman behind square-leg, so that a single ought to be assured and the chance of a four quite good. Moreover, it is a wonderful antidote to those poisonous short-legs.

Next time you see a batsman play the sweep and there are short-leg fieldsmen, watch how the one in danger recoils and ducks out of the way. It makes all the difference to these men's effectiveness.

Tremendous courage is required to hold ground facing a swinging bat. Tony Lock is one of the few men I can remember having seen stand firm and not even flinch against a full-blooded sweep, and often he regarded discretion as the better part of valour. In any case he would have little hope of stopping the ball if it were squarely hit. The top photograph on page 71 shows exactly what I mean.

The Art of Placing the Ball when Batting

It is unwise for a batsman specifically to make up his mind before the ball is bowled where he will hit it. That is, of course, unless there are exceptional circumstances, such as playing for the strike or when wickets are of no moment and only runs count, etc. Nevertheless, batsmen should always have prominently in their minds the thought that they will take advantage of openings in the field if opportunity occurs.

When taking strike a batsman should be able at any time to shut his eyes and visualise, just as though he were looking at a photograph, the exact position of every man on the field. Then and only then can he be mentally conditioned to the art of placing the ball.

Let me give two simple illustrations.

An inviting half-volley comes along just outside the leg stump. It can be easily forced just in front of square-leg or, with just a little more control, swept round to fine-leg. There is a fieldsman at square-leg and none behind. The greater scoring medium would be to sweep it fine. So when he sees that particular ball coming along, the striker instinctively knows the sweep to fine-leg will offer the greatest reward.

Now let us imagine a half-volley pitched on the leg stump. The batsman can safely and easily play it anywhere between the bowler and square-leg, according to his choice.

If mid-on is very straight and there is no man at mid-wicket, then he should go for the wide on drive past the fieldsman's right side.

Conversely, if that man were stationed rather wide and there was a gap between the bowler and mid-on, the sensible thing would be to aim for the gap, i.e. almost a straight drive.

These are clear-cut instances of where the batsman can play whichever shot he likes, and naturally he should select the most profitable one. If it happens also to be the safer one, so much the better.

But the important thing is that he should be on the look-out for the opportunity and not waste time playing the unprofitable stroke.

Any big gaps which invite scoring opportunities, especially those where the boundary is unprotected, should be pinpointed. A positive aggressive mental approach to batting is the only way to score at reasonable speed.

The man who thinks in terms of defence unless he receives a very bad ball is seldom ready to attack a bad one when it does arrive.

I saw a player go in recently and a survey of the off-side field revealed nobody between mid-off and gully. The first ball he received was a full-pitch which went past him 30 cm off the ground and about the same distance outside the off stump. He promptly covered up with his pads, put the bat over his shoulder and allowed it to pass. I was dumbfounded. It was almost impossible for the fellow to have got out from the ball no matter what he did, and almost any sort of a drive must have yielded runs.

It was, you see, purely a mental attitude. He wasn't thinking in terms of anything but defence.

And just because the ball is of good length or on the stumps doesn't mean it can't be attacked. The batsman has room to manoeuvre by the use of his feet. A ball on the middle stump can quite often be safely turned to mid-on, forced back past the bowler or calmly placed towards the covers, where many singles go begging. This applies particularly when the wicket is good and a batsman well set.

Many times various shots can be played off a given ball. Take one short of a length 45 cm outside the off stump. The batsman has the option of playing the shot down the gully, a square cut, a forcing shot into the covers or even a pull shot to mid-wicket. Why not play the one which appears to offer the greatest yield?

If there is a man on the fence at third-man, you know the gully shot will only yield a single. If cover is deep, the square cut and the pull may be the only possible fours. You may not be willing to risk one of them. You may think it safest to play the ball gently into the covers for one. But my point is that you must be ready with the mental picture of the field before the ball is bowled, and be prepared to act.

This is very different from deciding on the shot before you know where the ball will be pitched.

We have all seen chaps thrashing hard drives into the covers for nought when all the time they could have been walking singles with softer shots.

The art of placing the ball is not only skill in stroke play – it is pitting your wits against the other fellow – deliberately at times playing shots to try to draw a fieldsman away from a position that you want opened up.

The really fast scorer over a period is not the wild slogger. The latter will make an extremely fast thirty today and then fail several times. The man who will come out on top is the one who is constantly looking for scoring opportunities – who does not neglect to pick up the singles when nothing better is offering – and who is always waiting to punch the ball through holes in the field which the opposing skipper leaves open.

There is endless scope and variety for the batsman in this art of placing the ball, and nothing demoralises a fielding side as much as the batsman who takes the initiative and refuses to be chained down by the bowler's tactics.

This diagram shows the approximate areas covered by cricket terms. It is included so that readers may more easily understand the various references to different strokes.

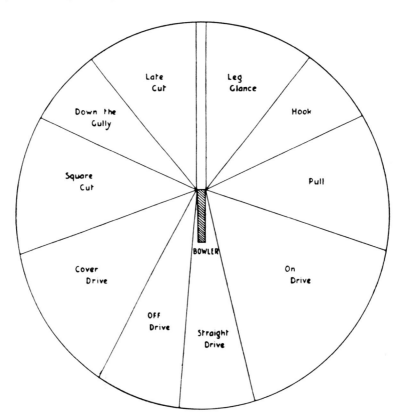

Ways of Getting Out

If one ignores the most recent pitfall whereby a batsman may be given out 'timed out' if he wilfully exceeds the time allowed for him to make his appearance at the crease (I would hate to be the fielding captain who appealed or the umpire who upheld such an appeal), there are nine ways of losing your wicket:

1. Bowled
2. Caught
3. Handled the ball
4. Hit the ball twice
5. Hit wicket
6. LBW
7. Obstructing the field
8. Run out
9. Stumped

In addition it must be stressed that when an injured batsman has a substitute runner, he can be out should his runner infringe nos. 3 or 7 above. The injured batsman himself, as striker, remains subject to the Laws.

During my first-class career, I was dismissed 295 times and it is interesting to record that the dismissals, expressed as percentages, worked out as follows:

Caught	59%
Bowled and hit wicket	27%
LBW	9%
Stumped	4%
Run out	1%

I do not expect that these figures will coincide with those of other players, but they highlight the fact that if a batsman can eliminate hitting the ball in the air his chances of survival are doubled.

I wonder how many players have analysed their faults this way.

It can be extended so that the 59% of catches is broken down into how many were in the slips, at cover, etc.

Statistics can be useful in lots of ways.

Bowling

It is probably true that there is more glamour attached to batting than to bowling, and I believe the majority of people go to cricket hoping to see a scintillating innings by one of their favourites. However, I would like to think they seriously and frequently reflect that there would be no cricket without bowlers, whose physical task is far more severe than that of batsmen.

When I have been watching men like Gregory, Lillee or Lindwall pounding away on a concrete-hard turf in a blazing sun, it has helped me to realise they possessed a tremendous love and enthusiasm for cricket. What else would drive them on to such exertions just for sport?

And there, I think, one might derive the first lesson in bowling. To have any hope of success in the big time, you must start off with perseverance and enthusiasm. And for that matter why should anyone want to play cricket unless he obtains pleasure in so doing and endeavours to provide an enjoyable spectacle for others?

I would hate to discourage any young bowler by regaling him with stories of how much practice he must put in to become great. But it would be equally foolish to mislead him into thinking he can acquire perfection without hard work.

The Grand Old Man of cricket, Dr W. G. Grace, claimed that he worked just as hard learning cricket as he did at his profession. 'Very quickly I found that there was no Royal Road,' he said.

According to those who saw him, C. T. B. Turner was one of Australia's greatest. He had three tours of England in which his figures were sensational by modern standards. They were as follows:

1888 314 wickets for 3,492 runs.
    Average 11.12.

1890 215 wickets for 2,725 runs.
    Average 12.67.
1893 160 wickets for 2,202 runs.
    Average 13.76.

In his own book on cricket Turner explains that he worked for the most famous of Australia's early mail carriers, Cobb and Co. His job necessitated that he rise at 4.30 a.m. to start the mail coaches for the various towns.

After that early work was completed he and a mate went off to practise bowling. For an hour to 90 minutes, four or five mornings a week for nearly three seasons, they did this, aiming at a single stump.

How many bowlers today spend more than half an hour a week at solid practice? Is it any wonder they lack the accuracy which is so essential?

This is the one branch of cricket which demands that the player 'scorn delights and live laborious days'. He must be prepared to toil really hard for long periods. There is no other way to achieve proficiency.

I feel a bowler has something in common with the distance runner who is prepared to sacrifice so much and train so hard in order to achieve his objective.

To do that the player must have a target – in other words he should set his mind on the job of becoming a great bowler because of the innermost joy and satisfaction it brings him.

I think that even professionals, who earn their living at the game and find it a painstaking job, start off by making cricket a career because they love it. After many years, when the game becomes somewhat routine and the flesh gets weary, one can perhaps excuse them if they fail to show the enthusiasm of the amateurs and sometimes give the impression of boredom.

Underneath the surface I am sure they con-

Triumphantly but modestly Jim Laker returns to the pavilion at Manchester, 1956, after having performed the most sensational bowling feat in history. He took 19 wickets for 90 runs in that Test match.

The Rev. David Sheppard (left) and Brian Statham (right) applaud him, with the admiring schoolboys following their idol. (Sport & General Press Agency Ltd)

tinue to love cricket even though it has become hard work, and the more they can maintain their keenness the better for the game and their own success.

Whilst tremendous pleasure can be obtained from batting, bowling and fielding, I feel that the greatest satisfaction any cricketer can have is to achieve a sensational match-winning bowling performance.

I suppose the most wonderful daydream any young bowler could have would be to imagine himself taking ten wickets in each innings to win a Test match for his country. Nobody has done it yet and I don't think it will ever be achieved. But I was there and saw every ball when Jim Laker took 19 wickets (nine in the first

innings and ten in the second) to overwhelm Australia at Manchester in 1956.

As he walked into the pavilion, every person privileged to see such a historic performance rose from his seat and clapped and cheered until Laker almost shyly and blushingly, burst into a trot and ran up the lane between the members to disappear into the sanctity of the dressing-room. Inwardly he must have been feeling the glowing warmth of satisfaction and achievement. In that moment we saw the culminating performance of his or anyone's career.

But who gave a thought to the years and years of painstaking effort and practice which had made it possible?

So young bowlers, set your sights high but with a full knowledge of the hard work which lies ahead. Be like my young godson who, in Australia's batting decline, left the television and announced his intention of playing Australia v England in the yard. An hour later he returned to say England were all out, and when asked who got the wickets, proudly said, 'I did – all ten.' That's the right spirit.

Batsmen may often save matches and sometimes win them, but more often it is the bowlers who are responsible for the victories.

Look at the list of English county champions. Almost without exception the winning side has had a strong attack, mostly backed up by splendid fielding. The same thing usually applies to the winners of Test rubbers.

There should be no illusions in anyone's mind as to the importance of bowlers, even though they may not get their fair share of the praise.

Are they born or made? Both, in the sense that some people are born with the ability to bowl fast or to spin a ball in a certain fashion, assets which scarcely any other living person could acquire no matter how much he tried.

I, for instance, could practise indefinitely but could never bowl as fast as Eddie Gilbert, who was perhaps a stone lighter and of very frail physique.

When Arthur Mailey had passed the age of seventy I saw him bowling wrong-'uns with a flexibility of wrist and disguise of intention better than any man then living. These things are born gifts. But to develop them to the point of Test match competence, the bowler must practise and practise and practise.

Bowling is not just a gift which can be mechanically exploited. Arthur Mailey could have had the finest googly in the world, but without the accuracy and the knowledge of tactics, etc., which enabled him to dismiss batsmen at a reasonable cost, that wonderful gift would never have had any value in the realm of international cricket.

To become a good bowler it is normal and wise for a youngster to determine what type of bowling is likely to suit him best – where his talent shines.

There have been notable exceptions of men who, late in life, altered their styles and subsequently became internationals. Clarrie Grimmett tells us he started bowling fast and I believe Fleetwood-Smith did likewise.

There was the case of Bill Johnston who preferred slow spinners but who deliberately stuck to fast bowling because it was the style best calculated to bring international recognition, having regard to the competition at that time. The selection achieved, he was able, later on, successfully to combine two styles. But such cases are rare.

It would have been stupid for any coach to try to turn Tich Freeman, with his small frame, into a fast bowler, and equally stupid for Bill O'Reilly to forsake his natural aptitude for spin just because his burly physique suggested speed rather than guile.

Usually a young man finds that he has some aptitude for one type or another and once this basic decision on style has been reached the hard work starts.

One of the first things a potential bowler should realise is that for every wicket he obtains, he is sure to send down a goodly number of balls and concede a certain number of runs.

The greatest bowler I ever saw was Bill O'Reilly, yet, in Sheffield Shield matches, he sent down 52 balls for every wicket he obtained and despite some amazing performances, each wicket cost him 17.43 runs. Grimmett's figures

were 55 balls per wicket at a cost of 25.29.

No matter how great he may be, the bowler must still be prepared to work for his success.

Another interesting point is that the wickets will come by various means. There are many ways of dismissing batsmen, but statistics show that over fifty per cent of the wickets which fall are caught.

That is another lesson. No bowler can expect to beat and bowl the batsmen all the time. The unplayable ball that pitches on the leg stump and takes the off bail is rare. Bowlers must learn to utilise their fieldsmen because of this fact that more wickets fall to catches than any other type of dismissal.

And without wishing to detract one whit from the bowler's art, let me also point out that a very large percentage of wickets fall simply because of an error on the part of the batsman and not because he is beaten or deceived by the bowler.

Every bowler can learn by observation. He should remember that the whole pattern of the game of cricket is, in the first instance, set by him. It is the bowler who (or in conjunction with his captain) originally decides where the fieldsmen shall be stationed, and he should endeavour to retain the initiative.

The minute a batsman forces the bowler to adopt a field he doesn't want, or to do something out of character, the bowler should realise he is either being outwitted, has faltered in length or direction, or in some way has allowed one of his best assets, initiative, to pass from his grasp. This interminable battle of wits is fascinating.

Great bowlers must be more than mechanical propellers of a ball. They should study the temperaments of batsmen, because no two men are entirely alike. You will find one who has unlimited patience and doesn't care how long he goes without scoring. Another will get impatient if he is tied down for long. A third won't be able to resist having a crack at an inviting full toss on the leg, and so on.

The bowler who can quickly assess his opponents and vary his methods to achieve the best results has a big lead on his less observant rivals.

This is no modern discovery. Away back in the middle of the nineteenth century that great Nottinghamshire bowler William Clarke had this to say: 'Bowling consists of two parts. There is the mechanical part and the intellectual part. First you want the hand to pitch where you please, and then the head to know where to pitch according to the player.' That is what I call putting it in a nutshell.

Attack should, in the main, be the bowler's creed. It is his prime duty to get the batsman out, and seldom do circumstances arise when that should not be his objective within the shortest possible time.

All bowlers have their own individualistic styles, but it is wise to observe and digest the methods of others. You may see something which can, with advantage, be incorporated into your own.

A thorough attention to detail is right and proper. Moreover it pays. Wickets are hard to get and the neglect of small matters may be costly.

Plan your field. But if the captain has a good reason for a change and insists upon it, obey cheerfully and do your best. He is the master of the ship and loyalty to one's captain is essential.

General Monash it was who said, 'I don't care a damn for your loyalty when you think I am right. The time I want it is when you think I am wrong.' What a wealth of truth is in that statement.

Displays of temperament merely sap your energy and reveal lack of control. If they appear in your opponents, learn to take advantage of them.

Most fast bowlers develop at an early age because they are endowed with great physical energy and strength. Their careers are not usually long.

Slow bowlers, on the other hand, seldom reach their peak until their mental powers, as reflected in experience, guile, etc., match their ability physically to carry out the brain's orders.

One great Australian slow off-spinner, Don Blackie, was first chosen to represent his country at the age of forty-six. Imagine that happening to a fast bowler.

Another thing which helps retard the spinner is that loose deliveries from him are punished more freely than those from fast bowlers, and a greater development of accuracy is required before full use can be made of him. An erratic fast bowler can sometimes get away with it. The erratic slow man very seldom.

There are basic essentials for bowling which I shall outline in detail later on. The two greatest are, of course, length and direction. They are the cornerstone on which most international reputations have been built.

But in the very top strata were the men who also achieved a great measure of success by deception.

One of a bowler's aims should be to deceive the batsman into thinking he is about to receive a certain type of ball, which, in fact, he doesn't.

Variations in pace, flight, spin, swing, etc., are very often the plaything of radio commentators and cricket writers who impute supernatural powers to humans. It is unwise to exaggerate what can be done. But there is undoubtedly a big field in what I term minor variations.

When a batsman is expecting a delivery at a certain speed and, in fact, it comes along faster or slower – when he expects a ball to turn 5 cm and it turns 10 cm – such happenings, if produced without any apparent alteration in the method of delivery, convey an element of surprise. They are the refinements in bowling of the highest class but must be developed only as adjuncts to length and direction. If these two are sacrificed, all is lost.

A Bowling Action

When a bowler has decided whether he wishes to try to become fast, slow, or medium pace, he should at the same time decide upon the most appropriate action for his delivery.

Maybe one should include the grip as part of the action, because it comes into it. However, I will deal with that separately.

The purpose of a bowling action is to enable delivery of the ball from a comfortable, well-

Maurice Tate (above) is just about to bring his right arm over as the weight goes through on to the front foot. For a medium-pace bowler this position is ideal.
(Sport & General Press Agency Ltd)

Top right. Bill Johnston's record entitles him to be considered as one of Australia's greatest left-hand bowlers. You see him here about to deliver a ball at the practice nets.
Johnston was loose-limbed and angular, and his arm had a long and delightfully free swing. He doesn't look as compact as Tate nor did he in fact possess quite the same control. But his pre-delivery position is very good and pacey.

Below, right. This photo was taken in 1955 after Bill Johnston had sustained a knee injury. The comparison between his action in this photo and the one above is quite remarkable. It is the difference between an action of gay abandon and one of caution.

balanced position, whereby the maximum efficiency is obtained from the co-ordination of fingers, wrist, arms, shoulders and body.

The run-up should be of the exact length required for the purpose – not too short and certainly not too long. It should be smooth and regular. There is no point in unnecessarily wasting your energy.

A fast bowler usually aims to achieve his maximum momentum at the point of delivery, though sometimes his run culminates, as in the case of Jack Gregory, in a huge stride or hop. In all cases the run-up is designed to get the body into the best position for delivering the ball, and this involves primarily a body or shoulder position which no description can portray so vividly as the portraits I have used in this book.

My favourite position for medium-pace bowlers is depicted by Maurice Tate on page 82, far left.

What a glorious wound-up position he had, with everything perfectly poised to put punch into the delivery.

The front shoulder must be pointed down the pitch before delivery. If the chest is square on, it retards shoulder swing and reduces 'life'.

Even so, the position of the chest can be varied slightly. Some bowlers think a better out-swinger can be obtained with the shoulders rather more square on to the batsman, and I remember Bill Bowes, who swung the ball very late towards slips, was squarer than the position I advocate.

Ray Lindwall (top right), as he approaches the bowling crease, gathers momentum for his final effort. A fine study in the co-ordination of body and limbs for speed. (P.A. Reuter Photos Ltd)

Below we see Lindwall about to complete his delivery. The left shoulder is held back sufficiently to retain control, but the wide shoulder swing and free right-arm action indicate the mighty effort going into the final burst. (P.A. Reuter Photos Ltd)

Another beautiful delivery position for a fastish left-hand bowler is shown by Bill Johnston, also on page 82, top right.

The position I refer to was during the early years of Johnston's career. In 1953 he sustained a knee injury which prevented him from delivering the ball with his previous freedom.

Underneath you will find another photograph of Johnston delivering the ball. It reveals only too clearly how the knee trouble caused him to alter the angle of his foot at the bowling crease. Obviously he is guarding this physical trouble. It is discernible in his whole action which no longer possesses the punch of earlier years.

For fast bowling I have selected Ray Lindwall as a model. There are two photographs. The first one (page 83, top) reveals the magnificent co-ordination of his whole body and limbs as he gathers momentum for the final delivery at the end of his beautiful rhythmic run-up.

The second one, below it, depicts the delivery stride, and one can almost sense the power and speed in the wide sweeping arc of the shoulder and arm.

The two photographs of Hedley Verity, below on this page, are perfect in showing poise, balance and concentration before delivery followed by a wonderful control position as the ball leaves his hand.

For a leg-spinner, Arthur Mailey had a splendid action, and opposite, on page 85 (top), he is shown coming into the delivery position.

England's great left-hand spin bowler of the 1930s was Hedley Verity. This photo below has captured his splendid pre-delivery position, obviously full of accuracy, concentration and guile.
(Sport & General Press Agency Ltd)

As Hedley Verity delivered the ball he retained his balance beautifully against a firmly braced right leg. One can see how the swing of the shoulders and the pull of his delivery arm across the body have assisted in imparting spin to the ball.
(Sport & General Press Agency Ltd)

One of the world's greatest leg-spinners, Arthur Mailey, just about to go into the final delivery position. He is evidently going to put the right foot some distance behind the crease. Ignoring that, note the lovely poised body position and fine left shoulder. Just before delivery as the right foot touched the ground, the left shoulder went slightly higher and the right arm lower to place him in the ideal position for putting leg spin on the ball. (Sport & General Press Agency Ltd)

The comfortable angle of Mailey's left shoulder is quite a feature.

And for a medium-pacer's follow-through it would be hard to beat the model of Alec Bedser (right) who has used every ounce of his shoulder and body swing to impart zip to the ball.

A quiet study of these action photographs can reveal much to the student.

Whilst text books generally teach that the run-up should be straight, I do not think this is necessarily correct. Alec Bedser always came up slightly from mid-off because he claimed it gave him a better side-on position for the delivery stride. And so it did.

Many famous left-handers have approached the crease from mid-on and bowled round the wicket so that they virtually swung round into position at delivery. Moreover, some tried to create a slight psychological advantage for themselves by emerging from behind the umpire.

All types of right-hand bowlers, in the delivery stride, seem to place the right foot parallel to the bowling crease. The actual delivery of the ball is made against a firmly braced left side, and

The greatest medium-pace bowler I faced was Alec Bedser. Below you see him in a typical after-delivery position.

He has bowled against a firmly braced left leg and side. The right shoulder has gone down and through as the left is swung clear. You can sense the power behind that shoulder.
(Hubert Davey)

A very good illustration of a bowler running on the pitch after delivery. He has bowled the batsman and must be almost a third of the way down the pitch – certainly as far as a good length ball from the other end – and his right foot is in a line between the two sets of stumps.

An umpire would be quite justified in taking action in such a case.
(The West Australian, Perth)

---

in this way the maximum snap is imparted in the forward movement of the shoulders in the delivery stride.

One coach has described the moment of delivery (especially for fast and medium-pace bowlers) as equivalent to the action of cracking a whip. Everyone knows how that is done, with the final movement concentrated on the actual crack. It appeals to me as a happy method of trying to describe 'timing' in letting a cricket ball leave the hand.

After delivering the ball, bowlers should quickly swing away off the pitch so that they do not damage it with their sprigs.

Sometimes a bowler is located who runs straight on after delivery and takes two or three strides on the pitch itself almost in a line with the leg stump. Any such habit should be broken without delay.

The umpire, of course, has the power to prevent a bowler cutting up the pitch, but apart from any such jurisdiction, there is the bad feeling a bowler may cause with the opposition and the possibility of his own teammates being seriously inconvenienced.

Remember, the bowlers of both sides can take advantage of a damaged pitch and there will be no bouquets from the batsmen of your team if you create a nice rough patch for the other side to use.

One who receives admonitions from the umpire for this infringement of the rules is not very popular. In addition, he may cost himself a wicket if he impedes the umpire's view. The bowler's umpire must stay behind the stumps, otherwise he cannot adjudicate on the LBW law, and if he can't see, his answer must be 'No'.

For most bowlers it is good advice to say, 'Keep the arm high.'

I know Clarrie Grimmett had a semi-round-arm, or certainly a low delivery, and he was a great bowler, but I am speaking in general terms.

Especially for the fast or medium-pace types, a high delivery assists lift off the pitch – a most valuable asset. No batsman likes the ball to come up sharply. They are all more at home when the height is comfortable.

One of the first things we say about a bowler who is on the decline is: 'Poor old so-and-so is on the way out – his arm is getting lower every day.' So don't let that delivery get too low.

Whilst on the subject of the height of the arm, it is perhaps worth mentioning that a woman is credited in some quarters with a change in bowling whereby the arm was first raised shoulder high.

John Willes is supposed to be the first man to use this form of bowling, and he in turn learnt it from his sister with whom he frequently practised.

So maybe the ladies have influenced the development of cricket more than we realise.

Spin bowlers normally have a slightly lower arm, depending on the action. There is some justification for believing it makes spin easier and also makes variation of spin and pace a simpler proposition.

Grimmett was notoriously low as will be seen from the photograph on this page.

When bowling fast with a lively run, many bowlers drag with their rear foot as they deliver the ball. A drag of some 30 cm to 45 cm is common.

For some bowlers (and I believe Lindwall was a good example) the drag of the rear foot seems to contribute towards balance and control.

But it seems to be a personal matter because many great fast bowlers did not drag at all, notably Wes Hall of the West Indies and Brian Statham of England.

Some bowlers deliver the ball with the rear foot right off the ground. I never feel that they

Charlie Grimmett, the little Australian leg-spinner, had a low delivery. It was not as low as this photo would suggest because the arm was higher when the ball left the hand. Still, he was lower than most and this may have accounted for the number of wickets he obtained LBW with his top-spinner. (Advertiser Newspapers Ltd)

have quite the same rhythm or follow-through as the draggers.

My former cricket foe, and friend, R. W. V. Robins, tweaked his leg-breaks so hard that he left the ground altogether with both feet, as the photograph overleaf shows.

There is no doubt he spun that ball, but lack of control was an occasional weakness and I am sure this action contributed towards it.

Whilst on the subject of drag I feel impelled

England leg-spinner R. W. V. Robins, spins himself off the ground in delivering one of his leg-breaks.
(Sport & General Press Agency Ltd)

to comment on the no-ball law relating to the bowler's feet.

During my playing days the law demanded that the bowler must have his back foot behind the bowling crease when delivering the ball. When a big dragger came along the umpires would make him put his foot down an appropriate distance behind the bowling crease to counteract this drag.

However, some people felt that the dragger was gaining an unfair advantage (though it could only happen with a weak umpire) and it was eventually decided to make the batting crease the line of demarcation for the front foot and ignore the bowling crease.

Regrettably, in my opinion, what is now known as the 'front-foot no-ball rule' became law. To adjudicate on the front foot certainly prevents any bowler from taking advantage of drag but whereas there were only a handful of such offenders, a great number of bowlers are hampered by the front-foot rule.

I fought bitterly (but unsuccessfully) against its introduction and all the ills forecast (should it be introduced) are obvious.

No bowler can watch where his front foot is going to land. He barely has time in the case of the back foot but at least he can make a calculated and pretty accurate judgment.

Match after match in modern cricket we see dozens of no-balls being called, most of them because of the most minute transgression.

The call is inevitably so late that it is a rarity for a batsman to have time for a free swing. This latter was always an exciting moment for spectators with the old back-foot law, now sadly confined to the dustbin. Cricket can ill afford the loss of any publicly attractive features.

Bowlers don't mind being no-balled when they are not penalised but the game sometimes becomes a bit of a mockery. When watching a cautious opening to an innings not long ago, with the total about 20, no-balls exceeded runs off the bat and 50 no-balls in a game is now quite common.

The problem of umpires watching the front foot and then looking up in time to make crucial LBW or 'caught behind' decisions cannot be solved, and privately, umpires admit it is a cause of some mistakes.

I can only conclude that lack of understanding and pig-headedness combine to allow this stupid law to exist.

Amongst experienced players and ex-players I am sure there is a vast majority who would prefer to revert to the back-foot law, and an overwhelming majority of spectators.

Rule changes of this nature take a long while to be evaluated and it could well be that the final answer is still some years ahead.

Every bowler should be able to analyse his own type of attack and devise a basic field which he thinks will suit it.

Obviously it can only be a starting point. The same field, for example, cannot be used for a right- and a left-hand batsman, a firm pitch and a sticky, and so on.

But there must be a plan, which can be altered as the need arises.

This is a phase of the game which normally

becomes a matter of discussion and co-operation between the bowler and the captain, but the bowler must have an original pattern even if the captain alters it. After all, the bowler is the man who knows what he is trying to do.

The captain is responsible for seeing that key fieldsmen are in the right place, but I would not say he is exclusively responsible. If a captain were stupid enough to place Tony Lock at mid-off instead of at leg-slip to Jim Laker bowling on a sticky wicket, then at least the bowler should call his captain's attention to this fact. It is vital to have the best catchers where they are likely to be fed, and so I say to bowlers, 'Don't waste your best fieldsmen where there is no work to do.'

And if a fieldsman does a fine piece of work it is good policy for the bowler, not necessarily immediately, but at the right time and place, to pass on a word of praise. Seldom does it pay to scold a fieldsman and that should only be done for carelessness, neglect and suchlike. In any event, it is the captain's prerogative. When a fieldsman misses an absolute sitter of a catch and you know he tried hard, no good purpose will be served by showing your feelings.

I remember an incident which happened early in my career. We were playing a Test match and in the opposing team was a very good and volatile fieldsman. His captain, who happened to be the bowler, put him in a certain place and said that he proposed to bowl a short one, the third ball he had at me in the over. He hoped I would conveniently pull a catch to this fieldsman. Of course, I knew nothing of the plan until later.

The ball came along and I obliged by smacking it right to him. Not only did he miss the catch but the ball went through his hands to the fence.

At the end of the over, the contrite fieldsman walked over to the bowler and dejectedly said, 'I just can't tell you how sorry I am about that catch.' He was greeted with an off-hand wave of the arms and a reply, 'Oh, don't worry about it, old boy. You've probably cost us The Ashes but don't let that bother you.'

Now I can understand the feelings of both

men, but I hardly think the fieldsman was given any confidence to do better next time by such a remark. In fact, it was he who told me about it years later. How much better to have said, 'Yes, it was rotten luck – the ball was travelling faster than you expected. Don't worry, we all drop them.'

Cricketers are human beings and, believe me, the man who drops a catch feels it worse than anyone else on the ground. I know only too well because I have dropped plenty.

It is axiomatic that every bowler should bowl to his field. 'You can't set a field for bad bowling' is an old saying and a true one. Even so, there can be bad bowling of different types.

Clarrie Grimmett was a great model to watch. His normal field was set for balls pitched on the stumps or on the off side. Only one man was used protectively on the leg side to take care of a ball pitched outside the leg stump. Seldom did it come along. If he made a mistake at all, Clarrie might bowl one a little wider to the off, where he had several fieldsmen, but when he erred on the leg side it was a surprise.

And, of course, he wanted batsmen to take the risk of trying to turn a ball off the stumps. The opening on the leg side was inviting. The number of LBWs in his bag contained quite a percentage of batsmen who tired of waiting for the loose one and took a chance.

When an innings starts or when a wicket falls, and a new batsman comes in, is a good time for the bowler to make a special effort. No matter how calm the player or how much he may say, 'Nerves don't bother me,' I have never met one who was not pleased to break his duck. There is very little numerical difference between '1' and '0' but psychologically the gap is huge.

Many a batsman has become jittery because he failed to score a single within a reasonable time, and has paid the penalty of a rash stroke to try to get off the mark or even of trying for a risky run. So peg a new batsman down and really put in a little bit extra to him.

Bowlers can learn a great deal by studying the type of scoring shots employed by batsmen. Especially is this so in a Test series where you

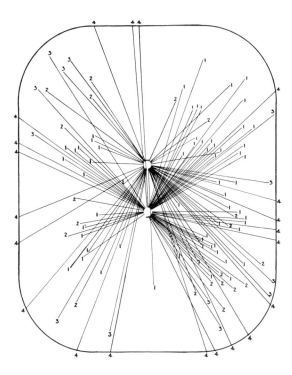

Typical scoring chart prepared by some scorers. They can be most helpful to bowlers and captains.

are likely to meet the same batsmen many times.

Bill Ferguson, doyen of all scorers, always produced a chart showing the scoring strokes played. It indicated the direction and the value of each one.

My first Test was against England at Brisbane. Sutcliffe and Hobbs opened, and before we went out Jack Gregory told me of a plan to get Sutcliffe caught on the leg boundary. He proposed to bowl a bumper at a given stage and he felt sure Sutcliffe would hook it in the air because, Gregory said, Sutcliffe always hooked in the air. Ponsford was given the job of policing the leg boundary.

Everything went beautifully except that Ponsford dropped the catch. But my point is that Gregory knew Sutcliffe's weakness and though the plan failed it was a plan and it was correct.

Of course, once the trap is sprung in one innings it will seldom work again quickly. The batsman uses his wits, too. Hence the necessity to try to ensure it does not misfire the first time.

Part of a bowler's responsibility is to help his partner. It not infrequently happens that two batsmen are together at a stage when one of them doesn't mind playing bowler 'A' but is rather a rabbit for bowler 'B'. Obviously then it is the job of bowler 'A' to see to it, if he can, that towards the end of his over he does not let 'B's' rabbit get to the wrong end.

One frequently sees that sort of thing when a great batsman, having been at the wicket for a long time and made a big score, is joined by a tail-ender. The fieldsmen make a special effort to stop the good player getting a single at the end of each over. But I doubt whether it is done often enough in the middle of an innings.

There are plenty of really good batsmen who don't particularly like batting against a certain bowler. I sometimes think this played quite a part in the success of great bowling combinations.

If it didn't in the way I have just mentioned, it was certainly true that one great bowler often made another one better.

Irrespective of the type of bowler you are, the same fundamentals of length and direction apply.

Length

This receives my vote for the no. 1 essential of bowling. But what is meant by length?

I suppose scientifically one would say it is the distance the ball travels after leaving the bowler's hand before hitting the turf. But in cricket parlance that is not really the picture.

A full-toss is a bad-length ball to any batsman. So is a long-hop. But then a long-hop to Jones might be a good length to Smith on account of their different physique. And a long-hop anyway is often an intentional bumper and a dangerous ball.

I prefer to think in terms of a 'good-length ball' and to define it thus – 'The type of delivery which has the striker in two minds as to whether he should play forward or back.' Pycroft described it as the ball which 'puzzles the judgment'.

As I said, it may vary according to the batsman. Likewise it will vary according to the bowler.

A fast bowler like Lindwall would need to pitch shorter than a slow bowler like Grimmett, and being faster he would have a greater margin for error.

Spin and swerve are equally useless unless harnessed to a good length. Any novice batsman can play a full toss no matter how much spin it carries. The only latitude I will give is to say that an over-pitched ball is less of a sin than a short-pitched one, especially when the ball is new and swinging or when the pitch is taking spin.

Whilst nobody can define a good-length ball in terms of metres and centimetres, an approximation can be ascertained in actual play. The young bowler can experiment at the nets by fixing a spot in his eye and then getting into the habit of bowling thereabouts.

As bowlers mature, the one who quickly assesses the right length for each batsman and bowls accordingly is the one who steals a march on his rivals.

A continuance of good-length bowling will often test a batsman's patience until he attempts a rash stroke.

On rain-affected pitches, the first commandment is, 'Thou shalt not be short'.

There is a great story of Wilfred Rhodes bowling on such a pitch against Australia. He was cut for four. Rhodes turned to the umpire and said of the batsman, 'He won't cut me again today.' And, so the story goes, he didn't.

And when I say a 'rain-affected pitch' I mean one where rain has penetrated the surface and the ball will bite. When a pitch is merely greasy after a shower of rain it often pays to drop the ball a fraction shorter. The ball tends to skid faster off a greasy surface than a dry one and will sometimes lift as well, so that catches in the slips or behind the stumps become more likely.

A cricket ball usually travels some 18 metres between delivery and contact with the bat. At

100 kilometres per hour that takes less than 7/10ths of a second. If by causing momentary indecision the bowler can reduce that time to even 6/10ths of a second, what a difference it must make in the batsman's ability to complete a shot successfully.

Some batsmen play forward all the time. Obviously to them the bowler would be well advised to drop the ball shorter, and to the deflector who plays back the reverse would apply.

How often does one hear an enthusiast say, 'Jones is so accurate he could drop the ball on a one-cent piece.' I have even read of an old-timer that 'he wore a hole in the pitch with his accuracy'. Don't you believe it. Try any bowler out with a sheet of newspaper and you'll be astonished how often he misses it. The one-cent piece story sounds fine but I'm afraid few bowlers can even approach it.

I finish my advice on length to the bowler: 'Keep the batsman in a mood of indecision if you can.'

Direction

Second only to length comes direction.

There is often a misconception about the meaning of direction. I have frequently heard it said, for example, 'Smith's direction is faulty. He is off the stumps too much.' From such a remark one would assume that direction meant bowling at the stumps.

With eight fieldsmen on the off side, a bowler should be torn to shreds by any good batsman if he continued to bowl at the stumps.

I cannot emphasise too much the necessity of combining length and direction. The former without good direction may have some virtue, but direction without length is hopeless.

Many bowlers aim to hit a spot on the pitch thereby combining the two qualities, but only incessant practice can bring about that control of both together which is vital to the top-flight bowler.

A bowler's ability to judge his length and direction is often impeded by the batsman's footwork. For this reason it is not uncommon to find a bowler who prefers to put in a proportion of his net practice with a wicket-keeper but no batsman. To some extent I think it aids the development of his judgment and enables him to see (especially when bowling breaks) both the exact direction and the behaviour of the ball after it leaves the pitch.

I would go further and say that all fast bowlers should indulge in serious net practice when there is no batsman. It allows them to go flat out without the fear of hitting a friend and colleague and with swing bowling it is of distinct value.

Few batsmen like to face fast bowlers in the nets anyway. They feel hemmed in and there is a tendency to back away, which in turn influences a teammate to ease up.

So for direction it should be – accuracy in any desired direction.

Bowling on a Sticky Wicket

When the pitch has become saturated by rain it may play easily because the ball comes off slowly (the type of pitch we call a pudding), or it may become extremely difficult.

The latter stage usually comes when the pitch is drying out, especially if there is a hot sun on it.

Easy or difficult, there are one or two 'musts'. One is to make the batsman play at every ball. Don't waste one. Another is to pitch the ball a little farther up than usual. It is a crime to drop the ball short on a wet wicket. Drag the batsman forward if you can without quite letting him smother the pitch of the ball.

And whatever you do, don't alter your normal delivery so that you lose accuracy.

Final Words

Bowling is a very strenuous business and calls into play muscles that otherwise don't seem to exist. That even happens when bowlers appeal or express their feelings by physical action.

If you doubt me have a look on the next page at the photographs of:

a] Tony Lock (below) offering up a prayer of thanksgiving for a wicket; and

b] John Drennan appealing for a catch.

Ask either of them to get into those positions in a gymnasium and they might find it hard.

The point is that these movements are made in the excitement of the moment.

A top-grade footballer can end the season in perfect physical condition. Let him go out and have half an hour's bowling at a lively pace and I'm prepared to wager he will be stiff next day or the one after.

It is wise to go quietly at early season practices. And it is good insurance, especially in England where the wind is deceptively cold, to guard against a chill in the back. Bowlers with bad backs get nowhere.

Those early practices are among the best to find out the value of body swing – of the virtue of coming into the delivery position with the body side on – left arm well forward. It enables a free, easy shoulder twist as the body swings round.

If the chest is square on, there is strain on the right shoulder and less chance of getting life off the pitch.

Look again at the illustration showing that glorious delivery position of Maurice Tate (p. 82).

There are times when a bowler must mark time or go on the defensive, but I preach offensive tactics whenever I can. I think it valuable for a bowler to take the initiative and try to hold it both for his own sake and the sake of the game.

Don't be misled by fancy stories of magic formulae. There is no secret that I know of to achieve 'pace off the pitch'. Tate had it because he had magnificent shoulders and wrists, and he co-ordinated everything to give the ball real punch at delivery. It was power and timing.

A great and very cunning bowler was once watching a youngster make heavy weather of things and he put years of wisdom into his wry comment, 'There is such a thing as observation.'

Watch and learn from others. Don't be afraid of trial and error. But there is no substitute for hard work and practice if you want to be successful. And just because you are a bowler, don't think there is no need for you to make runs. It is such an asset when the team can bat down to no. 11.

This was never better exemplified than when the South Africans visited Australia in 1952/53.

In the last two Test matches, in which they lost 30 wickets, only two men were dismissed under double figures. In the last of those two matches, not one man.

Australia lost 33 wickets in the same two Tests, ten of them under double figures.

Those extra runs at the finish can do so much to help a team to victory.

Tony Lock (below), noted for his volatile expressions on the field, almost turns himself inside out with joy as he sees first slip hold the catch to add another scalp to his belt. (Central Press Photos Ltd)

John Drennan, South Australian fast bowler, jubilantly does an Indian war dance as he appeals for caught behind against Ian Craig. The batsman doesn't wait for the verdict. (The News, Adelaide)

The Yorker

A true yorker is the ball which pitches in the block hole right at the bottom of the blade.

Many a batsman has made a ball into a yorker by leaving his crease and hitting over the top of it, or by going back and doing the same, but from the bowler's point of view that was an accident, and purely an error of judgment on the batsman's part.

A yorker is never easy to play. There is a natural tendency to hit over the top of it.

All fast or medium-pace bowlers should try one now and then. Lindwall developed it until he was able to regard it as one of his most potent deliveries.

All yorkers should be aimed directly at the middle stump. They are little use if pitched off the stumps because one cannot hit a catch off a yorker.

Perhaps the hardest of all is the swinging yorker, but it takes extreme skill and accuracy to control the ball so that it will finish up landing on the popping crease and also hit the stumps after swinging in the air.

Learn to bowl the yorker if you can but be prepared to get hit for some fours off the over-pitched balls in the process.

YORKER
This is the term applied to a ball which pitches on the ground exactly at the bottom of the bat.

LONG-HOP
Example of a short-pitched ball or long-hop. This gives the batsman ample time to see any break which spin may impart to the ball, and it minimises any chance of the ball beating the batsman by either break or swing. The batsman is given plenty of time to control his shot.

FULL-TOSS
The full-toss lands on the bat without first touching the pitch.

HALF-VOLLEY
The half-volley is pitched in such a position that it will strike the bat immediately after it begins its bounce. Normally this is too far up, but if the ball is swinging, especially late, it is far better than the long-hop.

GOOD LENGTH
The good-length ball is the one which does not allow the batsman to play either forward or back with any certainty.

Fast Bowling

To be a really good fast bowler one needs strong physique and stamina. The very big heavily muscled man is usually too tight and slow in his movements and the successful man is the one who is supple as well as strong.

I am sure it helps for a fast bowler to appear hostile in his run-up and delivery. A meek and mild approach to the stumps can't possibly engender the same apprehension in the mind of the batsman as the tear-away run-up and fearsome hop of a Jack Gregory.

Batsmen are human. They tend to react adversely to the attacker, and that is what a fast bowler should be.

His role is not that of the patient plodder but rather to batter down the defences quickly.

The series of pictures of Frank Tyson shown above illustrate, better than any words can, the ideal way for a fast bowler to fling himself into the task.

The bowler's run-up should be sufficiently long for him to work up his top pace, Eddie Gilbert's brief shuffle notwithstanding.

Keith Miller was a grand example of a man who could achieve full speed with an economical run of about ten steps. Many others ran 20 metres or so and felt they lost rhythm if there was any reduction, but I remain convinced many of them would have been just

As Frank Tyson commenced his long run (left), one could see the determination and the intention to work up to a crescendo of power.

As the ball was about to be delivered, tremendous shoulder width had been obtained, so that a full free swing was given to the arm. It would be well nigh impossible to imagine a more perfect position to obtain the maximum use of one's physical capacity.

When Tyson let the ball go (right), the very last drop of energy had been expended and his momentum carried the bowler into a position which is enough to scare the life out of a weak-kneed batsman. This must be one of the most astonishing photos ever taken. (Daily Mirror)

---

as effective with a run many metres shorter.

Frank Tyson, when he first came to Australia, had a tremendous run, longer than the pitch itself, but was wisely persuaded to cut it down and he immediately obtained better results. He had more energy left to bowl the ball. It was not all expended in running.

Amongst modern bowlers I believe Geoff Lawson would be a better bowler if he reduced his run-up by a few metres.

Don't forget every five metres extra in the run-up means another five metres extra in walking back to the starting point.

Gubby Allen had a smooth run-up and delivery and a fine shoulder action. This study (above) shows his splendid pre-delivery position. It was taken in Australia in 1932. The umpire is George Hele – one of the best Australia ever produced.

When the ball is new, the stumps should always be the target. Even if they are, there will still be plenty of balls which miss on either side and for which the field can be appropriately placed. And if one's length is faulty, over-pitch rather than under-pitch that new ball. It will have more opportunity for swing, and any snicks behind the wicket will be more likely to carry to the fieldsmen.

Gubby Allen was one who believed in giving the new ball plenty of air and he did so.

One of a fast bowler's weapons is the 'bumper'. In simple terms it means delivering the ball short enough to bounce chest, shoulder or head high, causing the batsman to make a difficult and often hasty defensive shot.

The ideal bumper is the one which will rise without being pitched too short. Anybody can make the ball bounce by pitching it, say, a third of the way up the wicket, but that sort of delivery is seldom dangerous. It gives the batsman ample time to see what is happening and quietly move out of harm's way.

Here we have the great value of height to a bowler. Obviously a man of 190 cm would bring the ball down from a sharper angle than a man of 165 cm and thereby gain more lift from the same length ball.

The bumper should normally be bowled at full speed, to give the striker as little time as

I doubt if any batsman ever faced a more fearsome sight than Wes Hall at full stretch. How would you like to see this figure (below) some 20 metres away coming towards you like an express train.

Note the chain and cross which he invariably wore around his neck. (Melbourne Herald Sun)

possible, and it should always be bowled directly over the stumps. Without any doubt that is the hardest one to negotiate. It is very difficult to stand in front of a ball coming, say, shoulder high, and play it down safely.

To a bouncer on the leg side or outside the off stump no stroke need be offered, but when it pitches on the stumps the striker must wait and watch the rise before deciding on his shot. Moreover, he is often undecided whether to get inside or outside the line of flight, and thus you get the bogy of indecision worrying him.

Bill Voce, playing against me in Sydney one day, pitched a ball on my stumps a third of the way up the wicket. I walked outside the off stump and turned my back on the ball, expecting it to sail harmlessly over the top, but I reckoned without the vagaries of turf. It hit the middle stump half-way up and a much sadder and wiser batsman retreated to the pavilion. Hence my dictum that a ball pitched on the stumps must be watched, no matter how short it may be.

Prior to 1932 the bumper was regarded as part and parcel of the game, and there were many players who hooked it supremely well – Sutcliffe, Victor Richardson and McCabe were three men who come readily to mind. Then came bodyline.

In this instructional work I do not wish to comment on bodyline other than to say it caused such bad feeling between counties and between countries that the ruling authorities saw fit to legislate against it.

Today the legitimate bumper is still permitted but its abuse is prevented by the instructions

Sometimes we hear about a fast bowler hurling himself at the batsman. This photo of G. O. Allen, taken just after he has delivered the ball, shows him in the act of hurling himself forward in a most remarkable and interesting fashion. It illustrates the force he has put behind the ball.

And incidentally what a glorious position the batsman is in. Stanley McCabe – one of the greatest.
(The Sydney Morning Herald)

---

to umpires under Law 42 which deals with unfair play.

Section 8 of that law says:

'The bowling of fast short-pitched balls is unfair if, in the opinion of the umpire at the bowler's end, it constitutes an attempt to intimidate the striker. Umpires shall consider intimidation to be the deliberate bowling of fast short-pitched balls which by their length, height and direction are intended or likely to inflict physical injury on the striker. The relative skill of the striker shall also be taken into consideration.'

Then follows the procedure the umpire shall take if he considers the bowling is unfair, including the penalties.

It is clear from the foregoing that bumpers are not prohibited. Nobody wants to turn the fast bowler into a namby pamby who is afraid to show life and spirit – who shrinks from a challenge. But the bowler can no longer use a planned intimidatory attack with all its consequences.

Following the bodyline season of 1932/33 various legislative attempts have been made to curb the excessive use of bouncers. The odium attached to this form of bowling caused some fast bowlers to be diffident about using the bumper legitimately for fear of incurring the umpire's sanction. At the same time fewer batsmen displayed any real ability to hook.

Instead of batsmen welcoming an occasional bouncer as a scoring medium, or at least a reasonable challenge (which I'm sure they did in the 1920s) the emphasis shifted to one of passive or negative defence.

A pity, I think, for the hook is a dynamic shot and necessary to the complete batsman. Moreover, a few well judged hooks deter the bowler from using such tactics quicker than anything.

This diffidence about fast bowlers using bumpers as an offensive weapon did not last long and in more recent years one or two have even boasted about their intentions in this regard. I have seen many matches in which, in my opinion, the umpires were far too lenient in their jurisdiction.

Perhaps the attitude of the bowlers has been encouraged because so many of the batsmen of the 1970s either couldn't hook or, if they did essay the shot, came up under the ball, due, probably, to their indoctrination into the defensive pendulum method of stroke production which severely limits the range of shots. Although I think the occasional bouncer should be a legitimate ball for the fast bowler to use, I totally support the attempt to keep it under control.

Even though helmets have lessened the physical danger to batsmen there should be a clear distinction between bowling skill on the one hand and intimidation on the other.

Fast bowling makes such demands upon the physical resources that it behoves the bowler to keep himself in splendid condition. Special consideration should be given to legs, back muscles and stomach muscles.

Perhaps of all places the most likely spot for a nasty muscle strain is in the groin. It has happened to many bowlers I've known. Overstretching at the crease or in the field is a danger. Such an injury can keep a bowler out for weeks or even become chronic. Tim Wall attributed regular exercises to strengthen his groin muscles as the reason why he was free from such injury in the closing stages of his career.

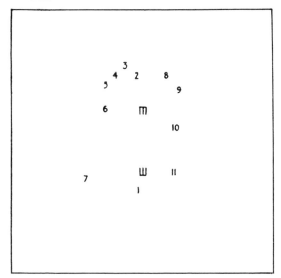

1. *Bowler*   2. *Wkt*   3. *1st slip*   4. *2nd slip*
5. *3rd slip*   6. *Short gully*   7. *Cover*
8. *1st leg slip*   9. *2nd leg slip*   10. *Short-leg*
11. *Mid-on.*

An attacking field for a fast bowler when the ball is new and the batsman is on the defensive. It contains no outfield and could not normally be maintained for long because it would provide too many scoring opportunities.

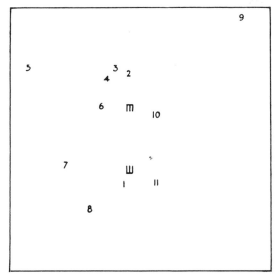

1. *Bowler*   2. *Wkt*   3. *1st slip*
4. *2nd slip*   5. *Deep third-man*
6. *Backward point or short gully*
7. *Cover*   8. *Mid-off*   9. *Deep fine-leg*
10. *Forward short-leg*   11. *Mid-on.*

This is a normal field on a firm pitch for a fast bowler with an old ball. Variations can be made in many ways, such as moving no. 10 deeper or behind square-leg or moving no. 6 round towards cover and so on. But the field shown is a sound beginning.

In modern cricket there is a tendency to bowl fast bowlers for long spells. Very often it is done for 'tactical' reasons. A fast bowler usually takes a long time to bowl an over and therefore is used to waste time. Obviously less runs are likely to come in a given time if fewer balls are bowled.

I deplore the tendency in the interests of cricket but more particularly of the bowler himself. Fast bowlers are at their best and most exciting when able to fling themselves into a burst of three or four overs, secure in the knowledge that a rest is around the corner.

And as a young fractious colt is tamed by overwork, so will the fire and temper of a fast bowler be blunted if he has to take on the hack work.

A good fast bowler needs the heart of a lion, but racehorse not draught-horse variety.

Just as the bumper is one of his best assets, so is a yorker, but the latter demands great accuracy or it may become expensive. Every yorker should be aimed dead on the middle stump.

Naturally a fast bowler endeavours to swing the ball, and if he can do so the batsmen have less time to counter than they have against the slower types. Without swing, the bowler hopes for a hurried shot which edges a catch to wicket-keeper or slips. The fieldsmen behind the stumps are looked upon as the potential wicket takers – the ones in front more as run savers.

No team is complete without a fast bowler to open with the new ball, and if there is any worthwhile breeze he should bowl with it to help his speed.

Field placing suggestions will be found on the previous page.

Medium-Pace Bowling

These medium-paced chaps really provide the backbone of most bowling sides. The title, of course, covers a variety of bowlers from fast-medium to slow-medium, left- and right-handers.

Periods have occurred in history when no medium-pace men were included in a Test side. England at The Oval in 1956 had Tyson and Statham (fast), Lock and Laker (spinners). Such a wealth of talent at one time is seldom available to gladden the selectors' hearts.

But it does not necessarily mean that it is always an advantage to have two very fast bowlers to open the attack.

I know all about the great bowling combinations of history. I saw Gregory and McDonald, Larwood and Voce, Miller and Lindwall and so on, but don't forget that one man must always bowl into whatever wind may be blowing.

In the combinations mentioned, McDonald,

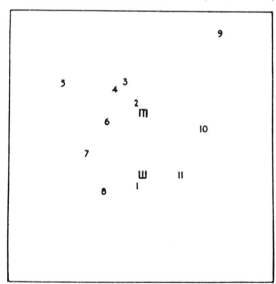

1. Bowler 2. Wkt 3. 1st slip 4. 2nd slip
5. Third man 6. Point 7. Cover
8. Mid-off 9. Deep fine-leg
10. Square-leg 11. Mid-on.

A strictly orthodox field for a medium-pace bowler with an old ball.

Voce and Miller took on this arduous task. Each was of superlative physique. Each had remarkable ability to swing the ball. Each would have been a wonderful bowler on his own with the wind. In other words the superb skill of these individuals enabled them to triumph over the circumstances.

Ted McDonald with the wind and Maurice Tate into it would have satisfied me beyond doubt as an opening pair.

We know what has happened in the past but it does not stop us theorising about what might have happened.

Medium-pacers must so often be prepared to

<hr />

A delightfully pleasant photo of Maurice Tate revealing the happy-go-lucky nature and charming personality of one of the greatest medium-pace bowlers of all time.

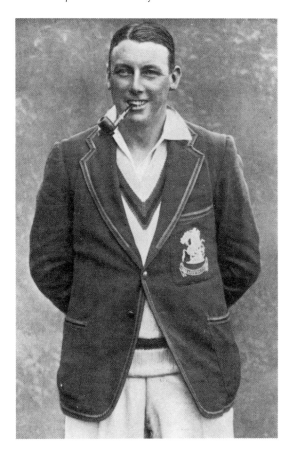

bowl with the wind or against it. They must be willing to take the new ball or be denied it. They must be prepared to attack or hold the fort as directed.

Accuracy should be their watchword above everything else. Certainly they may attempt swing, perhaps a measure of off-spin, a cutter, change of pace, etc., but at no time must it be at the expense of accuracy.

Even if a wet wicket comes along, the kind he has dreamt about, he must sometimes be content silently to watch the ball being handed to a fast bowler one end and a spinner the other.

I take off my hat to the courage and determination of the medium-pacer, the Maurice Tate or Alec Bedser type, whose stout hearts were only matched by their long-suffering bodies.

Off-Spin Bowling

Cricket history is studded with the names of great off-spin bowlers. One of the greatest was C. T. B. Turner, who played for Australia away back in 1888. His figures were remarkable. Touring England with Australian teams he took 689 wickets at an average of 12.2 and his 101 Test match wickets at 16.53 apiece are still the cheapest obtained by any bowler who took 100 wickets or more in Tests between England and Australia.

Those who know how good Grimmett was may reflect that his English Test wickets cost 32.4 each.

There was off-spinner Hughie Trumble who, in Test matches for Australia against England, took 141 wickets at an average of 20.8. Later, as genial host and Secretary of the Melbourne Cricket Club, he became a very widely known and much-loved character. His Mexican-type sombrero was never in danger of being stolen by mistake.

It is interesting to point out that of eight Australian bowlers who have taken 100 wickets in Test matches against England three were right-hand off-spinners, Trumble, Turner and Noble. Moreover, until the advent of Lindwall and later Dennis Lillee, they were the three most economical bowlers to be included in the list.

George Giffen also took over 100 wickets, and some say he bowled a proportion of off-spinners but I prefer to leave him more in the medium-pace category.

Coming to later periods we find Jim Laker, whose performances in the 1956 Test series against Australia dwarfed anything previously achieved by any type of bowler in Anglo-Australian Tests. In the whole five matches his figures were:

Overs	Maidens	Wickets	Runs	Average
283.5	127	46	442	9.6

In four of those Tests he was assisted by either a dry crumbling pitch or one taking spin after rain, and in those four games his figures were:

Overs	Maidens	Wickets	Runs	Average
247	114	43	378	8.7

One must be historically fair in commenting on the state of the pitches, but don't let me detract from the merit of his bowling. Those figures would be sensational on a metalled road.

There are two fundamental spins which mainly concern a bowler, off-spin and leg-spin. The former enjoys the great advantage that it can be bowled more accurately than any other type of spin. In fact, I think an off-spinner, providing he did not try for too much spin or variation, could bowl more accurately perhaps than even a medium-pacer.

Off-spin comes easily and utilises so perfectly the natural swing of the arm and positioning of the body. This partially explains the achievements of men like Rhodes and Verity, for they were really left-hand off-spinners.

Where pitches will take spin, or where they vary so much in character from day to day, the off-spinner cannot very well fail to achieve a reasonable degree of success. This, coupled with the economy, is why the type is so prevalent

Grip for the off-break as seen by the batsman just before the ball leaves the hand.

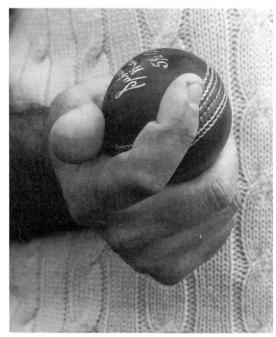

Orthodox grip for the off-spinner taken from a different angle.

and is given so much encouragement in England. Nearly every county has one, mostly a
good one at that.

There is no doubt the off-side LBW rule has
encouraged and assisted off-spinners. It was
partially designed to do so. And anyway, why
should a batsman be able safely to negotiate a
ball pitched outside his off stump by merely
putting his bat over his shoulder and covering
the stumps with his pads?

No one will ever convince me that this sort of
negative play is good for the game. Nor do I
believe it was in the minds of the game's in-
ventors.

The main leverage to obtain off-spin comes
from the index finger which, in delivering the
ball, is turned outwards and downwards by a co-
ordinated turn of the fingers and wrist. The ball
is spun from left to right, and the action of the
hand is very similar to that used in turning a
door knob. The second finger assists the first
finger in producing spin but does not actively
contribute much towards it, whilst the third and
fourth fingers really become a shelf for the ball
to sit on. The thumb acts as a balancing agent
and its position will vary according to the size
and flexibility of the bowler's hand.

Whilst obviously the fingers and the wrist are
the main instruments of transmitting life to the
ball, body movement and shoulder swing also
play a big part. It is essential to get that left
shoulder pointing down the wicket or even to
fine-leg in the delivery action. This will considerably assist the final swivel action into
delivery position.

Most people can bowl off-spinners but not
with a great deal of spin. Long, powerful, flexible fingers are desirable here, probably more
than for any other type of ball.

Some young and enthusiastic fellows who
had energy to burn started their careers by
bowling fast or medium pace. As the fires
slackened, they were able to turn to off-spin
with great success.

A notable case was the Gloucestershire
bowler Tom Goddard, whose career is a most
remarkable example of what can happen when
someone intelligently applies himself to a task.

*Jim Laker is shown just after the ball leaves
his hand, on the day he took all ten
Australian wickets for Surrey at The Oval,
1956.
(Sport & General Press Agency Ltd)*

Goddard was a fast bowler in his youth and
gained his place in the county side. He was tall
and a big strong type who seemed likely to
develop.

However, his effectiveness with this class
of bowling fell away and in 1927, with those
deliveries, he took a mere 24 wickets for
Gloucestershire and they cost 55.9 runs each.

The following season Goddard did not play
for his county. Instead he went to Lord's, where
he set about learning to use his tremendous
hands and long fingers in the art of bowling off-
breaks.

Jim Laker had an ideal run and delivery for the off-break. His action is pictured here. (Le-Roye Productions Ltd)

The following year he went back to Gloucester, and from then on he reeled off a succession of wonderful performances in English first-class cricket.

His figures are so astonishing, and could be such an inspiration to others, that I quote them below:

Season	Wickets	Average
1929	184	16.3
1930	144	19.5
1931	141	18.6
1932	170	19.1
1933	183	17.4
1934	126	24.0
1935	200	20.3
1936	153	20.3
1937	248	16.7
1938	114	23.0
1939	200	14.8

Then came the break from first-class cricket during World War II, but immediately afterwards Goddard confirmed his place as one of England's greatest bowlers and continued to hold it for five more years. Here are his figures:

Season	Wickets	Average
1946	177	17.4
1947	238	17.3
1948	125	21.4
1949	160	19.1
1950	137	19.9

That was virtually the end, for this great cricketer was born in 1900 and could scarcely be expected to go on after reaching fifty years of age. His skill brought him the honour of representing England in Test matches, as an off-spinner.

Just because a fast bowling career may be short does not mean there is no other pathway to fame in cricket. Off-breaks are less exacting to bowl in the physical sense and, therefore, this type of bowler has a better chance of staying in the game until he reaches, for cricketers, an advanced age.

It is far easier to throw an off-break than to bowl it. The bent elbow assists the rhythm. That is why the actions of quite a few off-spinners have been suspect.

It is also the reason why a young boy can get the feel of delivering an off-break by first learning to throw a tennis ball against a wall. The position of the hand and fingers, the snap of the wrist – they can be co-ordinated so beautifully in throwing.

An off-break can be delivered with the hand very high and the arm coming straight over. Variation can be procured by delivering from a slightly more round-arm position so that the angle of spin, when the ball hits the ground, won't be quite the same.

One of the most effective surprise deliveries which an off-spinner can develop is what I might term an undercutter. Ian Johnson bowled this ball particularly well. It is done by holding the palm of the hand under the ball and pointing skywards as the ball is spun and as it leaves the hand.

From this angle the ball may be spun in the identical way to an ordinary off-break, but on being propelled into the air it will be spinning like a top, i.e. parallel to the ground or horizontally.

The ball in landing will usually go straight on and, if the bowler is coming round the wicket, it will sometimes even cut away towards slips because of the angle of delivery.

Johnson had me stumped twice in one match off such a ball. He pitched outside the off stump and I jumped out to drive, allowing for a slight turn which did not eventuate. From that moment I was like a fish out of water, left hopelessly high and dry.

One difficulty with the under-cutter is to bowl it at the same speed as the normal ball. Actually it is a splendid method of bowling a slower ball, but if this particular ball is always slower it gives the batsman a clue to its identity, hence the need to try to maintain the ordinary pace, at least sometimes.

The chief avenues available to an off-spinner for getting wickets are LBW, bowled, caught at slip, leg-slip or by the wicket-keeper. A variety of fields are available according to conditions.

I like to see the off-spinner bowling at or just outside the off stump. Accuracy in this direction will make the batsman fight all the time, for he has to guard against many ways of losing his wicket. He must be prepared for the ball that will turn, and there are always the wicket-keeper and first slip waiting for a snick off the outside edge if the ball does not turn.

It is precisely to worry the batsman against such a possibility that I think off-spinners should always (on firm wickets) have a first slip fairly fine. The only time he should be dispensed with is when the ball is gripping all the time, such as on a sticky.

A diagram is shown on page 106 for the normal field where the bowling is directed just outside the off stump.

The bowler should try to drag the batsman forward on the defensive. If he can, there is always a prospect of the ball floating away, thereby causing the batsman to leave a fatal gap between the bat and the pads.

When the ball is turning a lot, a different field

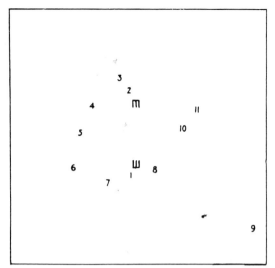

Field for a right-hand off-spin bowler on a good firm pitch. If there is any 'bite' in the pitch, nos. 10 and 11 could be moved in closer and no. 6 moved across behind square-leg.
1. Bowler   2. Wkt   3. 1st slip   4. Point
5. Cover   6. Extra-cover   7. Mid-off
8. Mid-on   9. Outfield
10. Short mid-wicket   11. Square-leg.

must be employed. Laker's phenomenal Test match performance at Manchester decided me to include a special chapter on it and in that chapter his field is shown, but, as I said, many field placings are open to the off-spinner.

His place in cricket is probably more secure today than ever before.

Leg-Spinner, Top-Spinner and Googly

The reason I have grouped these three together is because they are each bowled with the identical grip. It is only the position of the wrist at the moment of delivery which varies the direction of spin as the ball hits the ground.

The spinning agent in this case is the third finger. The first two fingers and the thumb are maintained in a comfortable balancing position but there is a wide gap between the second and third fingers.

As the ball is about to be delivered, the palm of the hand, for a leg-break, is practically facing the batsman, and as the ball is released the third finger is flicked up and over the ball, spinning it somewhere in the direction of gully or even point.

Maximum turn will be achieved if the spin is at right angles to the line of flight, but the normal ball of most leg-spinners carries a degree of top spin because it gives a slightly easier delivery position and, into a wind, will produce a measure of dip in the flight.

The combination of top and leg spins is the most prolific cause of stumpings. Such a ball will often lure a batsman into coming out of his crease for a drive only to find that the ball has dropped rather more quickly than he anticipated. Then, when he gropes for it, the leg spin completes the job by turning the ball past his bat.

Tremendous spin can be imparted by the use of that third finger in association with a strong flexible wrist, and therefore, when well pitched, this ball is extremely dangerous.

But it is the hardest of all to control and bad leg-spinners may be punished unmercifully.

Perhaps that is why they mature rather later, on the average, than other types. Perhaps also it is the reason why they are somewhat rare in English county cricket, where the old pros, whose job includes moulding the young bowlers, are notoriously averse to bowling which may be termed erratic.

But the success of men like Mailey, Grimmett and Benaud in the international sphere shows what can be done when you have mastered the art.

Some bowlers have developed what may be termed a purely finger-spin leg-break. This is accomplished by reducing the distance between the second and third fingers in the grip and by rolling rather than flicking the wrist on delivery.

The finger-spinner can usually attain a very fine degree of accuracy. An outstanding example was the Warwickshire bowler, Eric Hollies, whose record is eloquent testimony to his skill and the success of his method under English conditions.

A photo of Jack Iverson (left) practising at the Adelaide Oval, 1950, reveals quite clearly the peculiar way he held the ball. (Advertiser Newspapers Ltd)

denying that the combination of finger spin and wrist flick is the best, providing the wristy bowler has gained sufficient accuracy.

Occasionally a great bowler comes along who has some extraordinary ability to spin a ball in an unusual way. Such a bowler was Jack Iverson of Victoria, who sensationally burst into cricket and looked as though he was going to be a world beater.

He played for his State and in a short space of time took 78 Sheffield Shield wickets at an average of 21. In 1950 he was chosen to go to New Zealand with an Australian team and was easily the outstanding bowler, with 75 wickets at an average of 7.6. Unfortunately, following an injury, he retired from cricket not long afterwards.

Iverson had very big hands and was able to hold the ball between the first and third fingers with the second finger underneath it. With my small hands I can scarcely hold a golf ball that way, let alone a cricket ball.

But the harder, truer wickets of Australia demand more than finger spin if the ball is going to turn sufficiently to be dangerous.

A good finger-spin leg-break bowler is far better than a wild erratic flipper, but there is no

Below, left. The normal leg-break grip as seen by batsman when the ball is about to leave the hand.

Middle. Top-spinner at point of delivery. Same as leg-break but different wrist position.

Right. The googly is spun the same as a leg-break but the wrist is turned so that the ball comes out of the back of the hand and spins the opposite way in the air.

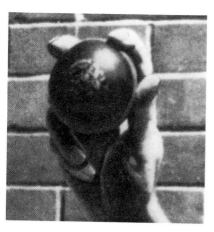

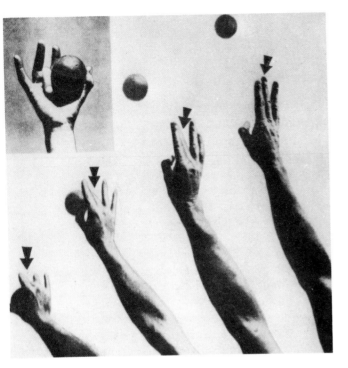

Iverson's unique grip.
Notice how the ball is flicked out
by the action of the middle finger.

As he delivered the ball, Iverson flicked the middle finger up one side of it and thus imparted spin. Most of the time he bowled googlies (apparently that was easier) but now and again the leg-break. To the batsman every delivery appeared to be a leg-break.

Iverson had great accuracy but the method of delivery excluded wrist spin and therefore he obtained negligible life off the pitch, which was his one real weakness.

I refer to the grip more as a curiosity than anything because I only knew one other person who could use it. But you never know in cricket. I would not discourage any 'freak' grip. Its owner may be a genius. The question is simply whether he can successfully use his method, orthodox or otherwise.

The normal leg-break grip and the delivery position are shown on page 107.

Whereas the palm of the hand faces the batsman at delivery for a leg-spinner, it faces the ground at delivery for a top-spinner and the fingers no longer point towards the batsman. They point towards mid-on and run practically horizontal to the ground as the ball is flicked out of the hand.

In effect then, a top-spinner leaves the hand a fraction earlier than the leg-spinner – or at least it is easier to bowl that way.

When we come to the googly it is merely a question of turning the wrist over until the back of the hand is facing the batsman at delivery. From this position the ball is spun exactly the same but it comes up from the third finger, over the top of the little finger, and thus is found to be turning in the air in the same direction as the off-break.

The great merit of a googly lies in the element of deception. Because the action is so fast at the very last moment with the finger and wrist movement combined, it is sometimes difficult for a batsman to be sure whether the ball is a leg-break or a googly. Obviously if he plays for a leg-break to a ball pitched 8 cm outside his off stump and it comes back the other way, he is in grave danger of being bowled.

Another virtue of a googly is that it usually comes along slightly slower than the leg-spinner. This was one of the main reasons why O'Reilly always maintained two fieldsmen at short-leg. He delivered the ball from a great height and whenever a batsman was deceived into groping forward a fraction too soon, he was in danger of spooning a catch. It is a difficult thing to keep your balance and hold your bat handle well forward when unwillingly dragged too far out.

The constant bowling of googlies without any element of surprise would defeat its own purpose unless one was a super exponent such as R. O. Schwartz. The bowler would, in effect, merely revert to an off-spinner without the latter's accuracy.

It may be of interest to mention here that O'Reilly preferred to bowl with the wind, which is contrary to the theory I expressed elsewhere. However, there was a very good reason for it. O'Reilly was not a googly bowler in the same

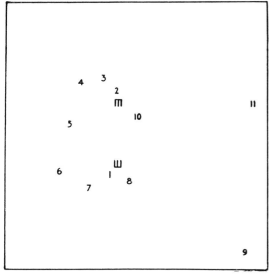

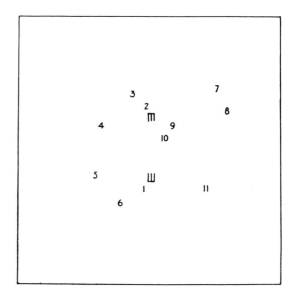

1. *Bowler* 2. *Wkt* 3. *1st slip*
4. *Backward point* 5. *Cover* 6. *Extra-cover*
7. *Mid-off* 8. *Mid-on* 9. *Long-on outfield*
10. *Short-leg* 11. *Square-leg outfield.*

This was a field regularly employed by
Grimmett, who concentrated on bowling over
the wicket, pitching on the stumps.

1. *Bowler* 2. *Wkt* 3. *1st slip* 4. *Point*
5. *Short extra-cover* 6. *Mid-off*
7. *Leg-side position, 20 to 30 m from the bat
midway between the umpire and the 'keeper.*
8. *Leg-side position, 20 to 30 m from the bat
and about 5 m finer than square-leg*
9. *Short-leg* 10. *Silly mid-on*
11. *Rather wide mid-on.*

This was the field normally used by Bill
O'Reilly. It was astonishing how many
wickets he obtained caught by nos. 9 and 10.

sense that Mailey was. He was a very tall man, delivered the ball from a good height and, with the normal leg-break, sent it straight from hand to pitch without any arc in the flight.

His pace was much above that of the average spinner – so much so that when the ball turned you had little time to follow it. Many batsmen tried to counter his pace and turn (which normally was not great) by playing forward, and became victims to his well-disguised googly, which was beautifully held back and bounced higher than the other ball.

Rather than let the wind take speed off his bowling, O'Reilly preferred to have it at his back. His spin was not sufficient to make much use of a head wind and therefore he was probably right.

Let me warn leg-spin and googly bowlers that this branch of bowling is by far the hardest to master – the googly in particular. The latter is a

tantalising ball to develop, for control is so very difficult at first, especially for the young boy whose hand is small and who will discover that he can bowl it a few metres but not the full length of the pitch. But don't be discouraged. Flexibility of wrist can make up for those small hands.

And don't try to bowl those googlies too often, even if you feel you have control over them. Always remember the surprise element.

A common fault with slow leg-spinners is the habit of bowling the ball at the ground with no arc at all. This denies any chance of flight. Moreover it tends to skid the ball off the turf without giving it any time to grip.

A boy can practise 'arc in flight' by bowling a tennis ball on the full against a brick wall so that

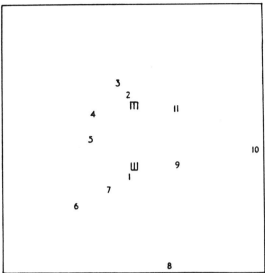

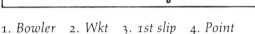

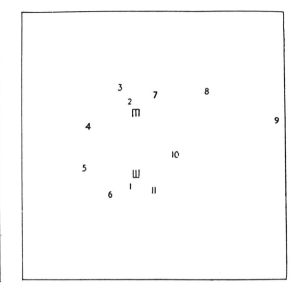

1. *Bowler*   2. *Wkt*   3. *1st slip*   4. *Point*
5. *Cover*   6. *Deep extra-cover*   7. *Mid-off*
8. *Long-on*   9. *Mid-wicket*
10. *Mid-wicket outfield*
11. *Square-leg near the umpire.*

Here is a useful field for a slow leg-break bowler who is not too sure of his control but who wants to keep the boundary shots within reason.

1. *Bowler*   2. *Wkt*   3. *1st slip*   4. *Point*
5. *Cover*   6. *Mid-off*   7. *Leg-slip*
8. *Leg-side position about 25 m from the bat*
9. *Outfield about square*
10. *Short mid-wicket*   11. *Mid-on.*

Here is an interesting field placing for a leg-spinner who wishes to attack the stumps, who is a little faster than normal and does not spin the ball very much. Fieldsman no. 7 may have to be changed to the gully position unless the bowler has very good control.

it flies upwards and back to him. It enables the youngster to get the feel of spinning the ball into the air rather than downwards on to the ground.

Don't overdo it or you will lose too much pace, but experiment and you'll be surprised what you can learn.

Diagrams are included showing basic fields for leg-spinners. Many variations may be used, according to conditions and, very often for this type of bowling, according to the tactics of the batsman.

When a new ball was allowed more frequently by the rules, it had the effect of pushing the leg-break bowler somewhat into the background. Captains thought it safer to bowl tight in between new balls and let the damage be done by the fast men. This in turn reduced scoring rates, and a leg-spinner dearly loves to have a few runs to play with to give of his best.

I deeply regretted this result of the new ball law. There is nothing so fascinating in cricket as a duel between the top-flight batsman and the good leg-spinner.

And what thrills there are with a tail-ender swiping away and hitting nowhere near the ball but always hoping to clock one over the fence.

I would like to see leg-break bowling encouraged beyond any other type. It demands great patience and has broken many a cricketing heart, but it carries a rich prize.

Left-Hand Spin Bowling

Most of what I have written about the science of bowling is just as applicable to the left-hander as the right-hander. The basic principles of bowling remain constant.

If a right-hand off-spinner is bowling to a left-hand batsman, it is equivalent to a left-hand first-finger spinner bowling to a right-hand batsman. In practice of course there is a preponderance of right-hand batsmen and so we more often find one of these opposed to the bowler.

Where the wicket is likely to take spin, it has been traditional to try to include a left-hander in the attack. There has been a long and remarkable line of English left-hand spinners such as Peel, Blythe, Briggs, Rhodes, Kilner, White, Verity, Lock, etc.

The 1956 series was remarkable for the fact that a right-hand off-spinner took the honours despite the presence of an extremely good left-hander in Tony Lock. Normally the latter would have been regarded as much the more difficult type because he turned the ball away from the batsman towards the slips, always regarded as the hardest ball to play.

There was a time when pitches and bowlers' footholds were all left uncovered against the elements. The rules were subsequently altered so that bowlers' footholds were covered but the pitch was NOT.

Whilst I quite understand the motive behind the change, which was designed in the interests of finance (and of course the spectators, too, in that it allowed play to proceed at the earliest possible moment), I regret that it has somewhat altered the balance of power between bowlers.

This rule gives rise to the likelihood of fast bowlers, from the firm footholds, hurling down express deliveries into a sticky pitch while the spinners look on. That is exactly what happened in Brisbane in 1936. Australia were caught under these very circumstances and dismissed for 58, Allen taking 5 for 36 and Voce 4 for 16. The greatest left-hand spinner of the day, Hedley Verity, was in the team but did not get a bowl.

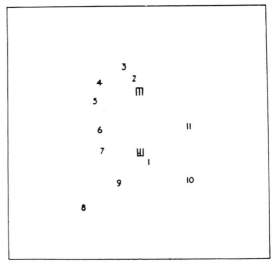

1. *Bowler*   2. *Wkt*   3. *1st slip*
4. *Backward point*   5. *Forward point*
6. *Cover*   7. *Extra-cover*
8. *Deep extra-cover*   9. *Mid-off*
10. *Wide mid-on*   11. *Short mid-wicket.*

A basic field for the normal first-finger left-hand spinner bowling over the wicket at the off stump on a firm pitch. This is the sort of field Jack White, with tantalising accuracy, employed so successfully against Australia in 1928/29.

I always feel that if the batsman has to face a sticky wicket then the bowler should be under some handicap, too. At least it would produce a more even fight.

There is a reasonable chance on an Australian sticky dog of applying skilful defence against a Verity but not much hope against a Voce, when nearly every ball flies straight up at your chin.

However, I fear the steps will never be retraced. We are more likely to have everything covered than everything uncovered in the future. That is in fact the position in Australia now. The financial demands of the game cannot be overlooked.

The slow left-hand spinner is an extremely accurate type and often fills the role of a stock bowler when batting conditions are easy. His normal task is to bowl to a strong off field as set out in the diagram on page 111 and to play on the batsman's patience. If the pitch is turning, he will be better suited bowling round the wicket.

There is not much difference between the fastish left-hander and the fastish right-hander. Perhaps a slight variation of field placing, according to whether the ball is moving into or away from the batsman, but that is entirely up to the bowler.

Occasionally cricket produces a phenomenon – a Fleetwood-Smith who was a faster, left-hand edition of the Arthur Mailey type. He presented, to right-hand batsmen, much the same problem as did Laker with his right-hand off spin. There was the added danger of a good wrong-'un. But then no Fleetwood-Smith type could ever hope to achieve quite the same accuracy as Laker. It is the old story of vicious third-finger spin competing against first-finger spin.

Also a left-hand googly bowler would, in my opinion, not be able to use a leg-side field of Laker's type nearly so well. Apart from the question of accuracy he somehow can't get the ball to lift so much and I think the 'chinaman' bowler should always concentrate just outside the off stump. Because of the extra spin he has a better chance of drifting the ball away farther to the off and thereby dragging the batsman off the straight line of defence.

Left-handers have one virtue. They are not so common as right-handers and therefore batsmen get less practice against them. I always liked to have a left-hand bowler on my side.

The Cutter

This term is used to describe a particular type of delivery and gives rise to a lot of misunderstanding.

The first time I encountered such a ball was against George Geary when he came to Australia in 1928. It appeared to me, as a batsman, that he was trying to bowl a finger-spin leg-break at medium pace and actually that was true. But in Australia he could seldom turn the ball sufficiently to beat the bat.

Alec Bedser's grip for a leg-cutter when bowled on a dry wicket taking spin. Second finger almost round seam; thumb underneath. Second finger does most of the work. Ball held more tightly than for swing bowling.

Alec Bedser's grip for a leg-cutter when bowled on a soft wicket. The fingers are in the same position as those of a normal leg-spin bowler. Second and third fingers do all the work.

When I went to England in 1930, we played Leicester and I found the same ball turned more often and to a greater degree. In fact, against Leicester on my next tour, in 1934, the score book shows Bradman bowled Geary, 65. That was a beautiful leg-cutter. It pitched on the leg stump and hit the off.

However, it was not until I played against Bedser that I fully appreciated how devastating a good leg-cutter can be. Although big Alec was a little faster than Geary, he consistently cut that ball across from leg to off whenever the wicket helped him and oft-times when it appeared not to be helping him.

All the batsmen of his period learnt to dread that wonderful ball which now and again came along, pitching on the leg stump and whizzing across near the off bail. It brought Bedser a host of wickets, and the number of times he just missed the stumps with it was legion.

At Adelaide in the fourth Test in 1947, he bowled me neck and crop with one of them. This particular ball dipped in from the off side and I had to go with it to defend my leg stump only to see it whip back and take the off. I still think it was the best ball ever bowled at me.

When they come at that speed leg-cutters are virtually unplayable.

As I think Bedser was the greatest exponent of this ball, I am reproducing opposite two photographs showing his grip. Actually the grip is the same in each case but the seam is held at a different angle.

The great bowler himself refers to his method of delivery in these terms:

'The term leg-cutter, describing this type of ball, comes from the fact that it is necessary to "cut" across the seam of the ball with the fingers at the moment of delivery. This imparts a type of leg spin which, of course, makes the ball leave or go away from the batsman.

'I use two different types of grip, one for dry wickets and the other on wet or rain-affected wickets.

'For the drier wickets, the ball seems to move more quickly if I "cut" or spin it off my second finger.

'To do this the ball must be held firmly, but great care should be taken that there is no tenseness of the wrist. If the wrist is at all taut at the moment of delivery, the ball will lose its effectiveness.

'On wet or rain-affected wickets I hold the ball in exactly the same way as the orthodox leg-spinner but deliver it at my normal pace, and cut or spin it principally off the third finger. I find this causes it to both lift and move away from the bat.

'The wrist and body action are most important, for it is necessary to put as much body into the delivery as possible if the ball is to be pitched on the correct spot.

'It is also imperative that the ball should be pitched well up to the batsman, forcing him to play forward.' (*Bowling*, Alec Bedser. Hodder & Stoughton).

Bedser further advocates that the ball should be bowled at the leg stump and says two close fielders on the leg side are essential. He should know.

Trevor Bailey was another player who was always trying cutters and often bowled them very successfully. This is what he has to say:

'There are two types of cutter – the off and the leg.

'To bowl a cutter the hand and the fingers are cut down the side of the ball, causing it to break on pitching, although it has not been actually spun.

'The seam of the ball is normally held upright.

'At the moment of release the hand and fingers are cut down the right-hand side of the ball for the off-cutter, and the left-hand side for the leg-cutter.' (*Cricket*, Trevor Bailey. Eyre & Spottiswoode).

So there you have the views of two experts on how it is done.

The great value of the ball is the speed at which it can be delivered. In fact, the ball cannot be bowled at all without moderate speed.

The turn is naturally restricted. Enough to beat the bat is regarded as very good but as the ball is usually travelling at medium pace or better, the extra speed makes it extremely difficult for batsmen to negotiate even a moderate change of direction.

Change of Pace

This is the term which is applied when the bowler delivers a ball either faster or slower than his normal delivery. It is not much use if undisguised.

If Tyson suddenly reverted to a googly or Grimmett tried to emulate Larwood that would be futile.

Changes of pace must be slight. Big changes are too easily observed. The objective is:

1. To deceive the batsman into playing the wrong stroke,

or

2. To make him play the correct stroke too soon or too late.

The bowler should endeavour to maintain exactly the same run and the same action. If the arm speed is quickened or reduced, the batsman will detect it.

Ron Oxenham of Queensland bowled a beautiful slow ball without any noticeable change of action. His normal delivery was slow-medium and he held the ball mainly between the first two fingers. For his slower one, he pushed it more between the second and third fingers. It left his hand the same way, was very deceptive and could only be picked up in the air.

Alec Bedser at times adopted the same method. He also used the more common practice of pushing the ball further into the palm. It is easy to prove that a ball held well forward in the fingers can be bowled faster than one held right in the palm, no matter how much effort you put into the latter, and it therefore follows that the palm grip has its uses just for this purpose.

Any bowler can deliver the ball from well behind the bowling crease instead of going right up to his mark. The ball, having to travel farther, takes longer to reach the batsman. I don't like the idea much, firstly because it is

Bruce Dooland, Australian leg-spinner who also played in the Lancashire League and for Nottinghamshire, delivers a ball well behind the bowling crease.
(Advertiser Newspapers Ltd)

easily detectable and, secondly, because the bowler often tends from such a delivery to bowl a bad length and pay the penalty.

In the case of a slow spin bowler he can certainly achieve variations of pace by letting the ball go slightly earlier or later in the delivery action. He will probably at the same time alter his break slightly and his arc of flight as well. This is all to the good if it can be controlled.

That wonderful bowler of the last century, Spofforth, was credited with having magnificent change of pace. W. G. Grace said of Spofforth: 'He was a master of the art of bowling a slower or faster ball without a perceptible change of action, and I question if anyone has surpassed him. There was the same run, the same action and the same elevation.'

That testimony is good enough for me.

Spofforth's secret was supposed to be the half-ball grip, a method which, I am told, C. T. B. Turner also successfully employed.

Instead of the first and second fingers being on opposite sides of the seam (and the thumb underneath) he had both those fingers on the right-hand side of the seam.

It is claimed that with this grip he could try his hardest and still could not bowl the ball as fast as he could with his normal grip.

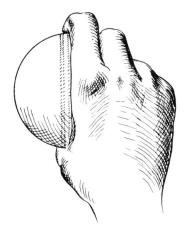

The half-ball grip which was commonly used by F. R. Spofforth and C. T. B. Turner to bowl a slower ball which the batsman did not detect.

Turner said it gave him the feeling on delivery that the ball came out between the thumb and the first finger.

Seeing that Spofforth in his five tours of England for Australia took 1,241 wickets at an average of 8.9, and he took 94 wickets in Test matches, I suggest he had some qualities which are worth looking into.

Anyway, I have tried this half-ball idea at the nets and believe it works. I know two or three bowlers who have experimented with it and they agree but find control the problem. There is no doubt the idea is possible and worth cultivating.

The thing is to know what you are aiming for, to make sure your arm goes through at the normal speed. And remember that deception is the key to success in change of pace.

Flight

In dealing with spin bowling, I have already referred quite a lot to the question of flight.

With all these cricketing terms there must be no ambiguity between writer and reader concerning their meaning. To my way of thinking, a well-flighted ball means one which will alter its expected course *in the air* by dropping more quickly or carrying on a little farther than the batsman expected. Or it may even be applied to a ball which only curves in its flight.

For instance, if an off-spinner sent down a slow ball which curled away outside the stumps and lured the batsman forward for a stumping, we may say it was beautifully flighted. Best of all is the one which curls away and drops at the same time.

But the most common usage is in reference to the ball which dips with an arc in its flight and causes the batsman unintentionally to hit the ball in the air.

If a leg-break bowler of the true third-finger, wrist variety is bowling into a good wind, there is no doubt that he can, with top spin, cause that ball to dip rather quickly towards the end of its airborne career.

One way is to deliver the ball before his wrist reaches his shoulder in the delivery swing. In

The above diagram shows how two balls can be delivered from point A towards the batsman's wicket X but by a variation of speed and trajectory the ball which goes higher in the air drops shorter than the other one. Also the bounce of the ball from the ground after pitching is likely to follow the pattern shown. Ball AB followed by ball AC would be a good attempt for caught and bowled. Ball AC followed by ball AB would be a good move for bowled or LBW.

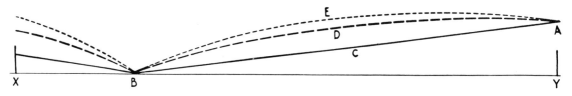

Here we see three deliveries A–B, all pitching at the same point, but obviously A–C–B would reach point B quicker than A–D–B and A–E–B. Similarly the latter would lift more after pitching. It is essential for the slow leg-spinner to fully understand the science of flight.

---

that way the ball can be well flighted even if it is aimed straight down on to the ground.

Flight must not be confused with seam swing. When someone like Lindwall or Bedser makes the new ball move from one side to the other, that is swing. It is not flight in the accepted sense.

And if anyone tells you a bowler of that pace flighted the ball, then we are not speaking the same language.

A bowler of Lindwall's pace cannot make the ball dip, or if he can it is microscopically small. We must get down to the spinners before flight begins to assume real meaning.

Leg-spinners can combine a drift to leg with the dropping ball, off-spinners a drift to the off with the dropping ball, whilst the top-spinner will dip more than any but the ball will hold its course and go straight. It will also probably bounce a little higher than the normal delivery and this aids the chance of a caught and bowled for an unwary batsman.

Flight is one of the more delicate refinements.

Many onlookers see flight which is non-existent, but when conditions are favourable and an expert bowler is using it, he has a tremendously valuable adjunct to spin. Mastery of it is well worth the trouble.

Use of Width of the Bowling Crease

The length of the bowling crease as set out in the laws is 2.64 m (8 ft. 8 in.). The stumps are 22.86 cm (9 in.) wide set in the middle. There is therefore a width of 120.6 cm (3 ft. 11½ in.) between the outer stump and the return crease on each side.

This small diagram which is drawn to scale illustrates it clearly:

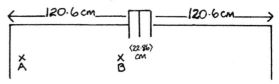

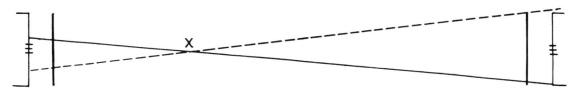

The direction of the ball in each case is perfectly straight. Each ball could land on the pitch at point X in a line with the stumps; but one would pass outside the off stump and the other outside the leg stump.

The rear foot at delivery may either be at point A or point B or anywhere in between.

Bowling over the wicket a bowler can obviously then alter his angle of delivery by the greater part of this 120.6 cm (3 ft. 11½ in.).

He should learn to deliver one ball from close to the stumps, another wide out and so on.

The normal usage of this width is for the bowler to go close to the stumps when he wants to run the ball away outside the off stump and to go wide of the bowling crease when he wants to push one in towards the batsman.

But this should not become an unalterable procedure because the batsman will soon observe the routine. Vary it so that occasionally a ball from wide of the crease will be sent straight through outside the off stump and so on. Don't get into a groove.

Going from over the wicket to round the wicket he can alter his angle of delivery by practically the whole 2.64 m (8 ft. 8 in.) and that makes a big difference when the ball has to travel some 20 metres (22 yards).

A drawing to scale of the bowling crease and the pitch gives a clear picture of how the direction of the ball may be varied without putting any break on it. See diagram above.

Over or Round the Wicket

It is appropriate that I should say a word on this aspect of bowling after referring to the width of the bowling crease. The two subjects are very closely related.

Most bowlers deliver the ball from over the wicket. It seems the natural and logical thing to do.

The ball in such cases is propelled with the arm over the stumps at the bowler's end – or very nearly so. Therefore the chance of getting an LBW decision with a straight ball 'pitched on the stumps' is obviously better than it is when the ball is delivered say round the wicket from a wide angle. In the latter case the ball may pitch on the stumps but be clearly missing them if it pursues a straight course.

Sometimes, however, conditions arise, such as a sticky wicket or a dry crumbler, where the bowler can turn the ball a lot. He may find that he has to deliver from a wider angle to counteract the break.

Have a look at the diagram (below) illustrating this point. Here is the identical delivery – same break, same pitch, but the one is bowled

The angle of break in ABC and XBZ is identical but the ball bowled over the wicket will miss the stumps, while the one bowled round the wicket will hit them.

over the wicket, the other round. See how in the first instance the provisions of the LBW law are not fulfilled. In the second they are.

Obviously the benefits don't end with the LBW law. The batsman also has to guard against being bowled or caught. Whereas the bowler may seek to limit his break when bowling over the wicket, he may be subject to no limitation coming round, and this extra turn can be a hazard for the batsman.

I have referred to the main reason why bowlers have cause to revert to round-the-wicket bowling. It does not follow that there are no other reasons. A bowler may just wish to introduce a little variety into his bowling or he may find that it gives him better control.

I feel that a round-the-wicket delivery by the orthodox first-finger spinner assists the bowler to swing his body and shoulder into the best possible position. Some bowlers have adopted this type of delivery in conjunction with a run-up which brings them behind the umpire. He is used as a sort of cover to hide the bowler at one point in his run. It shouldn't worry anyone, but I suppose a temperamental person might be inclined to let it distract him.

An orthodox left-hand first-finger spinner when bowling to a left-hand batsman may even go round the wicket just to keep him on tenterhooks with the ball which pitches on the off stump but, instead of turning, goes straight on towards first slip.

Many of the great left-handers of the Rhodes-Verity type bowled round the wicket just as often as over the wicket, whether the pitch was good or bad. It really becomes a matter of judgment on the bowler's part to say when the move is justified.

Example of typical run-up by right-hand off-spinner bowling round the wicket and coming behind the umpire.

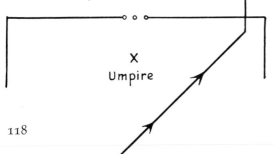

THINK I'LL BOWL ROUND UMP, SHE'S A BIT STICKY

The virtue of round the wicket seldom, if ever, applies to the right-hand leg-spinner. In his case the delivery position would make it very much harder for him to get an LBW decision against a right-hand batsman.

Of course there are always exceptions to orthodoxy and I am well aware of the famous occasion when Richie Benaud won a Test match for Australia by suddenly switching his leg breaks to round the wicket. The batsmen were well set and Richie was not achieving the breakthrough he was seeking when suddenly he conceived the idea of bowling round the wicket and pitching the ball in the rough created by the bowler's footmarks.

He managed to land one right on the spot, the ball turned appreciably and bowled the batsman round his legs.

One cannot help castigating the batsman for not making sure he had his pads in the right position to guard his stumps but full marks to Richie for his ingenuity and skill.

If you are the type of bowler who may need at some time or other to bowl round the wicket, don't wait until the necessity arises before trying it out. It is rather late to start learning the art when a wet wicket is encountered. One should have become accustomed long before that to the different angle of approach, the change in body position at delivery and the feel of running off the pitch after delivery at a different angle. Practise at the nets when wickets are firm to grasp the idea.

No-Balls

When the original laws were promulgated in 1744 bowling was underarm and, therefore, it is understandable that the only no-ball penalty was when a bowler overstepped the bowling crease.

In 1816 an amendment was made which provided that the hand should be kept below the elbow. This was to prevent 'throwing'. In 1835 the bowler was allowed to raise his arm as high as the shoulder and modern overarm bowling was legalised in 1864. The no-ball penalty if a bowler 'throws' has remained constant ever since.

I think it worth while pointing out that the no-ball law regarding 'throwing' reads: 'If either umpire is not completely satisfied with the absolute fairness of a delivery,' etc., he shall call no-ball.

Australian fast bowler Pat Crawford, practising at the nets, takes no care where he places his feet and commits the bad habit of overstepping the mark – leading to an error in match play – see the other photograph. (Central Press Photos Ltd)

Here we see Pat Crawford bowling in a match and about to deliver a no-ball. I have not seen any other picture where the bowler so markedly offended against both the old and the new no-ball rules.
(Associated Newspapers Ltd)

I am afraid some umpires interpret the rule to mean that they should not no-ball a bowler unless satisfied he is throwing. This is wrong, as you can see. The rule is quite clear that an umpire should call if he is doubtful. He does not have to be satisfied it is a throw but only uncertain whether it is a fair delivery.

Fortunately, the throwing evil is not very prevalent these days. Nevertheless, one occasionally sees a doubtful delivery and players should be corrected right at the start and not allowed to develop bad habits.

A bowler cannot secure a wicket with a no-ball, so the batsman gets a free swing at it.

The main offenders are the bowlers who overstep the mark during their delivery stride.

Perhaps there is some excuse for an occasional error on the part of a tearaway fast bowler who runs some 20 metres and hurls himself into the fray. But there is none whatever for the slower type – not even for the one who commits the offence by going so wide that his foot goes outside the return crease.

Every bowler should have a fixed run of so many steps. He should religiously adhere to it all the time.

Providing his run is properly measured and he invariably starts from the same spot, he should likewise finish at the same spot each time.

But still we find bowlers giving away innumerable runs (and possibly wickets) in a season through sheer carelessness or neglect of this simple precaution.

The unpredictable Keith Miller, even in Test cricket, would vary the length of his run quite a lot and seldom bowled a no-ball. But he was an unusually gifted athletic figure who obviously watched the bowling crease and adjusted his stride to it. His method cannot be recommended.

I don't ever remember Grimmett being no-balled. He regarded it as an unforgivable sin.

I am sure one of the prime causes of trouble is the way bowlers neglect their run-up at practice.

Haven't we all seen bowlers at the nets repeatedly going over the line and bowling what would have been no-balls in a match? Such a habit is bad for the run and bad from the angle that it alters the length of the pitch.

No good coach should condone it and bowlers who send down no-balls in a match get no sympathy from me. The two photographs on the previous page illustrate what can happen.

Swerve and Swing

As I have stated earlier, there are certain cricket terms which are hard to define. One is timing as applied to batting. There may be legitimate arguments as to the difference between a hook shot and a pull shot.

In the bowling line what constitutes swing and what constitutes swerve?

I do not set myself up as an authority on the English language, but for the sake of clarity of expression it is necessary to define the difference.

In my reasoning, swing is the term applied to the movement of a ball in the air caused by the shine on the ball and the angle of the seam – not by spin.

Swerve, on the other hand, is used in the cricket sense in accordance with the dictionary as 'diverging from its regular line of motion', but caused entirely by spin.

Strictly speaking we think of swing, in general daily terms, as a 'to and fro' motion. This fits in with the cricket definition because the swing of a cricket ball, caused by using the seam, may start in one direction, then suddenly change its course in the air before pitching and swing the opposite way.

Such balls are rare, and when they occur are well-nigh unplayable. Nobody can bowl such a delivery on purpose. The cause is apparently a variation in the position of the seam as the ball pursues its course, causing air pressure to veer to the opposite side. Thus the seam swing, which normally goes one way only, may occasionally change course.

The spin swerve, however, will constantly travel in the one direction until making contact with the ground.

Anybody conversant with the behaviour of a ball when vigorously spun will know that off spin causes a ball to deviate to the left and leg spin causes it to deviate to the right – that is of course as it travels away from its propellant source.

A right-hand bowler bowling off-spinners to a right-hand batsman will find they swerve away outside his off stump. Conversely the leg-break bowler will find his leg-spinners tend to drift outside the leg stump.

Top spin causes a ball to drop more quickly than it would otherwise do and back spin tends to make it carry further towards the batsman.

In the game of cricket we may forget back spin because no bowler can impart sufficient back spin to a ball to have any noticeable effect on its flight.

This swerving effect on a ball is far more obvious when some outside agency is employed to increase the speed and spin imparted to it. I can think of no better example than golf.

It is well known that to make a golf ball rise in

the air with a lofted iron one deliberately hits down on the ball, thereby imparting tremendous back spin which, coupled with the speed of flight, causes the ball to lift.

Frequently, when they land on a green, such shots will bite into the turf and the back spin will actually cause the ball to bounce back towards its striker.

The great bane of golfers is side spin, and the art of golf teaching centres around the mechanics of body swing, arm action, etc., all designed to eliminate those wild hooks and slices produced by unwanted side spin.

The baseball pitcher produces his out-curve by off spin. His out-dropper is a combination of top spin and off spin. And so on.

The scientific principles of swerve produced by spin are easily understood and the movement of the ball much more predictable than is the case with seam swing.

So far as swerve applies to a cricket ball, the problem is for a bowler to impart sufficient spin to the ball for it to become effective. Obviously he cannot reproduce the vicious spin imparted by a golf club or tennis racket or even that by throwing a soft ball.

However, my main purpose is not to estimate the extent of swerve. It is merely to clearly establish the expected behaviour of a ball under certain conditions.

The leg-break bowler of the Arthur Mailey type, who spins the ball viciously from the leg side towards slips, will find the ball drifting towards or outside the batsman's legs, whereas the Jim Laker type, with his off-spinners turning from the off towards the leg side, would find his deliveries drifting towards slips.

Therefore, in aiming for a given spot on the pitch, these spin bowlers must allow for some swerve in the air.

The stronger the wind blowing towards the ball, the greater the swerve. That is the main reason why slow bowlers should almost invariably bowl against the wind. It assists them to confuse the batsman with variations in flight.

From a batsman's point of view this swerve can be most disconcerting because the ball, should it bite at all on hitting the ground, will invariably break in the opposite direction to the swerve. And, naturally, one can never be sure that it will bite, in which case the ball will continue in the direction of the swerve.

When the ball swerves, a batsman very often finds himself impelled to go with the swerve and it then becomes difficult to cover any subsequent break back.

I recall a famous occasion in Melbourne in 1932. Lisle Nagel, 196 cm (6 ft. 5 in.) Australian off-spinner, found conditions to his liking and, playing for an Australian XI against MCC, bowled these off-spin swerves magnificently. They would swerve perhaps 30 or 40 cm towards slips and with the occasional ball breaking back from the off he had the batsmen bewildered. His analysis read:

10 overs, 32 runs, 8 wickets, and amongst his victims were: Wyatt, Sutcliffe, Pataudi, Leyland, Allen and Paynter.

My one and only Test wicket, that of Wally Hammond at Adelaide in January 1933, was gained the reverse way. It was a leg-spinner which drifted outside the leg stump. Hammond knew all about swerve but, on this occasion, instead of playing with the swerve and forcing the ball past mid-on, he tried to hit against the swerve to mid-off. This technical error on his part allowed the ball to get past his bat on the full and it then turned in to the stumps after landing on the footmarks at the crease.

I hope by these explanations I have been able to make readers understand the fundamental difference between what I term swing – mainly the ally of fastish new-ball bowlers – and swerve – the play-thing of the spinner.

They are quite distinct and each is of great importance in the bowling art.

Seam and Swing Bowling

Despite the claims of well-meaning theorists (some of whom have even gone to the extent of writing newspaper articles on the subject) that a cricket ball cannot be made to change its direction in the air, any knowledgeable practical cricketer knows that it can.

The bowler who understands the mechanics

of swing can make a new ball change its course in mid-air under practically any conditions. But give him favourable conditions and it is astonishing how far it will move on occasions.

For some reason which I do not profess to understand, a two-piece ball will swing ever so much more than a four-piece ball.

Very many years ago I played in a second-class game in which Australia's fast bowler Tim Wall opened the attack with a two-piece ball. He swung it so much that the game was a farce. Balls which started off towards the stumps finished up near the wide mark and batsmen were unable to make shots.

A conference was held and the ball changed to a four-piece one.

It is impossible to trace the precise discovery and development of swing. With underarm bowling it could not have been of any consequence and we may safely say that it played no part in cricket before the legislation of overarm bowling in 1864. But I can't find out who first discovered it.

There is little doubt great bowlers who played before 1900 such as Tom Richardson, Lohmann, Hirst, Spofforth, W. G. Grace and Ernest Jones swung the ball.

America's greatest cricketing son, Bart King of Philadelphia, confused the opposition with his swing bowling during his tours of England just after the beginning of the twentieth century.

We must remember that originally the laws of cricket only allowed a new ball at the start of each innings. Then came a change when a new ball could be claimed by the fielding side after 200 runs had been scored.

But possibly the thing which gave swing bowling its greatest impetus was the experimental change in 1946, which permitted a new ball after 55 overs (six-ball).

Different tactics were adopted. Fast or medium-pace bowlers operated as long as they reasonably could, whereupon, the fielding captain often resorted to negative bowling and field placing with other bowlers until a new ball could be taken again.

The spin bowler, being relatively expensive in terms of runs per over, was used sparingly.

Under such circumstances a new ball was coming up regularly after little more than 100 runs. Indeed, many instances occurred where it was taken below 90.

The batsmen were virtually facing all the time a shiny ball which would swing, especially in England where climatic conditions do not impose the same wear and tear on the ball. No wonder the bowlers worked on swing at every turn.

I am sure this legislation was responsible to some extent for the development of leg-side defensive bowling. Bowlers found themselves able to move the ball across the batsman's body with their in-swingers and to restrict the rate of scoring.

In retrospect the experiment may be regarded as unwise and I have heard many people condemn it.

But the rule was altered to encourage fast bowling which, many thought, was languishing.

The fast bowler, who had to be satisfied with one new ball in 200 runs in scorching dry heat at Adelaide when the turf was flint hard, not unreasonably thought he was harshly treated compared with the slow bowler.

The experiment did encourage fast bowling, which returned and dominated cricket to a large extent.

But a feeling soon grew that the slow bowler was being pushed too far into the background.

Gradually the rule was relaxed, and within ten years of the commencement of the experiment, legislation tended to reverse the trend so that spin bowlers would be encouraged.

If the experiment did nothing else but pinpoint the rleative virtues of fast and slow bowling, it will have been well worth while.

There is little doubt that a fixed number of overs is the right answer. The problem is to be sure how many overs in order to do justice to all types of bowling.

At the time of writing one of the greatest tragedies in cricket is the almost complete absence of slow leg-spin bowlers. There is more than one cause for this and without doubt limited-overs cricket must take a large share of the blame. Nevertheless it highlights the need constantly to review the situation and I believe a good case can be made out for legislating that a greater number of overs must be bowled before a new ball can be taken.

But getting back to swing itself. So many people have asked why a cricket ball will swing that I have decided to quote in full, at the conclusion of this section, a scientific explanation of the matter.

For this I am indebted to Dr R. A. Lyttleton, FRS, who dealt with the subject in a talk on the BBC.

For cricketers, the important thing is not so much to know why the ball swings, and how to make it swing. But if they know what causes it, surely they will be better fitted to try to bring about the necessary state of affairs.

Despite the scientific nature of Dr Lyttleton's treatment, I think it is most absorbing, and his explanations should, once and for all, answer the sceptics who say a cricket ball will not swing.

One of the most interesting parts of the matter is the knowledge that a cricket ball will not change direction in the air if travelling too fast.

I have long held the view that a bowler of Tyson's pace could not produce the degree of swing which was achievable by a bowler of Bedser's pace.

Scientifically it proves to be true because there is a pace at which maximum swing is procured, and it is well below the pace at which Tyson bowled.

Of course, that doesn't mean Tyson was any easier to play. A deviation of 8 cm off line at 130 or 140 kilometres per hour may be much harder to combat than a deviation of 30 cm at 60 kilometres per hour, because the time factor comes to the batsman's aid at the lower speed.

Certain conditions are shown to be desirable in order that maximum swing may be obtained. They are:
1. A new ball with a shiny surface.
2. A humid atmosphere, with cloud.
3. A wind blowing from the right quarter.

Grip for in-swinger (left). The seam is pointing towards fine-leg. Fingers are closed together and more to one side.

Grip for out-swinger (right). The seam is pointing towards first or second slip. This is the way the ball would appear to the batsman as it leaves the bowler's hand.

As these factors disappear, so will swing.

Although a ball may swing at first under the unfavourable conditions of heat, dryness and calm, only a few overs may be sufficient to take away the shine and all semblance of swing.

An interesting factor concerning a new ball is that a glossy surface, as distinct from polish, is no good.

There was a period in Australia when some cricket ball manufacturers, probably for reasons of economy, resorted to lacquering the surface of balls instead of shining them. The lacquer gives a beautiful bright, glossy finish. But that ball will not swing to anything like the same extent as one with the leather itself polished. Moreover, the lacquer surface gets broken as soon as the ball hits the ground and subsequently can be peeled off in strips. It might suit the manufacturers but from the bowler's viewpoint lacquering is a curse.

In England, on a dull day with a green pitch, the ball may move about to a considerable degree all day, even though as the ball gets older the seam normally tends to get battered down and become less prominent, thereby militating against swing.

The preponderance of seam bowling brought in its train a mania for polishing the ball, not only by the bowler but often by fieldsmen who handled it. The prevalence of this habit finally caused legislation to keep the practice within reasonable bounds and it is perhaps too early to say what the final outcome of such experimental legislation will be.

An interesting point about polishing the ball which may not be appreciated is that the bowler likes to have one side only shined up. A ball with one shiny side can be made to swing even though it has virtually no seam at all, but with no seam and two rough sides it probably couldn't.

Putting things in their simplest form so that bowlers will know what to do one may say the seam of a ball acts like a rudder. Point the seam towards slips and the ball will veer that way to become an out-swinger. Point the seam towards fine-leg, the reverse will happen and you will get an in-swinger.

The illustrations of finger grips (page 123) show the position quite plainly.

In delivering the out-swinger, a right-hand bowler may occasionally obtain better results by allowing his arm to stray slightly to the right. This would in effect minutely lower the height of delivery and give the smallest suggestion of round-arm. Moreover, as the ball leaves the hand, the wrist is turned ever so slightly so that the palm of the hand moves towards the direction in which swing is required. For an out-swinger this of course would be in the direction of, say, third slip.

When delivering the in-swinger, a bowler needs to keep his action as high as possible. There is, in fact, a common term in cricket that a bowler flicks his right ear at delivery. This is to indicate how close the arm goes to the head as it comes over the top. Again there is the suggestion of wrist movement, this time to turn the palm of the hand towards the leg side as the ball is delivered.

There should be no attempt whatever to spin the ball.

The fingers should merely go forward and down in the direction of flight so that the only rotation of the ball will be very slightly backwards parallel to the pitch.

The only effect of this backward movement will be to assist in maintaining the seam of the ball in the same plane during its flight.

The object of swing bowling is naturally to beat the bat by making the ball change its course through the air as compared with a ball breaking with spin after making contact with the ground. Providing this can be done, the batsman has to be exceptionally wary of being caught off the edge.

I cannot stress too much that lateness of swing is a batsman's real worry. What we term a cartwheel, that is one which uniformly swings all the way from the moment of delivery, is not troublesome unless it is very fast and moves a considerable distance.

In the latter case, it will quite often be well clear of the stumps and easily left alone.

But the swinger which dips late, the ball which apparently is dead straight three-quarters of the length of the pitch and then suddenly dips one way or the other, is the very devil. A late out-swinger which cuts away still farther off the pitch will defeat anyone.

There are certain things which swing bowlers should aim to do.

a] They should try to deliver the ball so that it will finish on the stumps after allowing for the swing, or

b] They should make sure that if condition a] does not apply, the batsman will at least be forced to make a shot at the ball.

One of the great sins of some new-ball bowlers is that they will continue to bowl cartwheel out-swingers at the stumps so that the ball finishes well outside the off stump and the batsman can safely watch it go by whilst another bit of shine has gone off the ball.

I know of nothing more exasperating to a captain than to see a new-ball bowler sending

The cartwheel out-swinger will get second-class batsmen who follow the swing, but the best players can usually see its path clearly and either play it or allow it to pass.

The late out-swinger which can defeat anyone, especially if pitched on the stumps so that the batsman is compelled to play for a straight ball.

The cartwheel type of in-swinger which is useful when it finishes on the stumps but not when it goes away well outside the leg stump.

The late in-swinger which obtains many batsmen's wickets bowled or LBW.

down ball after ball at which the batsmen are rarely compelled to offer strokes of any kind.

Another important thing is to keep the ball up. A long-hop with a new ball is mostly a bad ball and nullifies whatever swing may have been there. It considerably reduces the opportunity of the ball to swing by lessening the time it stays in the air.

A half-volley has a far better chance to achieve maximum swing, and a slip catch off a half-volley is usually going up to the fieldsman or at least it will have a better chance of carrying to him.

When the pitch is green and grassy the ball will not only retain its sheen much longer, it will also 'move' off the pitch itself.

The swing in the air may take effect but in addition there will be a further noticeable change of direction after the ball lands.

Those who have bothered to look closely at a green-top pitch at the conclusion of a day's play (especially in England) will have noticed that every ball has made a distinct mark where it landed and the pitch is dotted with minute indentations. It appears that the weight of the ball in contact with the earth is sufficient to crush some of the tender green grass shoots. This contact with grass or earth sometimes produces a trace of moisture to aid the pace of the ball and, according to the direction or angle of the seam of the ball when it lands, so may the direction of its flight be very slightly changed.

Seamers do not move off the pitch very much, but under very favourable conditions they may do enough to at least clip the edge of the blade and provide a catch in the slips.

The grip for swing bowling must always be in the fingers – never in the palm – and the bowler should be conscious of the ball going out of his finger-tips on release.

Tim Wall claimed that when he bowled particularly well and swung the ball late it was his fingers which tired first.

With regard to wind direction, it is generally agreed that a mild zephyr coming towards the bowler from the direction of the third slip will help the in-swinger whilst a breeze coming up between square-leg and the wicket-keeper will assist the out-swinger. The breeze seems to provide just the amount of 'resistance' which a bowler likes to feel he can 'push' the ball into. Too much breeze is no good because it retards his pace.

This wind factor is not unimportant when speaking about great fast bowling combinations. Take Larwood and Tate. The former wanted the wind behind him to assist his express speed. The latter would often be more effective bowling into a slight wind because of the aid to his swing.

Rain is one of the bugbears of a swing bowler. Once the grass gets wet it becomes impossible to retain the gloss on the ball for long. Any ball which travels out towards the boundary is sure to gather moisture and, though a towel or sawdust may be used to dry the surface, no amount of rubbing will restore shine to damp leather.

Should a bowler wish to sandwich a perfectly straight ball in between some swingers, he can easily do so by gripping the ball with the fingers across the seam which will then be at right angles to the line of flight.

Occasionally, a genuine seam out-swinger will come back from the off after it pitches. Nothing adequately explains why, but I liken it to the cutter, which is referred to elsewhere. I believe the angle of the seam relative to the ground sometimes causes this change of direction after contact with the ground.

Though bowlers make it happen occasionally, I have yet to find one who could bowl a genuine out-swinger with the break back except by accident. He might try a hundred times and not get one. Then suddenly it will happen.

The diagrams outlining the direction of the ball will help to clarify my explanations regarding swing in general.

I quote hereunder part of a talk given on the BBC by Raymond A. Lyttleton, FRS, of St John's College, Cambridge. He refers to the fact that a ball will '*swerve in the air*' and says that is what we mean by 'swing bowling'.

In the section entitled 'Swerve and Swing' I have tried to explain the difference between swerve caused by spin, and swing caused by other factors.

A ball will swerve even if it has no shine and seam (example – a golf ball which is hooked or sliced) but a ball will not swing without these factors.

Therefore, the article should be read, bearing in mind the cricket usage of the terms.

According to Newton's laws of motion, a moving object not acted on by any force continues to travel in a straight line. For objects near the earth's surface there is, however, always the force of gravity pulling directly downwards, and it is this that brings things back to earth. But there is no similar sideways force to deflect anything, and so as a rule the path in which an object moves freely will be expected to lie in a vertical plane.

But any cricketer knows that on occasion this no longer holds, and that the ball may move out sideways from this vertical plane, and do what is called *swerve in the air*. This is what is meant by the term 'swing bowling'. We are not here concerned with what a ball may do on striking the ground, but only with effects during its flight through the air.

It seems probable that swerve bowling has come into more frequent use during the present century, simply because the rule allowing access to the all-important new ball, not only at the beginning of an innings, but at the latest after 200 runs have been scored, was first introduced only in 1907. Hitherto a new ball made its appearance only at the start of each innings. The practical effect is that on the average a new ball is now available every 130 runs or so, as a few sample matches will show, instead of after the average length of an innings, which is more like 230 runs. [Note: this was the case when Raymond Lyttleton gave his talk. The rule has since been altered.]

Swerve occurs not only in cricket, but also in golf, tennis, and baseball, not to mention other games. But in these, swerve is produced by spinning the ball, whereas in cricket the ball can be made to swerve without imparting any significant degree of spin to it, solely because of the presence of the seam on an otherwise smooth surface, as we shall explain.

If by some magic cricket or any of these games could be played in a vacuum, then Newton's laws would operate directly, and no swerve at all could occur. So we must look for some effect arising from the presence of the air for the cause. It is not always realised just how large the forces are that are exerted by the air on an object. The atmosphere presses on everything with a force of around one kilogram per square centimetre of surface. So on a cricket ball, the opposing pressures on any two hemispheres are each about 40 kg. If by any means some kind of pressure difference, as between the left-hand side of the ball and the right-hand, could be brought about, so that these opposing forces failed to balance by even as little as *one part in a thousand*, a sideways force of 40 g would come into play. This is about a quarter the weight of a cricket ball, and so could easily make the path curve sideways appreciably. The deviation would be about 30 cm during the motion lasting half a second, which is roughly the time the ball is in the air for fast bowling.

But in order to see how any difference of pressure on opposite sides of the ball could arise, it is first necessary to understand in some detail what happens to the near air as the ball travels through it. We can see that the air must be pushed aside and parted as the ball moves along, but in fact, the air does *not* simply slide by the ball and join up again at the back in an otherwise undisturbed way. Whenever a fluid such as air streams past a solid body, the particles of fluid actually in contact with the body adhere to it and move at exactly the speed of the body itself. In other words, the air immediately in contact with the ball is at rest on its surface. On the other hand, not very far away, the air is quite obviously more or less undisturbed – just as for a boat, the water only a few centimetres away from the side appears to flow by almost undisturbed. On the forward part of the ball at any rate then, where it is breasting its way through the air, this means that in an extremely thin layer just outside the surface the motion of the air changes from that of the ball itself to almost no movement at all. For the speeds a cricket ball is bowled at, which range roughly from 60 to 130 kilometres an hour, this *boundary layer*, as it is termed, is less than a millimetre deep, but its thickness is least at the front of the ball and gradually increases round the sides. We can picture it as a very thin skin clinging to the ball at its inner side but slipping by with the air at its outside.

If the speed is extremely small, this boundary layer will cling to the surface almost round to the rearmost point before it finally leaves the ball in a narrow stream behind it. But when the speed is increased to anything like the rates that occur in cricket, things are very different, and the layer breaks away about half-way round the ball at its sides. Immediately behind the ball, however, the air is violently disturbed, and forms an irregularly eddying wake that gradually diffuses back into the ordinary air as it drifts away behind the ball. This wake is exactly contained within the boundary layer that streams off the sides of the ball. The existence of this turbulent wake can be demonstrated visually in the experiments in which the ball is held at rest and the air made to stream past it, by introducing smoke into the air immediately behind the ball.

Now imagine the speed of the air past the ball to go on steadily increasing. Then the place on the surface where this smooth boundary layer flow ceases gradually moves forward on the ball. But there is a limit beyond which it never comes. This is not quite half-way round the ball from the front – actually, it is about 80 degrees from the nose of the ball. The eddying wake streams off at a tangent from this part of the ball to form a gently widening region trailing away behind and gradually melting back into the undisturbed air. The energy to produce the turbulence in this wake is supplied by the ball's motion, which accordingly experiences a resistance slowing it down. One might think that resistance would come mainly from the drag of the air slipping by at the sides. But this is not so. The drag is negligible compared with the effect of the low pressure region immediately behind the ball, which can be thought of as a partial vacuum sucking the ball back.

If the speed is still further increased, an entirely unexpected thing happens next. The boundary layer now begins to creep further round towards the back again as the speed rises, before finally breaking away to form the edge of the wake. The wake behind the ball grows much narrower as a consequence, and measurements show that once this stage is passed the resistance to the motion begins to decrease quite abruptly. At sufficiently high speeds, the boundary layer reaches three-quarters the way round the ball, that is to within about 45 degrees of the rearmost point before peeling off.

For any particular size of ball there is a 'critical speed' at which these things begin to happen, and above which the resistance force suddenly starts to drop. For a perfectly smooth metal sphere the size of a cricket ball, the boundary layer begins to extend rearwards again when the speed reaches about 145 kilometres an hour. The upper limit, when the boundary layer has got round to the back as far as it can, occurs at about twice this speed. This is for a smooth ball. But for a rough ball, as we shall see, this critical speed may be considerably less.

Now increase of speed above this critical velocity is not the only way in which the boundary layer can be made to cling further round the surface. This can be achieved at speeds much less than the critical one by attaching small raised ridges to the otherwise even surface of the ball; in other words by roughness at suitable parts of the surface. At first sight one might think any such irregularity would so disturb the flow near the surface as to incite separation of the boundary layer, but, in fact, just the reverse happens. A thin wire ridge, for instance, placed transverse to the air-stream round the forward part of the ball, results in the boundary layer adhering further round than it otherwise would, for a given air speed, before lifting off into the wake. The breadth of the turbulent wake is again consequently narrowed, and more important still the air resistance opposing the motion of the ball is lessened owing to the surface irregularity. This is the reason why grooves and dimples are patterned on the surface of a golf ball. Were they not there, the ball could not be driven anything like as far, because air resistance to a smooth ball, at these critical speeds, is more than *four* times what it is on a ridged ball.

So we may conclude from all this that small irregularities on the surface can delay the separation of the boundary layer and narrow the resultant wake, thereby producing a *lower* critical speed at which the reduced air resistance suddenly enters. Having got these matters clear, we can now begin to think first of an actual cricket ball, and then of the effect that the seam can introduce in the kind of way.

The actual force of air resistance exerted on a cricket ball is surprisingly large. With a critical speed of about 30 metres per second, just *above* this the air resistance directly opposing the motion is about *half* the weight of the ball. But just *below* it, the opposing force becomes nearly *twice* the weight of the ball. The precise value of the critical speed depends very much on the condition of the surface of the ball, and for a rough ball might well be still lower. For instance, if it were 20 metres per second, that is about 70 kilometres an hour, the air resistance would be about a *quarter* the weight of the ball *above* the critical speed, and *equal* to the weight just below it. So for a bowler operating at and near the critical speed of the ball, considerable difference of trajectory would result from very minor changes in the starting speed. This shows that the claims one hears about the ball being flighted in the air, of its being made to dip suddenly, and such like, although not usually stated in precise terms, may nevertheless have a definite basis in mechanics. All these effects, and that of swing itself, depend on the fact that the density of the air is just right for them to happen. If it were very much denser or rarer, none of these peculiarities would enter. So if cricket is played on Mars, swing bowling and flighting the ball will be unknown in that thin atmosphere.

To come now to the effect of the seam. As you know, a cricket ball has a prominent band of six lines of stitches running parallel to each other right round it and holding the two halves together. This band is about 2 cm wide, and when the ball is new the four outer lines of stitches stand out about half a millimetre – that is, something approaching the depth of the boundary layer. Also, when the ball is new, the rest of the surface, nearly ninety per cent of the area, is smooth and shiny. As the ball is used, the seam gradually becomes flattened down, and the rest of the surface loses its shininess.

If we imagine the air streaming horizontally past the ball, with the general plane of the seam upright and in the direction of the motion through the air, then everything will be perfectly symmetrical on the two sides of the ball, and there can be no sideways force. But things become very different if the plane of the seam is turned to one side round the vertical axis. Suppose, for example, that the forward part of the seam is turned towards the bowler's left, so that the plane of the seam runs from mid-on towards the slips; that is, turned at say 30 degrees to the direction of motion through the air. It is at this point that we come to the crucial effect that the seam can have. The roughness provided by the stitches at the front, which are now slightly to the left, will operate to maintain the boundary

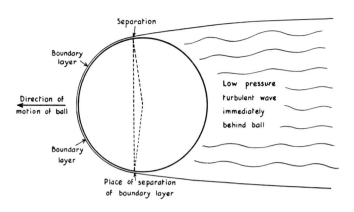

Ball moving below the critical speed. Symmetrical flow.

The extent of the boundary layer, and the general form of the turbulent wake behind the ball. The wake is slightly broader than the ball, and the pressure in it immediately behind the ball is lower than on the front part of the ball. (It is the net effect of the pressure on the whole surface that retards the ball.) The wake gradually melts back into the undisturbed air. (The drawing is not to scale: the thickness of the boundary layer is exaggerated in order to show it.)

layer flow more than half-way round on this left-hand side of the ball. But on the right, the stitches will be too far round at the back to have any influence on the boundary layer, which will already have broken away somewhere about half-way round the ball. The flow on the two sides is therefore no longer symmetrical, and we arrive at a situation in which a sideways force can occur. On the left, where the flow is undisturbed over a greater range of boundary layer, the total air pressure is less than it is on the right, and the ball accordingly experiences a force to the left that will deviate it sideways and make it move towards the slips. This force can rise to nearly half the weight of the ball on occasion when everything is just right for it. If the seam is turned the other way, with its plane running from mid-off down to fine-leg, the situation is reversed, and the sideways force is to the leg side.

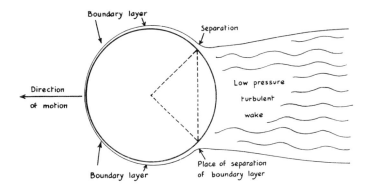

Ball moving above the critical speed. Flow necessarily symmetrical. The boundary layer now clings much further around the ball. The wake is now narrower, but the pressure in it immediately behind the ball is higher than in the first diagram, with the result that the retarding force (coefficient) is much less.

The boundary layer can also be extended in this way (for lower speeds) by slight surface roughness on the front half of the ball, and the resistance force similarly reduced. (The drawing is not to scale: the thickness of the boundary layer is exaggerated in order to show it.)

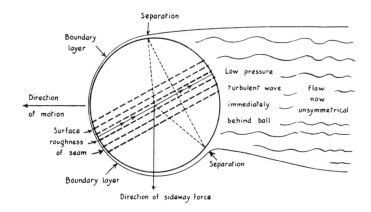

Ball moving below the critical speed, but flow rendered unsymmetrical by the effect of the seam. (The ball is being viewed from directly above.) The roughness of the seam at the front of the ball (on the left as shown here) makes the boundary layer cling much further round this side. On the smooth side the layer breaks away early on. The flow is not symmetrical. This produces an asymmetrical pressure distribution over the surface, and the resulting sideways force component makes the ball swerve.

The seam stays in position because of the backward spin given to it as bowled; the direction of this is indicated by small arrows along the central line of the seam. (The drawing is not to scale: the thickness of the boundary layer is exaggerated in order to show it.)

We can see also at this point that a rough ball will not swerve. This is because its surface roughness will operate equally everywhere to keep the boundary layer fully extended and quite symmetrical on the two sides, and there is no further effect that the seam can have. We can also predict that a ball sufficiently roughened on one side, but smooth on the other, could be made to swerve even if it had no seam at all.

We should perhaps explain how it is that the seam can remain fixed in the right position as the ball moves through the air and does not stray away to spoil the effect. The reason is simply the slight amount of rotation, almost in the backward direction, that is automatically given to the ball as it leaves the bowler's hand. The seam merely turns in its own general plane just as the rim of a wheel does. This, of course, may not always happen, and then the ball will not swerve.

One of the most intriguing features of swing bowling is the so-called 'late swerve', in which the sideways deviation shows little or no signs of occurring until late in the ball's flight, usually as it begins to dip downwards towards the ground. There are two possible causes that could bring this about; both could independently produce a late effect, and if operating together would combine to produce it in greater amount.

The first arises from the mere position of the seam relative to the air-flow past the ball. We have so far thought of the ball as travelling along a horizontal straight line with the plane of the seam vertical but turned slightly to one side. But, in fact, the later part of the flight, just before the ball reaches the ground, is inclined distinctly downwards at an angle of some 20 degrees or so, the exact value depending on the speed. If, therefore, the seam is in the most suitable position for swerve during this downward part of the path, it will necessarily be in a less suitable position at the early horizontal part, and vice versa. So by altering the grip, the bowler could take advantage of this changing direction of motion and obtain the best effect late in the flight.

The second independent cause could arise from the existence of this critical speed above which, as we have seen, the ball will not swerve at all because the place of separation of the boundary layer is already so far towards the rear that surface roughness in the shape of the seam can have no effect, and the flow is perfectly symmetrical on the two sides of the ball. The seam cannot affect this situation. But the resistance of the air will diminish the speed and bring it to values at which swerve effects *can* come into play. So, if the bowler starts the ball off at the merest fraction above its critical speed, swerve may occur in the later part of the flight only, when the speed has dropped below the critical amount, and the seam thereby given its chance to operate.

Clearly, by combining these possible ways of producing late swerve the greatest effect will be obtained. This would be a question of experimenting not only with the grip, but also with the speed, and obviously it would be a very elusive thing to get all the factors right, as is well known to be only too true.

The foregoing explanation of swerve is based on the results of practical experiments with various-sized spheres in the airstream of a wind-tunnel. Even under the more or less ideal conditions so provided, it is found that the critical speed is highly sensitive to the surface roughness, and also to seemingly minor irregularities in the airstream itself, such as the slightest degree of inherent turbulence. These factors are found to be capable of reducing the critical speed by fully fifty per cent.

There seems little doubt that it is features corresponding to these that explain why it is that a bowler may at one time succeed hugely in obtaining swerve and yet at another fail altogether to get the effect. There are strong indications that humid, sultry weather somehow affords the most suitable conditions, and one may conjecture that this may involve very small scale irregularities of motion in the air, or it may affect suitably the surface smoothness of the ball, or, of course, even do both. It has even been suggested that humidity might swell the seam stitches to make them even more effective in relation to the depth of the boundary layer.

Another strange thing is that an individual new ball, apparently indistinguishable from any other new ball, may not swerve at all, in so far as this can be established on the cricket field. So evidently the various factors, if indeed they have all yet been appreciated, combine together in an obscurely complicated way, and it is impossible at present to say in detail precisely what are the *best* conditions, of atmosphere and surface of the ball, conducive to the effect. In problems of this kind, when several factors may be operating to produce or hinder a single main result, the analysis of the underlying causes can be one of the most difficult things to carry out. Unfortunately, the theoretical treatment of such problems is beyond the resources of mathematical analysis, at any rate at the present time, and, of course, no amount of mere verbal discussion of the various factors can ever finally settle their individual contributions. The only remaining way to study the matter is by direct experiment, in which the various factors, supposing them to have been appreciated, are under control and capable of being varied at will. Such experiments are, in fact, at present being carried out by means of a wind-tunnel with the object of achieving a fuller understanding of this intricate question of swerve. With a wind-tunnel the air-speed can be adjusted to any desired value, while the ball can be dropped vertically through the stream to give a situation completely equivalent to a ball projected through the air. Beside the speed, the things that can be varied are the angle of the seam to the air-flow, the size of the stitches, the smoothness of the ball and, of course, of each side of it separately, and even the humidity of the air flowing through the tunnel. These are the factors that appear most likely to be involved, but possibly there may be others not yet thought of, whose existence will gradually emerge if it does not prove possible to interpret the results on the basis of the assumed causes only.

If all the factors can eventually be isolated, it would then become possible, instead of leaving it to chance whether a ball is suited to swerve bowling or not, to have a standard specification for a cricket ball, just as at present there are standards for size and weight. But perhaps this is a dangerous matter to bring up, suggesting as it does the possibility of secret researches to discover how to make cricket balls that will swerve, and also ones that will not.

Field Placing

Several charts are included in this book depicting suggested field placings for various types of bowlers. I want to stress that they are purely suggestions and must on no account be regarded as unalterable.

The placing of a bowler's field must always be dictated by four things:

a] The type of bowling;
b] The kind of batsman;
c] The condition of the pitch;
d] The state of the match.

Let me briefly enlarge on these.

A bowler may be classified as slow right-hand leg-break. It is still possible to be included in the category even though you have a low trajectory with little spin and concentrate on the off stump, or you have a high trajectory with lots of spin and aim at the leg stump.

A batsman who seldom drives but who relies upon deflections each side of the stumps is hardly likely to require men deep behind the bowler, whereas a powerful driver almost certainly will.

The field placings change out of all recognition when a sticky wicket is encountered as compared with a firm dry pitch.

Lastly, why should a fast bowler worry about having a deep third-man if there are two wickets to fall, 30 minutes left for play, and 200 runs to get? Obviously, runs would then be of no concern and how often has one heard of deep third-man taking a catch? He is predominantly a run-saver.

These matters are all a challenge to be studied as the game unfolds.

Dealing with an Off-Spinner

I am constrained to write under the above heading by the astonishing performances of Jim Laker in the 1956 Test series in England.

His figures in the five Tests were:

Overs	Maidens	Wickets	Runs	Average
283.5	127	46	442	9.6

At Manchester, in the fourth Test, his analyses read:

Overs	Maidens	Wickets	Runs	Average
68	27	19	90	4.7

The Australian batsmen at various stages appeared helpless and could not devise a satisfactory counter. But surely there must be an answer to a method of bowling which has been used ever since overarm bowling became legal.

Anyway, I am going to analyse the position as I saw it, and at least the attempt may be described as a mental exercise.

The game of cricket is constantly a battle between the wits of the striker and those of the bowler. The latter is of course supported by a wicket-keeper and nine fieldsmen, but no more. He will try to use them to the best advantage

a] to get you out;

b] to stop you scoring runs.

So long as he can keep these men where he wants to, the initiative belongs to the bowler and your chances of success are reduced. Force him to shift them and the initiative passes to you. His plan goes astray.

The game resembles draughts in the way you should look ahead.

The diagram, shown here, is the basic field which Laker used for his destructive spell of bowling.

Surveying that field it is obvious that the batsman's chances of getting out exist mainly through the agency of the wicket-keeper, fieldsmen nos. 3, 4 and 5, or being bowled or LBW.

A check of the Test match in question reveals, in fact, that of the 15 right-hand batting wickets which fell to Laker

4 were bowled

3 LBW

3 caught by no. 3

3 caught by no. 4

1 caught by no. 8

1 stumped.

The wicket-keeper and fieldsmen nos. 3, 4 and 5 are really the only ones in the picture when defensive shots are being played. The batsman's counter, therefore, must somehow try to minimise the chances of being LBW or

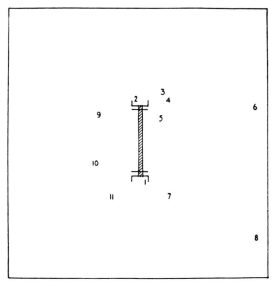

1. *Bowler* 2. *Wkt* 3. *1st leg-slip*
4. *2nd leg-slip* 5. *Forward short-leg*
6. *Outfield (square)* 7. *Mid-on* 8. *Long-on*
9. *Point* 10. *Cover* 11. *Mid-off.*

The above field placing was used by Laker for his sensational bowling performance. Rarely did he find it necessary to move a man.

Dealing with an off-spinner.

bowled, and an attempt must be made to disperse those short-legs or reduce their effectiveness.

Remember that the LBW law which was operating at that time only penalised a batsman when his legs were within the shaded area between wicket and wicket shown in the diagram of Laker's field.

We are dealing with a set of conditions under which the bowler is able to turn the ball considerably.

The batsman should, therefore, first resolve never to play forward defensively unless he feels certain of smothering the spin on the ball, and when he does to make sure the handle of the bat is always kept well forward of the blade. To play forward at the pitch of the ball without smothering it would almost certainly result in a catch to fieldsmen nos. 3, 4 or 5.

As an added precaution, he should endeavour to make sure that the front leg is always alongside the bat or even slightly ahead of it, to guard against any ball going off the inside edge on to the pad, thence to leg-slip for a catch.

Secondly he should resolve that when he plays back defensively, he will go well back towards the stumps – not play back just from the crease line – to give himself more time to see the ball.

Again he should try to keep the handle of the bat slightly ahead of the blade on contact with the ball and try to ensure playing with a dead bat so that the ball will drop down at the feet and not be impelled away.

To any ball pitched outside the off stump and therefore outside the shaded area, the danger would mainly arise if it turned into the stumps. Therefore, always cover the stumps with the pads and be ready to play for the ball turning into the shaded area, knowing that if it goes straight on outside the off stump, no harm will result. The only danger would be a snick to the wicket-keeper and this should not be hard to avoid.

To any ball pitched within the shaded area, the batsman's worry would be mainly against the ball which was not turning enough to miss the stumps because that ball would carry the bowled or LBW label. So always be ready to protect the line of the stumps.

If the ball was sufficiently short of a length to enable one to play back and it turned enough to miss the stumps, there must be a reasonable chance of letting it go. If it didn't turn that much, it should be playable without difficulty.

Up to this stage I have dealt only with the defensive measures which the bowler may force on the batsman. They would certainly be necessary because a bowler of that class must cause the batsman to play defensively on very many occasions.

However, my main interest would be in trying to adopt some form of attacking role to put him off his length and nullify the value of those short-legs.

Providing the runs come quickly enough or regularly enough without wickets falling, the batsman would call the tune sufficiently to force an alteration in the field.

The scoring possibilities which are evident against this field are numerous. Any ball pitched short of a length should be pulled straight into the faces of the short-legs, preferably at no. 4. These men would have no hope of catching a pull shot. They would be too busy protecting themselves to sight the ball.

A hard pull past no. 4 should often yield four runs because it would have a good chance of beating no. 6 on the fence.

Even the ball pitched short outside the off stump could be pulled between nos. 6 and 8, straight past no. 5.

There would be no attempt to cut with a horizontal bat unless the ball happens to be extremely short and quite wide of the off stump, because cutting against an off-spinner is dangerous. However, one should be ready to force the ball on the off side with a perpendicular bat (providing the stumps are well covered by pads outside the shaded area) because of the desirability of keeping fieldsman no. 9 where he is. In that position he is purely defensive, and an occasional studied placement either side of nos.

9 and 10 for a short run would be one's best hope of keeping him there.

Any half-volley pitched outside the leg stump would be swept away with a full-blooded swing straight at no. 4 and that ought to be perfectly safe besides yielding runs.

The real danger would be that ball pitching round the off stump. Here is where I think footwork would supply the answer.

At the top of these pages you will find reproduced a series of photographs from a movie film.

These show me making a controlled on drive from a half-volley and moving on down the pitch to run.

From that position a ball could not get between bat and pad.

The bat is turning over with the spin as it makes contact to ensure the ball is kept on the ground. Head and shoulders lean well forward into the stroke.

There is also a picture on page 136 depicting a forcing shot wide of mid-on. Moving forward out of the crease I have directed the ball wide along the ground. It is clearly visible just to the right of the wicket-keeper's head. This was in fact the stroke which brought me my hundredth century in first-class cricket.

With such an on-side stroke there should be plenty of singles to be picked up towards fieldsman no. 8 and, indeed, some twos and an occasional four between nos. 6 and 8.

This stroke could safely be played to any half-volley (or ball which was converted into a half-volley) which pitched in the shaded area.

Any ball which turned enough to beat the bat when such a stroke was attempted well down the pitch could hardly result in an LBW.

And it would have to turn tremendously to miss the pads on the leg side so that no wicket-keeper would have much hope of gathering the ball for a stumping.

But to assist the position still further, I suggest the striker taking up his stance 30 cm or more outside the crease when waiting for the ball to be delivered. This would be a potent weapon in trying to upset the bowler's length. It should enable the batsman to make half-volleys out of balls that would otherwise be of good length, and it should, if used judiciously, cause the bowler to drop one short here and there and so provide opportunities for the pull shots which I mentioned earlier. It should also

give driving opportunities from over-pitched deliveries.

Should the bowler counter by throwing the ball further to the off, he would immediately lay himself open to the possibility of being driven between the bowler and no. 11 (where there is a big gap with the bowler coming round the wicket) or even between nos. 10 and 11. Moreover, it would largely play into the batsman's hands because it would somewhat negate the use of the short-legs.

A very wide one on the off to try for a stumping could be protected by the pads and, anyway, would not demand a shot so that the bat could be placed behind the batting crease.

This, of course, is a counsel of perfection, and I am just as well aware as anyone who reads my theoretical exercise that such a batting plan would be subject to human frailty on the part of the batsman and to the counter plan of the bowler.

The latter's first move may well be to shift no. 5 to a position mid-way between where he is now on the plan and no. 8, but such a move would mean one danger fieldsman had been

The on-drive for a single against India which gave me my hundredth century in first-class cricket.

removed and would reduce the risks in playing a forward drive towards mid-wicket.

Under no circumstances should one attempt to hit the ball in the air except over the heads of nos. 3 and 4. A lofted drive in the direction of no. 8 to try to clear the boundary would be sheer suicide. And if there was obviously a batting plan to lift the ball into the outfield, no. 6 could easily be moved round towards no. 8.

This type of bowling under conditions favouring a spinner can never be defeated purely by defence. If no runs are coming the batsman must eventually lose.

And seldom can attack alone win the day. The latter, without a sound defence, must fail. The only hope is a judicious blending of the two.

By combined attack and defence the batsman has cause to hope that he will occupy the creases for a reasonable time, during which he will get a fair quota of runs. With everybody doing the same thing will come the best insurance against the team being overwhelmed.

The plan would require judgment, but it is a plan, seriously thought out along sound and well-defined lines, which offers some hope. A haphazard approach with no plan has no future.

And I hope this treatise will have served to stimulate thought in the minds of readers who will at least be able to formulate ideas of their own to meet this or any other type of challenge they may encounter.

The execution of a plan is much harder than formulating one, but what builder would think of commencing a structure without any idea what his next step was to be?

Batting is a scientific study. One must have a theory which is sound and then it is up to the individual to implement it.

These remarks are applicable of course only to right-hand batsmen. The problem is quite different for the left-handers who are faced with the ball which turns from leg – the ball which, in my opinion, is by far the hardest to play when it is properly pitched.

Even though I sincerely believe that the ball turning from the leg is the hardest to play, it is extraordinary that in the same match Tony Lock, then the best first-finger left-hander in

the world, bowled 69 overs and took only one wicket for 106 runs. At least it helps to prove that the pitch was by no means unplayable.

And so this chapter is written, using as a background the most famous bowling performance in history.

Its main purpose is to show that bowling and field placing must be analysed by the batsman. A coach with a blackboard could spend a profitable hour debating the various moves with his pupils.

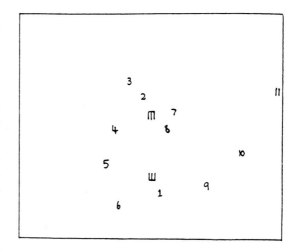

1. *Bowler* 2. *Wkt* 3. *1st slip* 4. *Point*
5. *Cover* 6. *Mid-off*
7. *Short backward square-leg*
8. *Short forward mid-on* 9. *Mid-on*
10. *Mid-wicket*
11. *Deep backward square-leg.*

The type of field placing often used by the flatter faster type of off-spinners bowling around the wicket.

They nearly always use the predominantly leg-side placing because, by bowling round the wicket at the middle and leg stumps, they can be more certain of containing the batsman's stroke play.

These bowlers don't appear to worry about flighting the ball but make their attack very positive and direct, trying mainly to get the bat-pad catch.

Fielding

If there is one department in cricket in which sheer natural ability is self-evident, I believe it to be fielding.

Take the volatile Learie Constantine. He just couldn't help being a marvellous fieldsman, no matter where he was stationed. Speed of foot, agility, balance, good throw, confident catching – he had the lot.

Poor fieldsmen can improve themselves – all fieldsmen can strive to do better – but some fellows are blessed with a marvellous ball sense which the rank and file just cannot emulate. You only had to see Davidson move towards a ball and immediately you felt aware that there was a man who moved beautifully by instinct. When you saw Neil Harvey running for a catch you had instant confidence that he would hold it. You could sense these things by observing their actions.

Too many players regard fielding as a necessary chore in cricket instead of an art in itself and a delight.

A man makes fifty with the bat and is applauded. But what if he misses a catch and the lucky batsman makes another sixty runs?

This must surely be one of the greatest catches ever made, and illustrates what a superb fieldsman Alan Davidson was. Because Davidson was a natural left-hander the catch was incredibly difficult.

Every time a catch is dropped it is equivalent to giving the other side an extra batsman. In fact, it is worse than that because the batsman has very often become accustomed to the light and pitch, and the bowlers become progressively more tired.

Runs lost by faulty ground fielding are just the same as runs made off the bat by the opponents, but again the job often becomes harder still in that an unnecessarily high total is set which is more difficult to overtake.

It is hard to measure in precise terms the value of good fielding but its benefits are none the less tangible.

When I first entered big cricket I spent most of my fielding time on the boundary and can honestly say I enjoyed fielding more than anything else. My enthusiasm went so far that sometimes I secretly hoped our skipper would lose the toss so that I could more quickly satisfy my desire to go out and field. Being young and full of energy I loved to have chases round the boundary, especially on the soft turf of England when skies were grey and I could go without a cap. There is a real thrill in a dash round the fence which culminates in a one-handed save and a return right over the middle stump into the keeper's gloves.

The in-fielding positions are probably more important, but I know that when I was forced, by virtue of being captain, to come into the covers or some close-in position, I never felt the same thrill as when outfielding.

One of the reasons may have been that an outfield has a more leisurely and restful existence. He doesn't work at quite the same pressure as the others.

That is why it is not a bad thing for fast bowlers to retire to the outfield at the end of an over – providing it can be conveniently arranged within the general pattern and does not delay the flow of the game.

This technique was developed by the Englishmen. At first it was criticised as giving the bowler unnecessary walking but the relaxation angle became better appreciated later on.

The South African team which came to Australia in 1952/53 gave the finest example of team spirit and co-operation in fielding that I have ever seen. They were not a great side in batting or bowling but they practised fielding with fanatical zeal and backed it up with superb physical fitness.

They finally drew the rubber with Australia, thanks largely to their wonderful fielding.

A poorly trained fielding side will neglect many refinements which the Test-class players should not. Here are some of them.

Throwing in from the Boundary

The fastest throw from boundary to stumps is naturally the one with the lowest trajectory providing, of course, it reaches the stumps on the full. But I have never seen any player with an arm so powerful that he could propel the ball from boundary to stumps without the need to give it some arc in the flight. With a short boundary, such as the side at Lord's, or Adelaide Oval, good throwers can land the ball over the stumps without much arc, but it is a different story from, say, the end of the Adelaide Oval when the throw may approximate 90 metres.

Under those conditions the outfield can usually return the ball with maximum speed by letting it bounce once on the way – by skidding

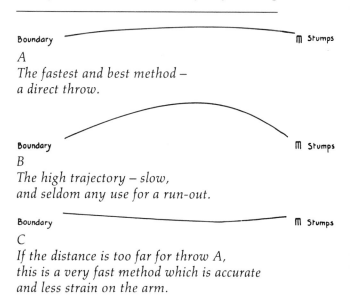

Boundary — ꟽ Stumps

A
The fastest and best method –
a direct throw.

Boundary — ꟽ Stumps

B
The high trajectory – slow,
and seldom any use for a run-out.

Boundary — ꟽ Stumps

C
If the distance is too far for throw A,
this is a very fast method which is accurate
and less strain on the arm.

it off the turf with a low trajectory. And that can be done with less effort than the throw on the full.

The various positions in the field demand quite different techniques for maximum proficiency. The man at first slip needs to be on the alert from the moment the bowler commences his run. On delivery he should observe the

---

Sir Leonard Hutton is brilliantly caught by Bobby Simpson of New South Wales. This must surely rank with the greatest of all slip catches.

Simpson has flung himself almost to the limit but in so doing has kept his eyes riveted on the ball. The body is perfectly balanced and supported on the left arm whilst the right hand is kept underneath the ball and clear of the ground to ensure a fair catch. Altogether the action is superb. Note also the bowler's position. He seems to be offering up a prayer that the catch will stick.

flight of the ball – eyes glued on it all the way. His job is to look out for a catch. The saving of runs is a secondary thought for him but, of course, his close observance of the ball makes him better able to stop any ball – catch or otherwise.

Fieldsmen near the wicket such as slips, gully, short-leg, silly point, etc., should stand evenly balanced with feet apart, ready to move in any direction. They must not move as the ball is being delivered.

I think it best for them to adopt a stooping position. It is much easier to get up quickly for a high ball than to bend quickly for a low one and also, from a stooping position, it is far easier to make a quick sideways movement

It is not important whether first slip is a good runner or not, but an outfield should be fast and he should be a good thrower. He has a more general survey of the whole scene and has room to manoeuvre according to the shot.

It is generally taught that every fieldsman must watch the ball the whole time but whilst in

general I agree, the outfield is the one man who may be permitted some licence.

Supposing a drive is made along the ground past mid-on and the outfield starts off in pursuit with obviously some 30 metres to go before reaching the ball. He can sometimes spare a momentary glance to see where the batsmen are so that he may judge whether the hit is merely a certain single, a certain two or a possible three, etc. He can observe whether one batsman is much more advanced than his colleague and so judge whether there is likely to be a danger end.

In such circumstances I sometimes tried to adjust my run (if I had the option) so that the batsmen would find themselves uncertain whether to run a second or not. To rush in and save the second run is very good but, depending on the state of the game, it may be a better thing, from the fielding point of view, to have the batsmen attempting a risky run. A little subtlety can occasionally be used in fielding.

However, when it is a case of trying to make a catch, there is no exception whatever to the rule – watch the ball all the way. This applies to all fieldsmen in every position.

An old saying is that the side which never drops a catch never loses a match and, whilst not completely true, there is a lot of common sense behind the remark. Percy Chapman's winning Test combination in 1928/29 did not drop a catch in the first four Test matches of that series and they won them all. In the final Test they failed to live up to this high standard and lost the game.

In attempting to make a catch I think it is wise to try to be well balanced and to keep the head quite still. I know this is impossible when a man is running flat out to reach the ball. But even if he has to run, he may be able to get under a catch and steady himself before it falls. Similarly with slips, they may have to overbalance in catching but I am quite sure they judge the ball more accurately if circumstances allow them to keep a still head till the last moment.

Nobody did this better than Tony Lock whose catching at short-leg or leg-slip was phenomenal. Unless he had to move his whole body to reach the ball, Lock's head remained motion-

I am about to catch a skier off Voce to end a Test match and am carrying out the theory of keeping the hands high, when possible, to take catches.
(The Sydney Morning Herald)

less, and I'm sure it contributed to the uncanny ease and certainty with which he picked up those lightning chances.

I'm sure also it is safer for outfields (assuming always that they have time) to catch at or above eye level.

Those who have watched crack baseball teams know how they get under a catch and never seem likely to miss. The glove is a tremendous help of course, but many baseballer-cricketers still use the same technique with bare hands. Neil Harvey was an arch-exponent of this. Victor Richardson was a wonderfully safe catcher and always took the ball as high as possible. It seems to allow a keen eye-focus of the position of the ball and prevents the blind spot which sometimes develops when trying to catch lower down.

A difficult catch is the hard drive chest high, so that you don't know whether to take it with fingers pointing towards the ground or the sky.

In the Nottingham Test of 1948 Godfrey Evans hit two such catches to me at extra-cover in the one over. Both times I was uncertain about which way to take the ball and dropped it. My chagrin was worse (except for relief at his dismissal) when Arthur Morris, fielding at mid-on, soon afterwards held a sensational catch to dismiss him.

All fieldsmen should take pride in returning the ball properly. It is a lovely sight to see outfields consistently dropping the ball over the stumps. What a contrast when the wicket-keeper is scampering everywhere to intercept erratic returns.

Even with the close-in fieldsmen, they should be very particular to return the ball chest high or waist high to either the wicket-keeper or bowler. Slovenly, shoddy returns reflect the mental attitude of a team, and it is galling to see a bowler putting everything into his work and then having to stoop and pick up a faulty throw-in.

That is one reason why I see virtue in the modern relay system whereby the wicket-keeper, standing back to a fast bowler, often throws the ball to slip or gully, who in turn passes it on with greater accuracy, or relays it through mid-off to the bowler. It is difficult for a wicket-keeper, with his big gloves and not much feel of the ball, to judge his distance when throwing. Some people don't like the relay and claim it wastes time. On the contrary, when it is done expertly there are occasions when time is actually saved.

Where to stand

It is always difficult to be absolutely sure of the correct fielding position but we may adhere to sensible deductions.

In the outfield I advocate that the man who is placed on the fence should stand at least five metres inside. I claim that from such a position no catch could go over his head and still land inside the boundary because he must have some time in which to observe its flight and move.

On the other hand he can certainly take a catch some five metres closer to the batsman than he could if standing right on the boundary line.

The depth of mid-on or cover is largely determined by the tenor of play, pace of the ground, etc. Cover normally would stand as far back as possible consistent with being able to save a single.

I had to occupy the position of mid-on to Clarrie Grimmett on many occasions and my job was to save the single, but I also had to make sure no four was hit straight past my left side. Such a stroke would have had to be an on drive or straight drive. It didn't matter if the ball got past on my right, because there was a man stationed on the fence that side who could cut off the four. But there was nobody behind me if it went through past the bowler.

So there was a small specialist problem. I had to use my judgment to try to save what singles I could in both directions but always making sure I allowed no fours to get past on the left.

All fieldsmen should closely observe their captain, for he is in control and must direct their movements. Very often he may desire a slight adjustment, without making it apparent to the batsmen. And what a reflection on the fieldsman when a captain is forced to hold up play and attract the attention of everybody just because this man was busy studying the latest cloud formation.

The depth of slip fields is often a problem. As a captain I mostly fielded at cover. From that side-on position I had a good sight of the ball and could judge its carry. Quite often I would ask slips to come up closer and many times was confronted (quietly and helpfully between overs) with their view that they were getting too close to focus catches.

Well, that's a fine point of judgment, but I always believed it was better to miss a catch than not to have the opportunity of catching it at all because the ball fell short.

Another important thing about slips is the width they stand apart. First slip should be well clear of the wicket-keeper.

The wicket-keeper should take what catches he can, and when he is standing back to a fast bowler he can cover a lot of ground. If a wicket-keeper is able to take catches which would have gone to first slip, then first slip is too fine. He should stand just so wide that in his judgment a catch won't go between him and the wicket-keeper.

Then, of course, the other slips adjust their position with him. In all cases they should stand as far apart as possible whilst making sure catches won't go between.

Also I like to see the slips splayed – in other words second slip a little closer to the bat than first slip and third slip a little closer than second slip. It is natural that the finer a slip catch the less resistance off the bat and the further the carry.

The gully fieldsman will have to adjust his place according to whether he is aiming to take a catch off a defensive prod, such as might happen on a sticky, or a full-blooded cut on a firm pitch. To take the latter very close in is no fun.

Cover is the place for a specialist, who should be able to move fast and throw well. The under-

An unusual happening. Those two wonderful Australian fieldsmen, Davidson and Benaud, muff a catch because they are too close to one another. The incident occurred during the Australian tour of England in 1953. (Sport & General Press Agency Ltd)

It seems obvious from the action below that the slip fieldsman was so close that he snatched at the snick from Sid Barnes. Don Tallon registers his agony at the miss. The only chance slip would have up there would be an outside-edge catch when the batsman played forward. (The Courier-Mail, Brisbane)

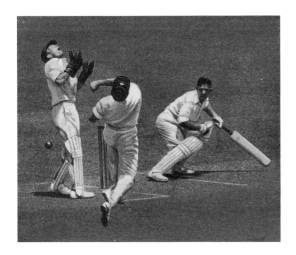

hand throw is valuable for him because he frequently has to get rid of the ball whilst on the run and no fieldsman is so likely to receive opportunities for run-outs.

Fieldsmen at cover, point, gully or third-man should remember that practically every stroke which is hit to them by a right-hand batsman will be partially cut and therefore will tend to curve from their right side towards their left.

They should endeavour, where possible, to field the ball on their right-hand side, so that any curl to the left can be controlled. But if the ball is being taken on the left side and goes away, you are in real trouble.

Many an inexperienced fieldsman at point has caused a laugh by failing to make allowance for this spin.

To a much lesser degree on-side fieldsmen will find the ball tending to go from their left-

The catch of a century. Richie Benaud is shown catching a tremendously fast square drive off Cowdrey in the Lord's Test of 1956. Benaud took some glorious catches (and some painful blows) in this position, in which he was fit to compare with the best of all time. (Sport & General Press Agency Ltd)

hand side towards their right. Only in the case of an off-spinner who is really breaking it will this curve be pronounced on the leg side and it is likely to be more so for shots hit behind square-leg.

All fielding and catching should be done with both hands whenever possible. Some fellows

DON'T USE ONE HAND WHEN TWO ARE SAFER

like to be flash and show how smart they are with one hand. It doesn't pay. Time enough to confine yourself to one hand when there is no option.

Care should be taken from the very first ball of the match to guard against mistakes. When a game is lost by one run or one wicket it is usually the last mistake which is remembered and that poor fieldsman hounded. Memories are sometimes short. It may have been a quite unnecessary piece of foolishness two days before that really caused the damage.

Close-in fielders must naturally keep still whilst the bowler is running up to bowl and on delivery. This is most important for men at, say, short-leg and silly point where any movement would distract the batsman. But mid-off, cover and the outfields should always start to move in as the bowler commences his run. It makes a tremendous difference to be on the move.

Imagine two chaps having a foot race – one having to stand still until the pistol went, the other being allowed a walking start. It wouldn't be a race at all.

So with fielding. A gentle move towards the batsman helps a lot in getting yourself balanced to go wherever you may have to.

And don't forget to back up. So many fieldsmen back up too late. They wait until they see danger developing before they move, whereas a sensible protective gesture a couple of seconds before may save much frantic rushing at the end.

This applies particularly to the need for a fieldsman to take his place at the bowler's wicket for a run-out. Most bowlers follow-through well down the pitch, especially the fast ones, and they are not in a position to conveniently turn and get back. Besides being easier for mid-off or mid-on to come in, the move saves the bowler the need for a sudden turn and the danger of ricking himself, to say nothing of a damaged finger from a hot throw.

Just because the ball is going to be thrown to the wicket-keeper doesn't mean that the need to back up has ceased. It may be thrown over his head, wide of him or it may bounce awkwardly.

When fielding a ball defensively, it is wise to use your body or legs as a protective shield. Get in front of the ball so that an unexpected bounce or turn won't get past.

But when it comes to the chance of a run-out this method may be too slow and something different is called for.

Very often there is no chance of positioning oneself at all. It is a case of do the best you can.

But sometimes (moving in from the outfield is a case in point) it is possible to adjust one's run and get into the finest possible position for an accurate throw in one continuous action without losing a fraction of a second.

The series of photographs on the next two pages illustrate the action.

No fieldsman has any control over the speed of the batsman's shot and therefore, by judgment, your own speed and direction must be so regulated that you reach the ball some 15 cm in front of and slightly to the right of the right toe. From this position the ball is gathered in both hands as the full weight of the body goes on to the right foot and it is transferred to the left as the throw takes place.

That was the old Wykehamist style. In the middle of the last century Winchester College was regarded for some twenty years as unrivalled by any school in England for its fielding prowess. In fielding, anyway, I am a Wykehamist at heart.

145

If these directions are closely followed you can move so that not a moment is lost in gathering the ball and disposing of it. The method can be used whether the fielder returns the ball with an underarm type of throw, round-arm or overarm. My throw from this position was round-arm. It seemed most convenient.

A little experimentation with the method of picking up with the weight on the left foot should quickly convince anyone how much slower it is. The fieldsman must take one extra step before throwing which could be fatal, because run-outs are more often obtained by a hair's breadth than a wide margin.

My method combines maximum speed and exactly the right position for an accurate throw. And those are normally the two essentials in a run-out.

A fieldsman can usually judge whether the run-out will be touch and go or whether the batsman is at his mercy (providing the return is accurate). Should it be the latter, always co-operate with wicket-keeper or fieldsman. Only when time is vital should you put everything into an effort to hit the stumps. Many a run-out has been a cinch but the fieldsman, by a wild throw at the wicket-keeper's shoe laces, has given him an impossible ball to take and the chance has been missed.

I mentioned earlier about my own love of fielding without a cap during grey days in England. Some players make a habit of going without a cap on hot sunny days. I think they make a mistake. The shield of a cap's peak is helpful during a long day in preventing eye strain, and it helps to guard against the possibility of losing a ball in the background.

On Test match grounds with large attendances the ball is difficult to pick up at certain heights. Many a catch has been missed because the fieldsman lost sight of it in the crowd.

In Australia, and in those other countries where the sun can be very fierce, the wearing of a wide-brimmed white hat is a sensible precaution. So is the use of a protective skin cream.

As I have mentioned elsewhere in this book I suffered severely from skin cancers after my playing days were over. My doctor assured me the damage was done through many long hours in the sun during my cricketing days.

Let me stress again that point about never taking your eye off the ball when it is a possible catch.

An interesting and valuable exercise at practice is to get someone with a bat to hit you catches which go over your head and for which you have to turn and run with the ball. Don't make them too high or too hard, but just get the feel of running with a ball which is coming over your head from behind. It is wonderful how it taxes both your eyesight and your judgment. Everything else must be subordinated to focusing your eyes on that ball

or you haven't a price to take the catch. Try it.

Slip-fielding machines can be procured and these offer useful practice. However, their value is rather limited because it becomes a relatively easy matter to tell which way the ball will go after hitting the wooden slats. You can

Practising slip catches by using the wooden cradle or slip-fielding machine.

thus anticipate its direction, something you can very seldom do with certainty on the field of play.

When considering the selection of players for a team I always have a soft spot for the keen, energetic fieldsman.

I'm afraid that some players are just lazy and won't take the trouble to try to improve. They prefer the extra half-hour in bed or consider some fielding exercise before a match just a nuisance.

In a crisis they are usually the ones who let you down.

Sometimes the situation arises where a choice has to be made between two fieldsmen as to which one shall take a catch. Perhaps two men can reach it with equal facility.

First, if the wicket-keeper is involved, let him take it. Should there be two other fieldsmen I think it should be left to the man in the better position. A man coming towards the ball for instance would normally have an easier catch than one running backwards, or a catch to the right-hand side would be easier than one on the left. These things happen in a split second, but if there is time to think leave it to the fellow with the easier catch.

Every fieldsman should remain alert and be as active as possible. There should be no standing with arms folded or hands in pockets. No leaning against the fence.

Talking to spectators or signing autographs over the fence are not the thing to do in big cricket. They may be harmless but they are distracting and tend to upset concentration.

Where there is a slip-fielding specialist in a team, he should be used in the slips. There is no position in the field (except the wicket-keeper) where catches are so numerous or so difficult.

Men like W. R. Hammond were worth untold value at first slip. Jack Gregory's influence on Arthur Mailey's bowling by his miraculous catching at first slip could not be measured.

Irrespective of one's attitude towards one-day cricket (or perhaps more accurately limited-overs cricket) even its most vocal opponents must admit that it has improved the quality of fielding.

In the first place selectors must be specially conscious of the need for fast alert fieldsmen and or this reason the slowcoaches tend to be left out.

When the game is in progress, particularly in the closing minutes when a tight finish becomes apparent, many chances of a run-out must be taken by the batsmen in order to achieve crucial runs. Superb fielding has won many a game.

One television station has initiated the re-playing of outstanding catches taken throughout a season and giving a handsome prize to the one adjudged the best. It is really exciting to watch say ten miraculous catches being repeated on the screen and to try and make a selection and they highlight the tremendous agility and skills of some of our players.

Returning the Ball to the Bowler

In an average day's first-class cricket a certain number of overs are bowled. The number will naturally vary according to the type of bowler around who is operating, but there may be 600 deliveries.

It is the job of the fieldsmen to protect the bowler and help him conserve his energy. To do this they should make sure the ball is returned to him at a convenient height.

Bad returns to the bowler causing him to bend down or move to one side to receive the ball help to make him more tired at the end of a long day.

Quite recently I watched a bowler who had just completed over 50 overs in the one innings, and was almost ready to drop, being forced to hastily stoop and pick up a nasty return which came from a fieldsman less than ten metres away. It was not because of any lack of thought or sympathy but merely because of a bad method of returning the ball.

In their anxiety to drop the ball softly right in the bowler's lap, so many chaps throw it back lolly-pop fashion. If there is an error of judgment and the ball falls short, it causes the bowler to stoop and pick up an awkward return.

Any risk of this can be avoided by adopting a different method or a different trajectory.

The first sketch below illustrates the better method.

These remarks are intended to apply only to returns from fieldsmen who are short distances from the bowler – say, 5 to 25 metres.

Run-outs

The query is often raised as to whether a fieldsman should aim at the stumps or at the wicket-keeper when going for a run-out.

For all practical purposes this question is confined to throws from somewhere reasonably close at hand.

A man on the boundary, for instance, should be quite satisfied if he can put the ball into the wicket-keeper's hands in close proximity to the stumps.

When it comes to the cover fieldsman (or his equivalent), in a sudden dash, I favour throwing at the top of the stumps to try to hit them. Many a run-out has been lost just because the wicket-keeper has had to take the ball. That minute fraction of a second has been lost, enabling the runner to make good his ground.

If the throw is made at the top of the stumps and it is wide on either side, it is still at the ideal height for the wicket-keeper. Those who advocate throwing at his chest overlook the difficulty involved in taking a ball and then having to make a downward movement to reach the stumps.

So I repeat – throw at the top of the stumps when the run-out chance occurs.

Fielding should be a joy and its value is incalculable. The score sheets and the record books have no way of assessing the runs saved by a brilliant cover specialist but, to those who understand and love their cricket, the man who shines in the field will always start with a big lead over the sluggard.

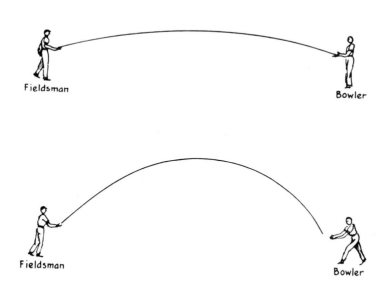

Fieldsman · Bowler

Wicket-Keeping

My own experience of wicket-keeping in first-class cricket was very limited because I only took over the gloves when our regular keeper was injured.

In the country, as a youth, I always had rather a liking for it but there were two reasons why I had no chance of getting such a position in the team.

First, my uncle was a very fine stumper and there was no thought of displacing him. Secondly, I was the team's leg-break bowler.

When I graduated into first-class cricket I was regarded as a batsman, and again the teams for which I played had their regular wicket-keepers.

So whatever my personal feelings in the matter, the chance never came my way but the inclination remained in my blood.

The main reason I interested myself mentally in this branch of cricket was because of my enthusiasm. I wanted to be in the game every moment I could and that of course is exactly what happens to the wicket-keeper. His job is tremendously important and exacting. There is no relaxation because every ball that his team sends down represents for him a need to concentrate. He never knows which one may spell defeat or victory as a result of his vigilance (or lack of it).

Great fieldsmen naturally play an important role in any team. A Gregory or Hammond in the slips, a Jack Hobbs in the covers or a Constantine anywhere can do much to uplift the fielding, but nothing has such an electrical effect upon the fielding morale as a wicket-keeper who brings off seemingly impossible stumpings and dives to hold phenomenal catches.

The very nature of the game means that these opportunities come his way so much more often than they do to other fielders.

It has been my good fortune to see many of the world's finest exponents of the art.

A magnificent study of Godfrey Evans at full stretch to intercept a wide return.
(Associated Press Ltd)

Further evidence of Evans' astonishing agility is shown in this photo as he attempts to run out West Indian star Frank Worrell.
(P.A. Reuter Photos Ltd)

Evans dives to try to reach a ball popped up by South Africa's Dudley Nourse. (Sport & General Press Agency Ltd)

Very early in my career I toured Canada and USA with a band of players whose wicket-keeper was lovable H. S. (Sammy) Carter – long since deceased. He was then an old man in the cricket sense but still wonderfully fast and skil-ful. Many long talks we had far into the night, and I revelled in hearing stories about his ex-periences in Test cricket going back to the days before I was born.

Before playing in a Test match myself I only saw two days' international cricket, and in that match (the fifth Test at Sydney in 1921) Carter kept wicket for Australia. The first ball Jack Gregory sent down went through to him and was taken right in the cup of the gloves, produc-ing that gorgeous soft dull sound which denotes perfect timing. I still remember that sound as though it happened yesterday and can recall commenting on it to my father at the time.

It was at once a lesson. There is perfect timing in the catching of a cricket ball just the same as there is in batting. Just as you get the sweet sound from a perfectly struck cover drive, so you do from the gloves.

How many thousands of times since 1921 have I heard the same sound, and when trying to judge the class of a young wicket-keeper, it is one of the first things I look (or listen) for.

From my first Sheffield Shield match with Bert Oldfied, to the 1932 tour with Carter and on to 1948, I was privileged to play with or against a line of wicket-keepers who have prob-ably been unsurpassed in history: Duckworth, Ames, Tallon, Langley, Evans and others.

Each had very special virtues and it is not my wish here to offer comparisons, except to refer to individual characteristics.

It is notable that the two outstanding qualities of great wicket-keepers are timing and footwork.

Godfrey Evans displayed more agility than anyone I can remember and he also possessed astonishing energy. In fact, his whole effervescent personality, his infectious humour and obvious enjoyment of the task, must have been a great inspiration to many English teams.

This enthusiasm is something every wicket-keeper could try to emulate, for, as I said earlier, no other fieldsman has anything like the same opportunities of inspiring his colleagues.

What special requirements does this job call for? Very high on the list I would place courage. Few men have stood behind the stumps during a long career without suffering severe physical injury.

In normal work the hands take a fairly heavy pounding. The early pioneers of the field, men like J. M. Blackham, wore gloves more akin to the present-day walking-out gloves. No wonder they initially had long-stops and that their hands finished up resembling gnarled oak. Broken fingers and busted joints were not by any means uncommon.

The wickets in the early days were ill-prepared and moreover there was some wild bowling. In the 1843 Oxford v. Cambridge match no less than 82 wides were chalked up. What a sensation that would cause today.

It is even recorded that Little Dench of Brighton, fielding at long-stop, had a sack of straw tied to his chest to prevent injury.

The modern heavily padded gloves, with finger-stalls and inner gloves, help to protect the hands from injury, but even today most wicket-keepers take the precaution of binding their top joints with adhesive tape to minimise the damage from a blow on the end of the finger.

It was freely stated that George Duckworth put a steak in the palm of his right glove to soften the blows when he was keeping to Harold Larwood. I cannot vouch for the accuracy of that but I do know the hands get very sore after a hard day taking fast bowlers.

But it is not damage to the hands which I am primarily thinking of when I refer to courage. Most wicket-keepers have received blows in the face or on the head to say nothing of plenty on the body. They are unavoidable at times even by the most skilful.

Wickets of all kinds, including sticky ones,

are encountered. There is the occasional mishap such as the ball flying up off the top of a stump when a batsman is bowled. One such happening badly cut Langley's eye and put him out of a Test match.

And apart from the danger of injury, the wicket-keeper must keep going and maintain his concentration throughout the longest and hottest days without flagging.

His job is not finished when the ball has been delivered, for then he frequently has to run up to the stumps and try to take a nasty, inaccurate return from the field, endeavouring to convert it miraculously into a run-out.

To force the hand and nerve and sinew to serve their turn long after they are tired out demands much moral as well as physical courage.

Fitness then is an important and valuable asset to any wicket-keeper.

Practice for Wicket-Keeping

The people who devise practice wickets seldom think of the Aunt Sally. Have a look next time you see a practice area and you will probably find in most instances that the rear net is so close to the stumps that there would be little room in which a wicket-keeper could operate.

Recently I saw a case where the batsman, playing back, actually caught his bat in the overhanging net with a resultant nasty crack in the face.

It is a good idea to have at least two or three metres between the stumps and the rear net so that a wicket-keeper would have room in which to move.

I can't think of any cricket ground where practice facilities for wicket-keeping to a fast bowler are provided.

Perhaps this inattention to practice facilities is one reason why you seldom notice wicket-keepers practising at the nets. They may also be fearful of damaging their hands or receiving an injury of some other kind, for undoubtedly wicket-keeping holds more hazards than other branches of cricket.

But nothing produces efficiency like practice, which is the best way to learn how to avoid those injuries.

I am a believer in sessions between the bowler and the wicket-keeper without a batsman, especially when the bowler is of the slow, tricky type, so that his stumper can get to understand the wrist and finger movement without having to worry about his opponent.

It is fatal if the bowler's own wicket-keeper can't spot his wrong-'un.

Equipment

The most important parts of the wicket-keeper's outfit must be the gloves – inner and outer. As an instrument is to the musician, they are the medium through which the player must display his art.

The inner gloves should be of chamois leather and put on slightly damp.

The outer should then fit snugly over the top. It is a mistake to have them sloppy, and unwise to use new gloves first time in a match. Normally they are stiff and require to be worked in by a fair amount of practice so that they become pliable and form a cup into which the ball snugly fits.

Then the gloves need to be faced. The rubber surface tends to become shiny and slippery so a preparation is often used to make it slightly tacky. Neatsfoot oil is commonly applied and so is eucalyptus. Mixed preparations are available in sports shops. The purpose is to have the rubber face properly conditioned, but be careful to see you don't overdo it otherwise this stickiness will be transmitted to the ball.

I have heard many a bowler use harsh language about a wicket-keeper who over-prepared his gloves. The black sticky substance is particularly annoying when it gets on a new ball and thence on to the bowler's fingers. And it militates against the ball swinging, too.

Should special pads be worn? Well, I have seen them with special heavily reinforced tops or even side levers down the outsides of the shins but I distrust them. I feel they make for clumsiness whereas speed is of supreme importance. Pads

are only the second line of defence anyway – the hands are the things that really count.

An abdominal protector must be worn. Not only does it protect the wearer from injury – it gives him far greater confidence.

Stumpings

Two points sometimes misunderstood are:
1. To avoid being stumped the striker must have some part of the bat in his hand or of his person grounded behind the popping crase. And the popping crease is the back edge (i.e. the edge nearest the wicket-keeper) of the crease marking.
2. The wicket-keeper must not take the ball in front of the stumps for the purpose of attempting a stumping unless the ball has touched the bat or person of the striker.

How often has one heard a spectactor complain about a batsman being out stumped because, so he claimed, the striker's foot was on the line. It may have been but he was still out. The marking of the creases is so designed that the distance allowed by the laws from stumps to batting crease is measured to the inside of the line. Therefore, the foot must be kept behind. On the line is not good enough. It is out. The rule, covering both points, reads as follows:

1. OUT STUMPED.
   The striker shall be out stumped if, in receiving the ball, not being a no-ball, he is out of his ground otherwise than in attempting a run and the wicket is put down by the wicket-keeper without the intervention of another fieldsman.
2. ACTION BY THE WICKET-KEEPER.
   The wicket-keeper may take the ball in front of the wicket in an attempt to stump the striker ONLY if the ball has touched the bat or person of the striker.
   Note. Ball rebounding from wicket-keeper's person. The striker may be out stumped if, in the circumstances stated in 1 above, the wicket is broken by a ball rebounding from the wicket-keeper's person or equipment or is kicked or thrown by the wicket-keeper on to the wicket.

Where and How to Stand

No hard and fast rules can be laid down under the above heading.

When slow or medium-pace bowlers are operating it is customary for the wicket-keeper to stand up at the stumps but he goes back to the faster types.

There is no doubt it is easier to take snicks behind the wicket (especially on the leg side) when standing back to a fastish bowler than when standing up. Likewise stumping opportunities become more rare as the bowler's pace increases.

Normally, therefore, it becomes a matter of judgment as to which position is likely to yield the better results.

Sometimes special considerations intrude. For instance, Alec Bedser always preferred to have his wicket-keeper at the stumps even when bowling in-swingers at top speed. For personal reasons Bedser gained confidence and felt better able to give his best, to exploit his technique to the full.

Godfrey Evans was so often his willing confederate in the English team and what a task he had. Many a time he made an incredible save on the leg side – often he took nasty cracks on the wrist or body, but occasionally he brought off an astounding stumping.

As one of the batsmen who were put to the test by Bedser's theory of a wicket-keeper at the stumps, I can vouch for its correctness in his case. He was a better bowler with Evans up at the stumps.

No batsman could afford to play forward and overbalance if he missed an in-swinger and I would have been happier as a batsman with Evans standing back.

Admittedly Evans did a marvellous job and very few men, if any, could have taken Bedser as he did.

But I have made a point. A wicket-keeper should stand where he thinks he can achieve the best result, co-ordinating his ideas with those of the bowler and the captain.

He must stand right up or right back. Halfway, or no-man's-land as we call it, is useless.

Wicket-keepers usually stand with the left foot round about the line of the off stump and in this position can obtain a clear view of the bowler's delivery outside that stump. However, there must be a degree of flexibility. He may stand a shade wider, for instance, for a right-hand bowler coming round the wicket than for a left-hander coming round, and so on. The main thing is to be comfortable, evenly balanced and to easily pick up the flight of the ball.

If standing at the stumps, he should be sufficiently close to remove the bails with a natural sweeping movement which does not demand any stretching.

When a ball is delivered wide of the wicket there is a natural tendency for the stumper to move across and slightly backwards. The latter should be resisted because it would take him away from the wickets and so make a stumping harder and slower.

Foot movements should be kept down to a minimum and confined to the essential ones for positioning the body and hands except where one has difficulty in reaching the ball at all.

A fault which is common with the lower-grade wicket-keepers is that they fail to move their bodies with the line of flight or even in advance of it. Let me clarify that point.

If a fast bowler sends down a big in-swinger which dips outside the leg stump, the wicket-keeper has to bear in mind both the saving of byes and the possibility of catching the batsman from a snick on the leg side. Therefore, immediately he picks up the flight and realises what the ball is doing, he should move to the leg side so that if possible he will be able to take the ball still coming towards his body. In this way he will be getting into the correct position to take the ball cleanly and he will have a margin on his left side to take the ball if it is deflected by a snick.

Don Tallon was an artist at this. He often went so fast and so far that he still took the ball on his right-hand side. But he took many snicks on his left-hand side which other players would never have reached.

The same principle holds good for out-

In this photo we see Les Ames taking a return from the field. By the attitude of the fieldsmen, especially the one backing up, the ball appears to have been thrown from the covers – moreover the ball is already in the wicket-keeper's gloves even though the batsman has only just reached the crease. Therefore I cannot understand why the wicket-keeper is not up at the stumps, unless he hadn't time to get there. At least it illustrates how essential it is for a wicket-keeper to be right at the stumps when a run-out chance occurs.
(The Herald, Melbourne)

---

swingers, namely to move across and still take the ball coming at the body if you can. But, of course, this is an easier proposition as the ball is visible all the way. There is no blind spot with the batsman's body obscuring the vision as there must be with an in-swinger outside the legs.

And don't forget to let those hands 'give' with the ball, especially off fast bowlers.

Always take the ball, if possible, with the fingers pointing towards the ground and see the hands give slightly as they take the ball. This is to minimise the risk of injury.

Most damaged joints and many broken fingers are caused by accidental blows on the ends of the fingers.

I know there are times when the fingers cannot be held down, the most difficult of all being the delivery which comes straight at the chest, but at least unnecessary injuries should be avoided.

Long experience and even instinct will prepare a wicket-keeper for the type of delivery which might produce a stumping chance – notably the unbalanced forward stroke.

In those crucial moments when split-second judgment is called for, there must be lightning speed and precision. Above all, certainty of taking the ball. Don't snatch at it in your excitement.

It is absolutely vital for the wicket-keeper to watch the ball right into his gloves. He should get his body in front of the line of flight when taking the ball, except when deliberately staying inside for a stumping chance or to avoid being hit.

No player on the field can be so helpful to his

Here we see Godfrey Evans about to attempt a stumping on the leg side. Note the concentration, the alertness, the impression of speed and the excellent balance.
(Hulton Picture Library)

bowler and his captain as the wicket-keeper. He is the man who sees exactly what every ball does. Whether it swings in the air or turns off the pitch – the slightest thing must be noticed.

The man at square-leg may see the striker play at but miss a ball near the off stump and form the opinion that it swung away to the off. He may be quite wrong. The ball may have gone straight through, the batsman just simply playing inside it. But the wicket-keeper won't be fooled.

Similarly he can instinctively tell which type of delivery is causing the batsman most concern and can quietly pass on useful tips to the bowlers between overs.

Then, of course, a vital part of the job is to take returns from the field and assist in run-outs. With wild and inaccurate throws the task

becomes far more onerous and dangerous than it need be. Many a blow has resulted from a fast throw which landed on the roughened footmarks near the stumps.

Should there be any chance of a run-out, the wicket-keeper should take position behind the stumps as early as possible and never take the ball in front of them.

It is the fieldsmen's job to throw correctly and the wicket-keeper should do everything he can to encourage and persuade them not to make him an Aunt Sally.

Because of the gloves, he is able to catch a ball with more certainty than anyone else. For this reason, whether it be a snick on the off or leg, or even a skied mis-hit, I strongly believe in allowing the wicket-keeper to take any catch he can reach.

I don't mean he should dive a metre to try and intercept with one hand a catch which would otherwise go comfortably to the two hands of first slip. Obviously my statement should be sensibly interpreted.

In the modern era I sometimes feel the emphasis has erroneously shifted towards placing unwarranted importance on how few sundries are recorded.

The primary job of the wicket-keeper is to take catches, make stumpings and play his part in run-out opportunities.

Here again we often find praise lavished on the man who, for instance, catches five and stumps two during a match as against his *vis-à-vis* who catches two and stumps one.

The proper comparison should of course be in regard to the chances missed.

If wicket-keeper A has ten chances, takes eight and misses two whilst wicket-keeper B has five chances and takes them all, clearly the latter has, percentage-wise, performed a more praiseworthy job. No player can take catches which are not offered.

Due regard must be paid to the one who makes chances possible by his agility or anticipation.

Godfrey Evans missed a few chances because he never shirked attempting the impossible to reach a ball. But I have seen cases where a wicket-keeper made no attempt to fly for a wide leg-side snick and in my own mind I have felt sure he wasn't prepared to risk failure.

As for sundries or extras, these are very often caused by erratic bowling or a nasty pitch.

If a hundred runs are scored on a sticky wicket you may be sure the wicket-keeper has been kept very busy taking some nasty flyers, whereas 500 runs on a lovely pitch may well indicate that few balls have passed the bat. It is all a question of keeping things in their proper perspective.

Lastly, the wicket-keeper sets the pattern for proper returns to the bowler (or nearby fieldsmen) to ensure that the bowler does not have to stoop and pick up the ball.

All of which adds up to a man-sized, responsible job. But what satisfaction at the end of a hard day to know that the score sheet reads no missed chances, no sundries and an indefinable contribution to the whole pattern of victory.

Running between the Wickets

One of the most exhilarating experiences for a cricket spectator is to watch a partnership between two batsmen who never miss an opportunity of picking up the cheekiest of singles.

Good running is largely a matter of judgment and experience. When two great players such as Hobbs and Sutcliffe have enjoyed countless hours together at the wicket they build up a marvellous understanding and a confidence in each other which makes the task appear simple.

But the hallmark of a really good runner is that he shall be able to run well with anybody. That can only be achieved by a strict observance of sound principles.

My initial education was on hard wickets in the country which are not nearly so conducive towards developing good runners as turf wickets. The ground is very often rough so that the bat cannot be slid along the turf at the conclusion of a run – the running surface alongside the pitch is uneven and the average country player just hasn't had the experience.

He doesn't get the same opportunities as the first-class player and I, like my country colleagues, was considered a bad runner when first I reached the city.

I had enough speed but my calling and judgment were so bad that a special effort was made by Tommy Andrews, one of our ex-internationals, to improve my knowledge on a short tour in which we played seven matches.

It was arranged that we should bat together whenever possible. I ran him out and he ran me out but the matches were unimportant so that didn't matter. The lessons were absorbed and stood by me in later life.

It is generally accepted that the striker is responsible for calling when the ball is hit in front of the wicket, whilst the non-striker shall call for a stroke behind the wicket. However, that must be regarded as a generalisation only. Either party must obviously have the right to deny his partner's call if he sees it is too dangerous.

Take a drive into the covers. The striker plays forward, moves into his shot and begins to advance down the pitch as he calls. But his partner slips a trifle in starting to run and notices that cover has made rapid progress towards the ball, which is seen going to his right hand, and the signs point towards a swift return to the wicket-keeper. The non-striker thinks he has no hope of making his ground.

He would obviously be foolish to go on with the run just because theoretically it was the right thing to do, according to the text book. He would have a duty to call 'No' immediately so that not only would he be protecting himself but he would also give his partner ample time to stop and return to the crease.

In such a case it is important that the denial of the striker's call must be loud, clear and prompt.

Under all circumstances initial calling,

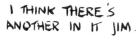

whether by striker or non-striker, should be restricted to one of three words, 'yes', 'no' or 'wait', and every call must be decisive.

You might say, 'How can the call of wait be decisive?' Well it can be in this sense, that the other person is effectively stopped from continuing a run pending some development.

Supposing a hard cover drive is made wide of the fieldsman, who can only hope to field it one handed. Both batsmen make preliminary moves towards running, but the striker realises that a hard drive to cover is more likely to produce a run-out than one hit slowly. He therefore prefers to wait and see whether the ball is cleanly picked up or whether the fieldsman mishandles it before being willing to commit himself.

Cases like this usually produce a dangerous run or an easy one, depending entirely on whether the ball is fielded cleanly.

So the value of the 'wait' call in this instance is to protect the non-striker from any danger of a run-out and at the same time warn him to be at the ready should the opportunity occur to continue the run.

There are lots of ways in which the two batsmen at the wickets can help each other. Assume a ball is cut down the gully and the batsmen set off for a run. By the time they cross on the first run, the non-striker should be able to form a fairly clear judgment as to whether the stroke will yield more than a single. So on passing the striker (whose back is towards the

ball) he may say, 'Probably two,' or some such guiding remark. This immediately gives his partner the cue to run quickly at the end of the first run and be ready to decide immediately whether he is willing to come back towards the dangerous end for a second. The call for that second run would be the prerogative of the runner who would be returning to the wicket most likely to be endangered.

The one unforgivable sin in running is indecision. There is nothing worse than a shilly-shally in mid-pitch with neither man knowing what the other proposes to do – the sort of thing a friend of mine describes as a 'perfect misunderstanding'.

If in doubt say 'No'. Only in exceptional circumstances is one run worth the risk of a valuable wicket.

After much experience with another player, expert runners can largely dispense with calling because of mutual understanding. I rarely heard Hobbs or Sutcliffe call. But that is a counsel of perfection and if one is to err at all it is far better to overcall than undercall.

Pay due regard to the speed of your partner. It is essential to make sure as far as possible that each run is just as safe for him as it is for you.

That wonderful judgment of pace and distance which some men possess can be developed up to a point, though not everyone can hope to attain it. But everybody can acquire a certain basic knowledge of procedure which should invariably be followed.

LEFT
The non-striker need only have his bat within his ground as the bowler delivers the ball. Once the ball has been released he is then in position to 'back-up'.

RIGHT
Showing how the non-striker should 'back-up' just after the bowler has released the ball. The metre or two gained by judicious backing-up will very often be the means of preventing a run-out.

1. The non-striker should always back-up. He does not have to stand behind the crease. So long as the bat is grounded behind, that is sufficient. I made a practice of standing outside with the bat inside as demonstrated by the photograph above; and I moved off immediately I saw the ball in the air after it had left the bowler's hand.

Some players have adopted the habit of moving off as the bowler completes his run. The danger of this method is that the bowler is quite entitled to retain the ball (as his arm goes over in the delivery stride) and knock the bails off at the bowling end. If the non-striker is then out of his ground he is run out.

Some people frown on this practice as being sharp, and think the bowler should first issue a warning. I cannot see this at all. The non-striker, by backing up too far or too soon, is in effect cheating. He is gaining an unfair advantage which may save him being run out in a photo finish the other end.

The law clearly provides that the non-striker may be run out at the bowler's end if he prematurely leaves his ground, and I have seen it happen in Test cricket. Hence my dictum — watch for the ball in the air before leaving the safety zone.

2. The non-striker should always stand two or three metres wide of the return crease on the opposite side of the stumps to that from which the bowler is delivering the ball.

3. The striker should always run closer to the pitch than the non-striker. Let me make this point clearer. To a right-hand batsman, with a left-hander bowling over the wicket, the non-striker would stand on the off-side of the pitch. Should the striker play a cover drive which, by virtue of his movement, takes him over to the off side, he too will run down that side. He should then run as close as possible to the pitch (without running on it, of course) and the non-striker should be on the outside of him. With such an understanding there is no danger of a collision or doubt about which lane in which to run.

It would be wrong in such circumstances for the striker to cut across the pitch after making his shot, just in order to run down the leg side. But if he jumped down the wicket to play an on drive, he may find it easier and more convenient to continue down the on side. There can be no absolutely hard-and-fast rule about which side of the pitch the striker should run. That is so often decided by circumstances. It is the non-striker's job to give his partner ample room and to protect him.

4. In making good his crease each batsman should ground his bat short of the popping crease and slide it over. This is particularly important when attempting to avoid a run-out or when making a quick turn for a second run. There is no need for the feet to reach the crease.

The right way, facing the fielder.

The wrong way, back to the fielder.

They may well stop a good metre short and that is ground saved. In fact, having regard to the starting position of the non-striker when he may stand outside his crease, and the distance he saves the other end, he only has to run some 16 metres.

5. As a general principle, run the first one fast in case there may be a chance of another. This must be interpreted with common sense. Plenty of shots are made where it is clearly impossible for more than one run to be scored. It would be absurd in such cases for the batsmen to charge wildly up the pitch looking for another run and merely help deplete their physical resources. On the other hand a glance to fine-leg where there is a fieldsman on the fence may well provide two runs if there is a semblance of misfielding, and the striker would need to get to the bowler's end quickly, turn and be ready for the chance.

6. Having completed a run and in the process of turning for a second, always turn towards that side of the ground on which the ball is struck. This may sound complicated but it isn't. The photographs above show what I mean.

A right-handed striker who makes a cover drive should, on turning for the second run, ground the bat with his left hand and turn towards cover. When making an on drive he would ground the bat with his right hand and turn towards the on side.

You may think such a point is trivial. It is not. Most run-outs occur by the narrowest of margins and these refinements are the very things which make all the difference.

Good running is a joy to watch and an even greater joy to implement. Its dangers lie in slow starting and indecision. If both batsmen run immediately the ball is struck, it is amazing what they can achieve and how difficult it becomes to run them out.

And don't overlook the great value of running between wickets as an adjunct to disorganisation of an attack and a fielding plan.

So long as the covers may remain deep and short runs are not taken, so long will they enjoy the advantage of being able to cut off fours which otherwise might get through. Judicious short running may pull them in and provide major scoring opportunities.

With a left- and a right-hand batsman operating together, the constant scoring of singles causes the field to change over and forces the bowler repeatedly to change his direction. No bowler likes that and very few can prevent it having some effect on their accuracy.

Batsmen should observe which fieldsmen are quick, which are slow, who can throw fast, who can't, whether a man is right- or left-handed, whether he is approaching the ball on his throwing side or not. There is literally no end to the subject.

Quite recently I was amused when two chaps were going for a run and the striker called out so loudly we heard him in the pavilion, 'Come two – he has a glass arm.' The same result could have been achieved without embarrassing the fieldsman and revealing to the fielding captain what he had observed.

Even more amusing was a happening in a second-class game in America. A ball was hit to third-man and it appeared to the onlookers that a second run could have been taken quite easily. However one of the batsmen, a big burly negro, loudly said 'NO', and declined to run. There was immediately some barracking from the crowd whereupon the big fellow said to his partner, 'Let them do the hollerin' out there, we'll do the judgin' right here'.

Even though a run-out appears inevitable, never give up. Many a batsman has made his ground safely because the wicket-keeper, in his excitement over a chance, has fumbled the ball, or when the fieldsman has failed to gather cleanly or thrown wildly in his urgent attempt to beat the batsman. If you give up the chase, you give added time and confidence to the fielding side who are less likely then to fall into error.

Should you accidentally drop the bat in running, it is mostly quicker to keep going than to stop and retrieve it. The bat can be safely picked up after the run is completed.

Despite every precaution run-outs will occur. More often than not no doubt exists as to who is to be the victim. But occasionally, through a misunderstanding, both batsmen find themselves in the middle and a run-out for somebody is inevitable.

If one of them is a recognised first-class bat and the other a rabbit, the latter should immediately sacrifice his own wicket by making certain he gets into the position which ensures he gets trapped. That is one of the rare cases where, in the interests of the team, the better batsman has a right to be selfish and allow his partner to be sacrificed.

Finally, don't forget to learn the rule about a substitute runner. You never know when (*a*) you may need one or (*b*) when your partner may need one and you will have to run with him. It would be a pity if you were run out simply because you didn't realise that when striking, both you and your substitute are vulnerable. The striker may be out stumped or run out even though his substitute runner is behind the crease. And the striker may be out if his substitute is guilty of 'handling the ball' or 'obstructing the field'.

It takes a long time to become a really first-class runner, but I do urge all players to realise the importance of this phase of cricket. There is great pleasure to be derived from it, apart altogether from the rewards.

Nothing could better illustrate the right way to slide one's bat along the ground in trying to beat a run-out than this photo of Keith Miller – stretched to the limit. It also shows fine action by Godfrey Evans who has whipped those bails off like lightning.
(The Sydney Sun)

Captaincy

Circumstances quite naturally decree that few men get the opportunity to captain an international cricket team. I suppose it is the highest honour which the game has to bestow and it entails heavy responsibility. The leadership on the field is important but there are many other ways too in which the captain's influence and example are vital.

It is essential that a captain should enjoy the respect and confidence of his team. Not only must his cricket record be such that he is looked up to as a player but his private life must be beyond reproach.

When the captain is bent on a good time, his teammates quickly find out and there is a resultant deterioration in morale and discipline. But when the boys know their skipper is literally wearing himself out for their sakes and that of the game, they will strive to the utmost, even when disagreeing with his decisions. Loyalty, built upon admiration and respect, is a powerful force.

A good captain must be a fighter: confident but not arrogant, firm but not obstinate, able to take criticism without letting it unduly disturb him, for he is sure to get it – and unjustly too.

It is customary for cricket teams to be chosen by a selection committee, but the controlling administrative authority normally reserves the right to veto the selection of any player on grounds other than cricket ability. This shows that sheer sporting prowess is not regarded as the sole qualification for a player.

In the early days of international cricket it is understandable that the demands on a captain were not so heavy as they are now. The mode of travel was more leisurely, and newspapers reported in a more conservative, less sensational, style. The players were allowed more privacy. In fact that state of affairs was true in some measure up to the start of the First World War.

Things gradually changed in the 1920s. The advent of moving pictures was followed by the sound film and the newsreel theatre. Then came radio and the introduction of ball-by-ball broadcasts. The day of the specialist cricket reporter arrived. Instead of a few regular newspaper men covering a Test match, the number has grown into a small army.

Now we have television and it would be a brave man who could forecast what further miracle of scientific invention may come along to cast its impact on the game.

Television is at once the most wonderful and fearsome creation. It not only takes the spoken word into the homes of millions but it portrays so vividly, with the telephoto lens, every action and gesture of a player. No longer can anyone feel secure that a momentary outburst of temper or feeling will remain unobserved.

There has already been a claim that expert lip readers can tell the innermost thoughts of a batsman who mutters under his breath some unprintable epithet. The insidious part of television is that the subject may overlook that he is being televised.

The strain of this constant glare of publicity is bad enough for the average player. For the captain it is far worse.

International tours are acknowledged as having considerable political significance and players have been awarded honours because of their contribution to the cause of mutual understanding and goodwill between nations.

International leadership can only come as a result of apprenticeship in lower grades, and any player who aspires to such a position, or who realises he may be destined for it, should use these formative years to the best advantage in acquiring the knowledge which still stand him in good stead later on.

It is impossible to manufacture an ideal captain or to lay down precise qualifications for one. However, as a general principle I think it is far easier for a specialist batsman to handle the position than a bowler, an all-rounder or a wicket-keeper.

The difficulty with a bowler is the constant fear that he will bowl himself too much and thereby incur an undercurrent of dissatisfaction amongst his colleagues, or underbowl himself because of undue modesty. Moreover, pre-occupation with his personal responsibilities on the field makes it difficult for him to exercise the same critical observation of all details which a batsman can.

A wicket-keeper suffers from the disability that he must minutely concentrate on every ball, even from the moment the bowler's run commences. Adding to that burden the task of captaincy is really too much. It does not matter in fixtures of lesser importance, but I think it is an unfair responsibility in the international field.

A great captain does not have to be his team's finest player. Nevertheless it must be to his advantage that his selection is in no doubt. The man who is not sure of his position can scarcely have that freedom of mind which a captain needs. And the man who has the ability to uplift and inspire his colleagues by performance on the field must have an advantage providing, of course, other qualifications are equal.

Whilst my remarks are directed very largely towards the highest plane, it is the sum total of effort which thousands of club cricket captains put into their jobs which does so much towards moulding the outlook of the average cricketer. Their influence for good or evil on this great game is incalculable. The public sees what happens on the field and largely forms its judgment by such observation or even on performance.

One of England's most successful county captains is reputed to have said, 'The public are not interested in the team which runs second.' That may have been a harsh verdict but it is not without truth. Even so, the words were possibly spoken more with a purpose in mind than with a regard to strict accuracy. The captain was trying to instil into his men that their job was to win, not play for a draw.

One must applaud such a motive. Cricket needs initiative and enterprise from its leaders. These attributes are the very core of attractive play, and one of the greatest dangers to cricket is that so many matches drift along to a stage when they become boring to everybody. It is not enough to try to win matches towards the end. The same spirit should be evident from the commencement.

I can never remember taking the field in any match without setting out to win. There were plenty of occasions when we were outplayed. Sometimes we had to be content with or even fight desperately to achieve a draw. But only once can I remember deliberately allowing a match to drift into a draw. It was the fourth Test at Adelaide in 1947. Australia held the Ashes and were leading two to nil in the series. We only had to make a draw of this particular game to win the rubber and retain 'The Ashes'.

From the outset we tried to win but on the last day the position was that England were 247 runs ahead and had two wickets in hand. With Compton and Evans at the wickets, the former, being the no. 1 batsman, tried to keep the strike. Evans refused to run for his own shots late in the over so that Compton would have the bowling as much as possible. The situation was such that Evans batted 135 minutes for ten runs. England, of course, wanted us to make a present of quick runs to Compton so that they might have time to dismiss us later in the day.

I refused to allow the initiative to be taken from me in this way and, therefore, deliberately kept a deep field and held the scoring rate down. If England were not prepared to take a risk, why should I present them with a chance to win, having regard to the state of the rubber?

The match petered out in a rather dismal fashion and I fear the spectators obtained poor entertainment, for which I was extremely sorry, but I felt England should take the initiative to try to win. It wasn't my job to do so on that occasion.

These unfortunate situations arise occasionally but how much better to see both sides striving for a result.

I like to see a captain who is prepared to use a close attacking field. The modern trend is to dispense with outfields when the ball is new and take the risk of giving away runs in the hope of picking up wickets.

A captain must use judgment as to how long it is to be maintained or whether, in fact, it is justified at all.

I'm afraid so many opening batsmen are defensive minded that it nearly always pays. I don't believe that defensive batting is always best against the close field when the ball is new. As a captain, I would prefer to see my opening batsmen prepared and willing to play shots unless forced on the defensive. When fieldsmen are close to the bat they have to be rather exceptional to cope with full-blooded shots. They are there to catch snicks and mishits or defensive prods.

So, whilst approving attacking fields, I don't think captains are enterprising enough in combating them. Instructions to opening batsmen to take advantage of no outfields would probably disperse many of these fields quicker and more successfully than is the case today. The 'occupancy of the crease' theory can become a curse. It is frequently an excuse propounded by those deplorable batsmen who seek to improve their batting averages at the expense of attractive cricket and their team's welfare. Captains should be very firm in instructing players to carry out their policy.

Much of a captain's best work is done in the dressing-room, at the practice nets or at least off the field of play. The arena is where one sees the culmination of his planning.

One thing I strongly advocate is that all captains should thoroughly study and understand the laws of cricket. They are fascinating and will repay the time spent on them.

The history of cricket, its whole background and evolution, traditions and so on can be gleaned from the marvellous volumes which have been handed down to us by historians, cricketers, statisticians, etc.

Every prospective international captain should be an avid reader. Not only will it help him on the field but he may find that his counsel

I made a study of the rules and passed an umpire's examination – not because I wanted to be an umpire, but because I felt that, as a player, I should be fully conversant with the laws.

and guidance are sought in the conference room regarding the future development of cricket.

It is astonishing how many great players make no effort to enlarge their knowledge. They are the losers.

How many men have you heard say that they don't believe in interfering with the laws of the game. They don't really know what they are talking about. If taken literally they mean we should still be using curved bats and have two stumps, 60 cm apart so that the ball could pass between.

The younger player is only emulating his father when he looks at a photograph of some great player of an earlier generation and says, 'How could he be any good with a stance like that?' or some equally cutting observation. How much better if he could, very early in life, extract the virtues of the methods of previous generations and adapt them to modern ones. The captain, most of all, can get things in better perspective by a thorough knowledge of history.

The problems on the field of play involve

judgment and experience. At the very outset a captain may win the toss and be faced with the decision whether to bat or not. If it is a Test match, he will probably bat. The pitch is usually at its best on the first day, there are perhaps three or four days to go in which the vagaries of the weather are more likely to help the side which bats first than their opponents, and the game is sudden death.

A county match may be quite different. The question of points at the end of the season can dictate the policy.

Assuming the team winning the toss has a very strong bowling side and must win (a draw being no use) to keep them in the fight, the captain may well take the risk and give his opponents first knock to obviate any danger of having runs to spare at the end.

Here is an example of how circumstances can work out. Team A wins the toss and bats, making 300. Team B makes 200. Team A bats a second time and the captain declares at 200 for five, leaving B 300 to get. At stumps on the last day Team B is 140 for nine. Match drawn. In that case 160 runs are available to cover the last wicket and time has saved the side.

If Team B batted first and made 200 and say 150 (all out) second innings, Team A could well have won the match with two or three hours to spare.

These sort of long-range calculations must sometimes be considered by the captain before committing himself to bat or not. A wrong decision then may involve the danger of a tricky declaration later on.

Credit is seldom given to the wise move which smoothes the later path.

This question of deciding in advance how a wicket will play is not an easy one. After years of experience one can easily be trapped, and I am sure that even some groundsmen don't know what will happen before the first ball is bowled. One has to consider the nature and hardness of the soil, then quantity and type of grass, the amount of moisture in the pitch, the atmosphere (whether the day is hot and dry or dull and humid) and so on. And nature has a nasty habit of altering her mind about what she will do after the captain makes his decision.

The critics always adjudicate after they see what did happen but the unfortunate captain is given no such licence. He is so often judged by the result, not the wisdom of a decision.

Quite recently a young captain having his first season in that capacity won the toss and sent his opponents in to bat. The results were not what he had expected and he was rather severely criticised. Naturally he was somewhat perturbed but I reminded him that history mostly records its verdict according to the result of an action and not according to whether it was correct by all the known factors at the time.

Happy is the man who can learn this lesson at a tender age in an unimportant game.

Remember the unfortunate English captain who sent Australia in to bat at Leeds after he won the toss? Bardsley was caught first ball. Macartney gave a slips catch off the fifth but it was dropped, and he proceeded to make a century before lunch. The skipper was in trouble.

But what if that slip catch had been held? He might have been a hero. You see, it was not his decision that mattered, it was the result.

A captain is often faced with the question of when to take a new ball. At 5.30, his fast bowlers tired and two men well set, he may prefer to wait until tomorrow. Or should he?

The batting order, unless agreed by prior arrangement with the selectors, can often be much more important than is generally realised. I am a great believer in having set positions for players. It is better that the openers know their job and are accustomed to it, and that other players get into the regular habit of going in nos. 3, 4, etc.

Circumstances inevitably dictate a change now and again, but as a general rule I am in no doubt that the alteration of a regular batting order tends to be disturbing to the individual. In addition to the player's personal habit it has the virtue of allowing the same fellows to bat together more often and so get accustomed to their methods of running between wickets. It also enables the building up of a regular policy such as having an enterprising attacking player in a certain position, a left-hander at say no. 5, and so on.

Openers must possess a sound defence but I think at least one of them should be capable of aggressive batsmanship. I am greatly in favour of no. 3 being a stroke-player. To start on the defensive so early seldom pays dividends. It is the policy of a draw and cricket is first and foremost a game to be won.

Whilst captains should not have to bother themselves about the small routine things, they are nevertheless responsible. The rules, for instance, lay down a maximum of two minutes between batsmen. Some players seem to think this time *must* be taken, and I have often noticed the incoming batsman standing at the entrance gate waiting until the dismissed player has left the arena before he enters.

This, of course, is unnecessary and a captain should make it clear to his team that he wishes each new batsman to take his place at the crease as soon as possible. The sum of these small matters adds greatly to public entertainment.

Circumstances may arise whereby a captain does the right thing by prolonging a match. If the result is a foregone conclusion he may do his team a major service by resting his regular bowlers and entrusting the dismissal of the opponents to less experienced men.

When to close an innings sometimes presents a tricky problem. Fine judgment must often be exercised. The risk of losing must be balanced against the possibility of a win – the time factor being all-important. Due appraisal must be made of the relative skills of the two teams. Whether a wicket will be easier or more difficult with the passage of time, e.g. a wet wicket under the influence of sun.

I am certain England lost one Test against Australia because the closure was delayed too long. England badly wanted runs and the skipper was reluctant to close.

But the extra runs he gained in the last half-hour were as nothing alongside the wickets he might have taken on that sticky dog. As it was, the pitch dried out over the week-end, we made a big score and won.

There are captains who overwork their fast bowlers at the start of play and ruin them for the day. Others take them off by the clock even though meeting with success. It is a great mistake to tire a fast bowler out in one long spell. He seldom recaptures his zip that day. The only time it is justified is when the captain feels he has a major prize within his grasp if he can push home an early advantage and is willing to risk using his bowler right up.

Reasonably quick bowling changes are normally sound policy. Any change at all may cause the batsman to fall into error just because of the difference in pace, flight, etc. – not necessarily because the new bowler bowls any better.

One of the greatest arts of captaincy is in being able to anticipate a batsman's weak spot. How often do we see a player spoon the ball in a certain place and immediately a fieldsman is placed there. Seldom does a second chance occur because the batsman has been warned.

If only the captain could sense it coming and have his fieldsman there the first time.

I cannot over-emphasise the importance of field placing in captaincy. When a bowler is a fully experienced international with a set type of field he may not need any help, but for a young bowler just entering big cricket, nothing can ruin him quicker than bad field placing which enables fours to be hit at random. The bowler becomes demoralised – thinks he is no good and loses all confidence.

An intelligent captain who will give him a sensible protective field and save him from punishment, who will advise him and know just how and when to use him, can do much towards deciding his future career.

At all times the captain should set the pattern, take his team into his confidence and let them know where they are going.

I knew one captain who would sit in a corner of the dressing-room and refuse to watch his team batting. How he was able to direct his batting intelligently from such a position, I don't know. It is the sort of attitude which stems from a stupid childish superstition.

A discussion between a captain and his men during the progress of play can often prove helpful. The bowler's strategy may be pin-pointed or ideas put forward which will help later batsmen. No captain has so much knowledge that he cannot profit by listening to others, and he is a wise man who will consult senior colleagues occasionally. The wicket-keeper in particular is often in a position to pass on valuable hints.

There are so many ways in which a captain must be constantly thinking:

Whether the field placing is just right.

Whether the bowler needs a spell.

Whether the pitch calls for a different type of bowler.

There is virtually no end to the problems.

How right was Sir Frederick Toone when he said, 'Cricket is a science, the study of a lifetime, in which you may exhaust yourself but never your subject.'

I don't know any game which entails such a severe and prolonged strain on the skipper, but, like the master of a ship, he must exercise control and accept the responsibility.

Coaching

When the 1952/53 South African team came to Australia, I went to see them play for the first time in Adelaide. At the end of the match someone asked me what I thought of their batting and I replied, 'If I had not known they were South Africans I would have thought it was an English team, their styles are so similar.'

This is due to the great influence of English coaches in South Africa.

There is no doubt that Australians as a whole are more individualistic and original in their batting styles.

Watching a Test match between England and Australia an experienced observer would not need to know the players or see the colour of their caps to realise which side was batting.

Maybe the playing conditions in the respective countries have something to do with it but in my view the major factor is coaching.

Most Englishmen are coached from an early age. Not only that but the coach is very often an ex-professional who played for his county over a long period and in turn was coached at the start of his career.

Australians, by comparison, normally receive less coaching. When they do, particularly at the club level, the coach is frequently one of the team. He is possibly a batsman who received no coaching himself as a boy.

Inevitably this lack of coaching means that players develop along more natural but less orthodox lines. The coaching which does take place is directed rather more towards what to do with the ball than how to do it. There is not so much insistence on the left elbow forward or the straight back lift in batting.

Regrettably in a large proportion of schools there is often no coach or sportsmaster who has any special knowledge, and his assistance to the boys can only be of a general character.

Recently very strenuous efforts have been made by the major Australian associations to improve this state of affairs. The use of films for instructional purposes, the holding of clinics for schoolboys, the organisation of schoolboy competitions and such like are being encouraged and this is good, but the effects cannot be apparent immediately.

Professional cricket as practised six or even seven days a week in England has never really existed in Australia. There has not been enough cricket to sustain it, but the gap is narrowing.

Apart from the occasional player who spent a season with the Lancashire League (and this was usually done to gain experience as much as money) all Australian players earned their livelihood at some other occupation, be it bank clerk, agent, electrician, etc. It was often difficult to convince English people of this situation. Many players in fact suffered in their private occupations by giving much time to the game. Lack of promotion, as compared with colleagues who put in more time at their jobs, was sometimes the result.

Since the advent of World Series Cricket the Australian scene has changed a good deal.

Several of the leading players contract with the Australian Cricket Board to make themselves available for the cricket season. For this they are guaranteed a fee or retainer. In addition, if selected, they are paid quite handsome Test match fees and, with the advent of two international teams visiting Australia in the one summer, playing one-day games as well as Tests, the match payments can amount to a substantial sum.

The Board also pays money into a provident fund for the players as a nest egg when their playing days are over.

On top of that a much more liberal attitude by the Board to players writing for the press or participating in sponsorship opens up a lucra-

A typical Australian boyhood scene. My son, John, is batting in the yard, with an old piece of wood for a wicket and his schoolmates looking on. The wicket-keeper is a full-blooded Aborigine. This picture gives some idea of the primitive conditions under which Australian boys often learn to use a bat. It is difficult to teach them technique on such a pitch, but it is great training in watching the ball.
(The Sun New-Pictorial, Melbourne)

tive avenue for players to augment their income.

As I write these comments the leading Australian players who participate in most games must be earning a handsome reward, and I am sure have no justifiable complaint on the score of finance.

The real problem is continuity and permanence. No player can ever be sure his form will justify selection. There is always the risk of being sidelined through injury. The ravages of time will see to it that the best of players can scarcely hope to remain a Test player for more than ten years or so.

Finally there are the problems of home and family.

So, whilst I can understand players making the best of things and taking advantage of cricket opportunities, the wise ones will not overlook the obvious need to build a more permanent and less hazardous occupation in the meantime.

In a country like Australia, where the wickets are hard and fairly true, there is not such a premium on correct batting technique as there is in England. Many of our young players find on going overseas that they have to make certain adjustments and play more correctly to cope with the ever-changing conditions abroad and all Australians need the experience of an English tour to tighten up their defence.

I was not coached as a boy. There was nobody to coach me and facilities just weren't available.

It is not to be wondered at, therefore, that I do not think it essential for a player to be coached in order that he may rise to become an international. Given natural ability and the opportunity plus the desire to learn, one can reach the top.

Nevertheless, I very strongly believe in coaching, *providing it is carried out intelligently.*

Some coaches try to alter a player's basic natural gifts, which is quite wrong unless there is some glaring fault certain to bring disaster. There is no sense in making a bowler grip the ball a certain way to bowl a leg-break if he can spin it better and obtain greater accuracy by his own unorthodox grip. It is dangerous to suppress originality and enterprise just for the sake of orthodoxy. The greatest bowler I ever saw was O'Reilly. His grip was not the kind a coach would have ingrained into a youngster, but thank goodness O'Reilly didn't alter it.

Coaches must have the sense to understand when there is need for correction and when it is better to keep quiet.

And they must be sure not to overcoach. May I quote Denis Compton who, in commenting on coaching, had this to say:

'If a young player with a good eye and a gift for the game has some unorthodox shot which is nevertheless always successful, it is wrong to coach him out of it. To do so deprives the batsman of the initiative and the onlookers of the pleasure they get from watching some originality.'

The text books may say a batsman's back lift should be straight. Within reason that is true – for defensive play anyway. But mine wasn't, and if I had been compelled to take my bat back on a perfectly straight line when intending to play the pull shot, I could never have done it. I might as well have given the stroke away.

The basic technique of a straight bat is sound for defence but there should be all possible emphasis on attack, on the aggressive outlook. And if technique is going to prove the master of the player and not his servant, then it will not be doing its job.

Think of some of the great batsmen and you will find very few who did not depart in some major degree from orthodoxy.

Sir Leonard Hutton and Sir Jack Hobbs were two renowned masters of style and correctness (though you may be surprised to know Jack Hobbs was not coached). But what of Denis Compton, Bill Ponsford and men of that ilk? They were ever ready to back their judgment and eyesight if the occasion demanded.

No hard-and-fast rule can be set. I repeat, coaching is only good if intelligently applied.

One of the coaching problems is to find suitable wickets. As I have often remarked, 'You wouldn't attempt to teach a man billiards on a table that wasn't level.' I'm afraid some of the people charged with the responsibility of providing practice wickets on suburban grounds think any old piece of turf upon which a roller has been used will suffice.

It is an unfortunate outlook. Many a young player has had his confidence shattered by a nasty blow in the face. A bumpy pitch and a fast bowler and you have the first ingredients of 'backing away', the greatest mistake any batsman can make.

And, as W. G. Grace maintained nearly a century ago, it is much harder to produce attractive stroke players when the pitches are bad.

The faster and truer they are, the easier your batsmen will learn the fundamentals of stroke play.

Unsatisfactory turf pitches are the main reason why I see a good deal of merit in hard wickets. I learnt my cricket on concrete, with coir or canvas mat covering, and know its limitations. There is no substitute for good turf. But to teach young lads the rudiments of stroke play it is most helpful that there should be some uniformity in the behaviour of the ball.

Some of the experimental pitches which are a combination of rubber and bitumen (or similar mixture) offer considerable promise. They have the advantage that no watering or rolling is required and the cost of maintenance is negligible.

The advent and growing number of indoor cricket coaching schools have brought into being artificial pitch coverings of various kinds.

They are proving to be extremely valuable for coaching young players and even the senior players often use them when weather conditions prevent the normal outdoor practice.

The main limitations I see in the artificial pitches are that they seldom allow for the really fast bowler to go flat out and that the bounce of the ball is predictable.

One of the prime hazards of a turf pitch is that no batsman can be absolutely sure how high the ball will rise, a problem never exhibited more than in the 1932/33 bodyline season.

From time to time evidence is forthcoming that Australian batsmen do not show to advantage when confronted by a wet wicket. This is usually followed by suggestions that wet wickets should be provided for practice in Australia. The people who propound the idea have seldom had any experience of batting under those conditions.

In England a wet wicket does not necessarily mean a bad one. In fact, very often a dry wicket over there is materially improved by rain.

The English turf seldom takes on any real viciousness. The ball will turn, but turn slowly. It will lift, but not alarmingly, and there is definitely some possibility that a sound technique and a certain amount of ability will enable one to overcome the conditions.

The chances of doing so in Australia are much more remote. There one finds the ball will turn quickly and fly up very abruptly. It becomes as much a question of self-protection as of batting technique.

Few players are willing to take the physical hiding which survival entails unless the occasion demands it, and frequently a reasonable score is more likely to be compiled by a few minutes' lusty swinging than by scientific play.

So when it comes to preparing wet practice pitches, I frankly doubt whether the average player would be willing to risk life and limb for fun.

Would you like to run the risk (not a remote chance but a distinct probability) of being hit on the jaw by a cricket ball doing 100 kilometres an hour?

And if you say, 'Well, let only the slow bowlers have a go,' the answer is that when it comes to matches you are almost sure, under today's playing conditions, to find yourself up against a quickish bowler.

The groundsman, too, dislikes players bowling on wet wickets because in Australia the ball cuts up the turf so much, and that same practice strip very often has to be used for weeks on end.

In theory the idea sounds fine and in England it probably happens often in the natural course of events, but in Australia I'm afraid the batsmen are unlikely to face it for pleasure.

One thing I do strongly advocate is that all major grounds should have separate practice areas, not on the playing arena but at the rear of the players' dressing-rooms.

At Adelaide there is a delightful arrangement whereby the players may conveniently go down the steps at the rear of the stand and within fifty metres they are able to enter a cyclone enclosure which is self-contained and entirely set aside for practice and coaching. This is used before big games, and is also used on mornings before play begins and during the day whilst play is in progress.

It is especially helpful in that batsmen, say nos. 5 and 6 can go and have a lengthy practice whilst nos. 1, 2 or 3 are at the wickets. In that way they play under exactly the same light and probably on a pitch resembling in character the one in the middle.

For touring teams it provides a convenient opportunity for practice during the day for those players who are not participating in the current match. These things are denied to players where the only practice facilities are on the playing arena.

Practice areas should always have a safety harbour where players can pad up without the constant need to watch out for the ball, and authorities should be careful to see the nets are foolproof. Just one hole might bring a casualty such as the broken jaw Bill Alley suffered one day when a full-blooded hook from the chap next door went straight through and felled him.

It is a good idea to use the practice nets for really solid practice. Far too many players use them for exercise only.

It always annoys me to see a batsman hitting balls away out of the net, making no attempt to improve his game and being a thorough nuisance to the bowlers and the other players who have to retrieve the ball. That is not the place for slogging.

Batsmen should see to it that they get opportunities for batting against the type of bowling they dislike or find difficulty in playing.

Bowlers should measure out their proper run and treat the matter seriously. This is to their own advantage and anything else is unfair to the batsman who can hardly improve his technique against bowlers who are fooling.

There is a tendency these days to neglect fielding practice. I don't think an outfield needs to have much work, especially in catching, because too many catches at the one time can make the hands sore and cause you to flinch. But there should always be a few. The infields need plenty. Slip-catching machines are a useful adjunct even though they have their limitations. One soon gets accustomed to the machine and can tell which way the ball will come off it. That is exactly what you can't do in a match. Therefore, I think it is better for slip fields to practise with a man throwing the ball to a batsman who is deflecting it.

But irrespective of whatever else he may do and whatever specialised training he may indulge in, I think there is nothing better than constant playing with a ball.

I don't care whether it is a tennis ball, a golf ball, baseball or any other medium. Nor do I mind the size and shape of the bat. It may be not even a bat at all, but only a golf ball and a piece of wood. The thing is that playing with a ball of any kind teaches ball sense. You acquire a sort of automatic knowledge of what reaction there is when a ball with a certain spin on it hits a solid object.

The more one can do things instinctively and have less cause to worry about what a ball might do – the more you can be certain of your judgment of its flight in the air instead of distrusting yourself – the greater will be your confidence.

If a player is consistently compiling big scores

No coach would have taught Constantine to play this shot. But what a pity if the cricket-loving public of the world had been denied the chance of watching his unorthodox, exhilarating play.

and has sore hands, he may have good reason for reducing his net practice. But normally, I don't care who the player is or how great his skill, there is no substitute for practice.

Watch others, note their methods and learn by observation and example. Coaches themselves must be very careful not to stultify the natural gifts of youngsters and must realise they can't turn every player into a robot.

Whilst watching net practice I have recently seen some bad examples. A youngster played a delightful pull shot and was promptly carpeted by the coach because he dared to hit a ball from outside the off stump to the on side. What do you think that did to his initiative?

Another boy was forced to stand with his feet together when his natural stance (with feet apart) was ideal – that is, ideal for playing cricket but not for his coach.

And then there's the chap who insists that every drive shall be made after the ball passes the front leg. I wish some coach could show me how to play an on drive that way. I can't do it.

It is a mistake to fog a boy's mind with a

multiplicity of complicated instructions, which means he forgets the much more important and simple basic principles.

And so I could go on about the question of using judgment. The coach must be careful because he is usually the old master teaching a pupil, but the protégés should also think and be sure they don't slavishly accept everything as being correct just because someone tells them so. They in turn must play their part.

In the final analysis, the best teacher is yourself. Analyse things sensibly – work out what suits you personally – practise and observe.

No coach on earth can give you ability or judgment. He can only tell you what to do or how to do it. The execution rests entirely with you.

When Martin Donnelly (the great New Zealand left-hand batsman) first went to England, the team worked out on the boat going over how they would play, in theory.

After getting away to a bad start and putting up some poor performances their captain said to them, 'I've listened to all you fellows talking theory since we left home. Go out to the nets this afternoon and forget all that and for goodness sake just look hard at the ball and hit it.'

I cannot emphasise too much my belief that 'watching the ball' and 'concentration' are of greater importance than all the theories.

Finally, I should add that in Australia the difficulty of finding a suitable coach for a state association is very real and so is the problem of adequate financial recompense.

Fortunately governments these days seem more understanding than they were years ago of the basic needs of sport and greater assistance from these quarters appears to be forthcoming.

It is a sad but indisputable fact that the public who in this modern age pay to watch cricket confine their presence to a greater degree than ever before to the top games and the top players.

I have a photo at home of 10,000 paying spectators watching a Saturday afternoon grade match in which I was playing at Hurstville Oval in NSW. Modern grade attendances are so meagre that it pays, financially, to throw the gates open.

Sheffield Shield takings in Australia don't remotely pay the cost of staging the matches.

We are left with, in the main, Test matches and the one-day internationals. And even then, massive sponsorship support and television income are essential to meet the huge demands of travel, accommodation, administration costs and players' remuneration and still leave a reasonable sum to end up in the coffers of the State Associations so that they may maintain the essential structure of the game.

There is strong opposition in some quarters to certain types of business organisations being allowed to sponsor our major sports. It will be a sad day for cricket if no sponsorships are forthcoming, particularly if prevented by legislation, and the game withers on the vine for lack of finance.

The top administrators of cricket have my sympathy because of the difficult path which lies ahead in so many directions.

The Leg-Before-Wicket Rule

There is no doubt that the leg-before-wicket law has been, over the years, the most controversial rule in cricket.

It was originally introduced because batsmen began to take what was considered to be an unfair advantage of the bowlers by preventing the ball hitting the stumps through the use of their legs.

I am sure a detailed history of the LBW law will prove interesting to those unfamiliar with it. And I'm afraid the ranks of those who do not understand how the current law operates are far greater than is generally realised.

Quite recently I was astounded to find a captain of a first-class team, a man who had been playing for years, who didn't know how it worked.

And there are quite a few men in administrative positions who don't.

Many laws and measurements in cricket have been altered from time to time but most of the changes have been tangible. For instance, when the size of the stumps was increased, you could see and measure the difference.

When a man is clean bowled and his middle stump goes flying, there is no need to ask if he is out. The evidence before your eyes is clear.

Not so with LBW.

Unfortunately, the very nature of this law demands that any decision under it must always come within the category of someone's opinion.

After a ball has been delivered seldom does anybody but the umpire watch precisely where it was pitched. He must be able to decide that fact in order to make a decision under the law.

It is a question of his judgment, and no matter how certain he may be, the bowler or the batsman may disagree with his verdict and be equally convinced they are right. Neither side can ever prove its case. Frequently not even the television camera can give a positive verdict.

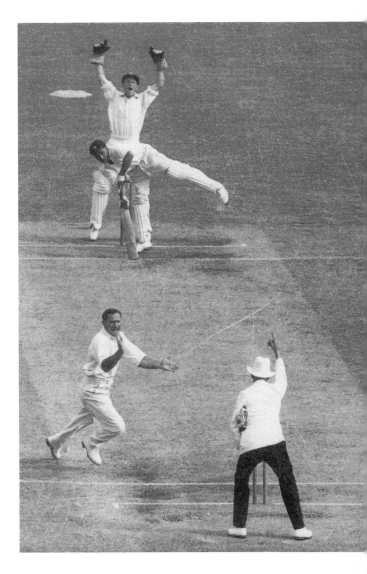

Indian captain Amarnath is out LBW to Sid Barnes in a Test match at Melbourne. The appeal of the bowler is obviously confident and aggressive and there is no doubt about this decision.
(The Herald, Melbourne)

The umpire is the only man in a perfect position to adjudicate on an LBW, but how often are his decisions criticised. Sometimes spectators (and even journalists) sitting at right angles to the pitch voice their opinions in no uncertain manner without any justification whatever. Regrettably this is a feature of cricket likely to remain permanently with us.

When the first code of laws was drawn up in 1744, it was evidently designed to cope with all likely happenings in accordance with the method of playing cricket up to that time, and it was quite possibly a revision of an earlier code, written or unwritten. But the interesting thing is that those laws made no reference whatever to leg before wicket.

Bowling was underarm, bats were crooked like hockey sticks and one can visualise the batsman standing clear of his stumps at all times, hence no rule being required.

The first law relating to LBW was passed in 1774.

Referring to it, that renowned player Beldham is quoted as saying, 'The law of LBW was not made nor wanted till Ring, one of our best hitters, was shabby enough to get his leg in the way and take advantage of the bowlers, and when Tom Taylor, another of our best hitters, did the same, the bowlers found themselves beaten, and the law was passed to make leg before wicket out.'

The wording of the original law was – 'The striker is out . . . if he puts his leg before the wicket with a design to stop the ball and actually prevent the ball from hitting it.'

This rule had to fail in terms of modern draftsmanship because nobody could say what the 'design' of the batsman was, nor what was meant by 'puts his leg before the wicket'.

Investigation of the facts strongly suggests that the indefinite nature of the original LBW rule caused much trouble and that Beldham may not have been strictly correct in saying the law was not 'made nor wanted' till Ring took advantage of the bowlers. Ring was born in 1758, therefore he commenced his adult career playing under the 1774 rule.

Beldham himself was not born until 1766 and could scarcely have remembered the introduction of the rule.

It is a reasonable conjecture that some umpires interpreted 'before the wicket' to mean the same as a subsequent ruling that the ball had to pitch between wicket and wicket, and Ring may have defended with his pads to balls pitching off the stumps.

The dissatisfaction with the LBW law in those days can be gauged from the fact that no less than nine revisions were made between 1774 and 1831.

In 1788 the word 'design' was omitted but the proviso added that the ball must pitch straight. This was changed when in 1793 a reversion was made to the 1774 law, but in 1799 they went back to the 1793 wording once more.

History records that about 1836/39 there was a difference of opinion between Dark and Caldecourt, the two leading umpires of the day, on the interpretation of the LBW rule. The question was referred to the MCC Committee who then decided that, for a batsman to be given out, the ball must pitch between wicket and wicket.

At the first meeting of the County Cricket Council in 1887 there was a great discussion about LBW, and Lord Bessborough is quoted as having said that he favoured a return to the old law of fifty years ago. He, therefore, evidently felt that the law as it once stood differed from the ultimate MCC decision about the ball pitching between wicket and wicket.

It seems fairly clear that he and many others thought the batsman should not defend his wicket with his pads, irrespective of where the ball pitched, and that such was the original intention of the law.

Lord Harris, Chairman of that first meeting in 1887, said he was inclined to think 'an alteration in the LBW law would be valuable and of importance'. He also reported that 'gentlemen of the older cricket world were decidedly of the opinion that some alteration was required in the law of LBW'.

I think we may accept it as quite clear there was general dissatisfaction with it in 1887.

The precise nature seems to have become crystallised on 8 February 1888 when, at a special meeting of the County Cricket Council, a Mr Ellison moved a resolution which was carried eleven votes to three. The resolution called the attention of MCC to the unsatisfactory effect of the LBW law and recommended 'that it be altered so as to secure that a batsman shall be out if with any part of his person, being in a straight line between wicket and wicket, he stop the ball, which in the opinion of the umpire would have hit the wicket'.

It is vital to clearly understand the implications of this recommendation. So long as the obstruction took place between wicket and wicket, *it didn't matter where the ball pitched.* Outside the off stump, outside the leg stump, it made no difference.

And note particularly that the resolution was carried by the huge majority of eleven votes to three.

It went on to MCC who, in cautious vein, appointed a Sub-Committee to investigate. The Sub-Committee eventually reported but made no recommendation regarding LBW, mainly on the grounds that they thought further opportunity for discussion should be given and that 'stopping the ball wilfully with the legs was done by a very limited number of cricketers'.

They obviously did not condone the offence, and one might reasonably ask whether murder should go unpenalised providing not too many people commit the crime.

Also, one might ask why there should be laws to give a man out for:

a] Handling the ball;
b] Hitting the ball twice;
c] Obstructing the field.

In my playing career I only saw one man given out under any of the above three headings.

Why? Because the laws provide specific penalties for doing these things and therefore players dare not take the risk.

But the MCC did pass the following resolution, which is so important that I make no apology for quoting it in full a second time in this book:

'That the practice of deliberately defending the wicket with the person instead of the bat is contrary to the spirit of the game and inconsistent with strict fairness, and the MCC will discountenance and prevent this practice by every means in their power.' Presumably that meant by every means other than the most effective one, namely legislating against it.

The Committee also recommended that instructions be given to umpires to report any batsman whom they observed deliberately defending his wicket with any part of his person.

They expressed the hope that these steps would prove adequate to prevent the evil complained of. If not, they said, stronger measures may be necessary. That was in 1888.

The evil remained unabated without MCC taking further steps, and dissatisfaction continued.

In 1901 the MCC Committee was convinced that action should be taken and voted eight to five in favour of a change. They called a special meeting in May 1901 at which it was moved that the LBW law be altered to provide that the striker be given out LBW 'if with any part of his person (except the hand) which is between wicket and wicket, he intercept a ball which would hit his wicket'. The wording was slightly different but it meant the same thing as the 1888 proposal.

The resolution was carried by 259 votes to 188, a majority of 71, but did not become law because a two-thirds majority had not been obtained.

Certain statements made at that meeting are of interest. The mover of the resolution, the Hon. Alfred Lyttelton, said that Mr Warner (later Sir Pelham) had referred to the Australians ('undoubtedly the most competent to judge in this matter after ourselves') as being against the proposal. But, added the Hon. Alfred, 'we have a reply from the Australians, received within the last two days, in favour of the proposal'. It was apparently not an official opinion but at least it indicated a measure of Australian support.

Another is that the late Lord Hawke said he would have to abandon the way he was taught to play if this law was carried. The law was not carried.

Mr A. G. Steel, who seconded the movement to reject the proposal, said he did so mainly because he objected to the LBW affecting the leg side. He did not so much object to the off side.

Although the laws were not altered, the Minor Counties were subsequently asked to test the value of the suggested alteration by using it in the 1902 season and it was agreed to try it at Lord's in MCC and Ground matches.

At the end of the season the editor of *Wisden* wrote to the captains of the Minor Counties and sought their opinions. Tabulation of their replies gives a most extraordinary combination. A concise summary reveals as follows:

a] Against. The proposal has had no effect upon altering the result of matches. There were two unsatisfactory decisions. Too much responsibility for umpire.

b] Against. There is not enough in it to make it worth the alteration. Too much scope for umpire.

c] No opinion. Thought it easier for umpires but believed rule not thoroughly understood.

d] Against. Says no help on good wickets. Too much help on bad ones.

e] Against. Mainly on grounds of unsatisfactory umpiring.

f] I think it is a good rule but it has not had a fair trial on account of the number of wet wickets and because umpires decided under one rule one week and another the next [evidently umpires officiated in both first and second-class matches which could certainly have made their task unenviable].

g] Against – same reasons as a]

h] The rule had the desired effect of stopping men playing with their legs.

i] No opinion – because trial insufficient and law not uniformly interpreted.

j] It made no practical difference to the game.

k] Not a success owing to the great amount of rain, but I think it would help very materially to shorten the innings in a dry season when wickets get crumbly.

From these opinions it seems clear that the trial season was very wet. *Wisden* refers to it as a deplorable summer. The rule was not thoroughly understood and umpires were insufficiently briefed. A trial in second-class games only was a mistake.

The following year a resolution was put to MCC to increase the size of the wickets. When seconding the proposal Lord Harris referred to the previous LBW experiment and said the umpires at Lord's did not adapt themselves to it.

I think the inconclusive nature of the trial is self-evident and the expressed objections to it nebulous and unconvincing.

It is important to emphasise that the trial covered both the off side and the leg side.

That was the end of any LBW change for some time. Meanwhile the preponderance of pad play caused the LBW decisions to keep mounting as per this table:

Year	No. of Wkts Taken	LBW	Percentage
1870	1,772	44	1 in 40
1890	3,792	219	1 in 17
1910	6,702	451	1 in 14
1926	8,528	957	1 in 9

By 1926 one can clearly see what a mockery was being made of the recommendation made by MCC Sub-Committee in 1888 not to alter the LBW law because 'stopping the ball wilfully with the pads was done by a very limited number of cricketers'.

When one man in every nine was being given out under the then existing rule that the ball had to pitch between wicket and wicket, it is a fair assumption that a far greater percentage were constantly defeating the bowler by defensive pad play to balls pitched off the stumps and therefore immune from the law.

In 1929 the Advisory County Cricket Committee decided to experiment with what came to be known as the 'snick' rule. It recommended that the striker be given out LBW even though the ball may have first hit his bat or hand providing, of course, the other requirements of the law were fulfilled. This was first tried in the County Championship in 1930 and was continued for a further two or three years purely as an experiment but finally was dropped.

It was a bad rule because it penalised the batsman who was at least trying to hit the ball, and had in fact done so.

Came 1932 and bodyline. In a letter to MCC I advocated a change in the LBW law to include the off side because I believed it would be a sensible counter to leg-side bowling and because basically I thought it would be good for cricket. And significantly, Harold Larwood, the spearhead of the bodyline attack, recommended the same thing.

At the annual meeting of the MCC in 1934 the President said, 'There is a strong feeling that it would be in the interests of the game if steps were taken to limit or prevent the use of the legs in guarding the wicket,' a strange statement, because no less than forty-six years had elapsed since the MCC Committee had officially *decided* to 'discountenance and prevent this practice by every means in their power'.

This time some legislative action was taken. It was agreed to give a trial in 1935 in the first- and second-class county matches to an LBW law whereby the striker could be given out, providing the interception of the ball took place between wicket and wicket, even though the ball pitched outside the off stump.

Commenting on the change, the editor of *Wisden* expressed the view that the leg side should be included. In other words he wanted to try the 1888 proposal.

It was interesting also to read that practically all the older school of cricketers were in favour of the change – most modern cricketers against.

After a year's trial the editor of *Wisden* enthusiastically welcomed the new rule in these words, 'Those who watched cricket day after day in variable weather on all kinds of pitches could see how the game benefited from the alteration.'

In county cricket, out of 1,273 instances of batsmen being out LBW no fewer than 404 were under the amended law.

Some of the great players of that era who had opposed its introduction freely admitted the change had been a success. Most county captains approved.

It was agreed to try the altered law in all cricket during 1936 after which *Wisden* pronounced the experiment so great a success that 'its adoption as a law of cricket is assured'.

It became law in 1937 by a *unanimous vote*.

But the saga of dissatisfaction continued. Batsmen still blatantly used their pads to protect their stumps and so long as the point of contact was not between wicket and wicket they were safe. And of course this applied whether the striker attempted to hit the ball or not.

In 1970 an experimental law came into being to provide that if the striker made no genuine attempt to play the ball, he could be given out LBW even though the point of contact was outside the off stump, and when the revised 1980 code of laws was adopted, this experiment became law.

The LBW law as set out in the 1980 code now provides:

The striker shall be out LBW in the circumstances set out below:

A] STRIKER ATTEMPTING TO PLAY THE BALL
The striker shall be out LBW if he first intercepts with any part of his person, dress or equipment a fair ball which would have hit the wicket and which has not previously touched his bat or a hand holding the bat, provided that

i. The ball pitched in a straight line between wicket and wicket or on the off side of the striker's wicket, or in the case of a ball intercepted full pitch would have pitched in a straight line between wicket and wicket and

ii. The point of impact is in a straight line between wicket and wicket even if above the level of the bails.

B] THE STRIKER MAKING NO ATTEMPT TO PLAY THE BALL
The striker shall be out LBW even if the ball is intercepted outside the line of the off stump if, in the opinion of the umpire, he has made no genuine attempt to play the ball with his bat, but has intercepted the ball with some part of his person and if the circumstances set out in A] above apply.

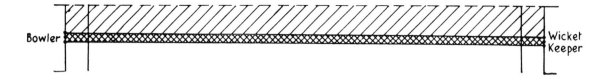

The striker making no attempt to play the ball.

The striker shall be LBW even if the ball is intercepted outside the line of the off stump if, in the opinion of the umpire, he has made no genuine attempt to play the ball with his bat but has intercepted the ball with some part of his person and if the circumstances set out in paragraph A] above (page 179) apply.

To make the interpretation of the rule clearer, I refer you to the drawing which visually shows the position.

In the season 1939/40 the South Australian Cricket Association tried as an experiment in its district A and B grade matches, the very resolution that had been carried by the County Cricket Council in 1888 and again by the MCC in 1901 (but which failed to become law because a two-thirds majority was not obtained).

This law provided that a man could be out LBW to balls pitched anywhere (off side or leg side) so long as the obstruction occurred between wicket and wicket (commonly termed the bowler's territory). This was precisely the same experiment as that carried out by the Minor Counties in 1902 and upon which I have reported earlier.

At the end of the 1939/40 season the captains and umpires were asked to report on the experiment. There were twenty captains involved. They gave opinions ranging from 'Very good. Should be retained', to 'A failure', with many of them giving detailed explanations of their views.

It was generally conceded that (1) a longer trial period was required so that the umpires would be better able to interpret it, and (2) the rule should be uniform in all states and in all grades of cricket in order that it could be properly tested.

But allowing for these side issues a fair summary of the opinions of the captains was:

Twelve believed it was an unqualified success.

Two thought it an improvement though not marked.

Four thought it made little or no difference.

Two considered it did not succeed and should be discontinued.

Of the 36 umpires who adjudicated in the matches and who were asked whether the experimental rule was a success and should be retained, no less than 30 said yes, four said no and two were indecisive.

The *Official South Australian Year Book of 1939/40* refers to the experimental LBW law as having proved successful. When it was discontinued after the war, the official statement said: 'The Committee considers the continuation of the experimental rule re LBW would be beneficial to the game if generally adopted.' However, the Committee considered it injudicious to continue the experiment whilst their players had to bat under a different law in first-class cricket.

It will be seen therefore that, whilst the experiment was tried in South Australia and voted a success, it was discontinued because of opposition from the other states *which had not tried it* and which refused to experiment despite the evidence from South Australia.

I think the foregoing information extremely valuable for any legislators who are trying to assess whether or not further experiments should be tried.

The whole incidence of the LBW law is still a live topic. Some wish to go back to the law which was operating in the 1920s, though why they should is beyond me. The history of that law proves it to have given general dissatisfaction.

As an offset, some of those advocating a reversion to the law operating in the 1920s are prepared to see an extension of the size of the wickets by, say, the addition of a fourth stump.

If an old diehard cringes at the thought of never again being able to see a man bowled middle stump, the same result could be obtained by making the three individual stumps bigger.

I was a strong advocate of changing the LBW law to embrace the off side and believe the change was justified and proved of value.

The one thing about it which has bothered me is whether it has been responsible for developing a less attractive style of batsmanship.

Two former England captains, R. E. S. Wyatt and G. O. Allen, both men of great wisdom and experience, claim that the off-side LBW brought about what has become known as the 'forward prod'.

What they are driving at is that back defensive play (and to a large extent attacking shots off the back foot) have largely gone out of the window because the first movement of batsmen has become forward to try and nullify the chance of an off-side LBW.

I played two tours of England under the old law and two tours under the off-side LBW. The change in the rule made no difference to my success or my style of play but it could fairly be argued that my type of batting was established and I just didn't change it.

I must concede that the arguments of Wyatt and Allen are sound and that batting methods have changed, probably because young players are now coached in the new forward mode.

This has got nothing to do with ability, but only style.

After having taken some fifty years to obtain an improvement it would seem a retrograde step to put the clock back completely and revive the old complaint.

Writing in *Wisden* in 1956, Bill Bowes, Yorkshire and England fast bowler, wrote:

'My own early recollection of first-class cricket, every time I bowled a ball just outside the off stump, was seeing Jack Hobbs, Sutcliffe and the rest "shouldering arms". Without playing a shot, they put bat above their heads, pads in front of the stumps, and allowed the bowler to waste his energy.'

Do we want to go back to that?

Some favour a further extension on the off side only – others wish to bring the leg side into the picture.

Many blame the current spate of leg-side defensive bowling on to the last LBW alteration. I find it hard to understand how a rule which only benefits the bowler when he pitches the ball outside the off stump can possibly be cited as causing him to regularly pitch it on or outside the leg stump.

I have always wanted to see the rule extended on the off side so that a batsman would be given out to any ball which is pitched outside the off stump and which he prevents from hitting his wicket except by bat or hand.

For clarification look again at the diagram on page 180. For the off-side LBW to be really effective I think a man should be adjudged LBW if the ball pitched in either the heavily shaded area or the lightly shaded area and providing the interception took place anywhere in that whole area – not only in the heavily shaded area as it is now.

I believe it would encourage off-side bowling and help to eradicate the obnoxious leg-side bowling, although the latter may have to be dealt with in other ways as well.

If the 1937 change in the LBW law on the off side is regarded in some quarters as being unsuccessful, the reason is, in my opinion, that the law did not go far enough and not because it was in the wrong direction.

One really needed to play under both rules to fully appreciate this.

An interesting opinion comes from Alf Gover, Surrey and England fast bowler, who was thoroughly acquainted with the practical side on the field and who also had a wide experience through his conduct of a coaching school. Writing in *Wisden* 1956, he says:

'The art of batting as practised in the 1930s has disappeared. Stroke play is almost non-existent against bowling which is principally aimed at the leg stump and leg-side fielders. Young players brought up under such conditions have no fair chance to develop strokes.'

He then advocates extending the LBW law outside the off stump, claiming it would bring back the googly, leg-break type of bowler.

'I write from the experience of having played in both 1930/39 and the post-war periods,' he added.

If the full off-side experiment were tried it would need at least two or three years' trial. One season would not be enough.

There are many difficulties confronting those people who seek to alter the current LBW law because they feel it is unsatisfactory.

The ability to reach a consensus is almost impossible.

For instance a leg-break bowler won't favour a suggestion which helps the off-break bowler because he thinks his own position is being relatively weakened. Batsmen will seldom support any alteration at all which is designed to help the bowlers. Fast bowlers won't have a bar of, say, one new ball per innings (as was the case originally) because it would detract from their effectiveness and cause more use to be made of the spinners.

I have long been an advocate of extending the present LBW law and my detractors have not missed what they think is a great chance to castigate me by claiming I am in favour because (a) my playing days are over and (b) to safeguard some of my batting records.

I can ignore the charge under (b) as being so narrow-minded it is unworthy of discussion and merely a sneer at my integrity.

As for (a) it is on record in black and white that I first advocated a change in the off-side LBW to help the bowler as far back as the 1932/33 season, fifteen years before I retired. The off-side change was tried in 1935, became law in 1937, and I played under it for more than half my cricketing life.

But let us get down to the fundamentals. Is there reason to consider changing the present law, and if so, why?

My belief is that spectators have no desire to watch cricket where the batsman is constantly saving his wicket by the use of his pads.

The game should primarily be a contest between bat and ball, and the public wants to see attractive stroke play by skilful batsmen on fast true wickets.

Legislators have a big responsibility to see that the game is played in a manner which will please and attract spectators, for without them it will die.

The one-day games have established beyond any doubt that the public will come in increasing numbers when they can be sure they will get a result and the batsmen will attack.

The one-day limited-over games in this regard present a peculiar mixture. Their underlying weakness is that bowlers don't have to take wickets in order to win matches. They only have to restrict the scoring rate of the opposition to less than that of their own team. Hence the emphasis is on negative defensive bowling.

Originally this threw up ridiculous situations such as for instance almost everyone (including the wicket-keeper) being placed on the boundary in the concluding moments of a tense finish.

But experience is a great teacher. Already more enlightenment has emerged in that controls are exercised over field placings. That they are necessary and successful is beyond doubt. It would not surprise me if they were further extended.

The great weakness I referred to earlier is offset by the absolute necessity for batsmen to make shots. In limited-over games one doesn't have to endure the spectacle of anyone continuing to bat at the rate of 10 runs an hour. Such types have to mend their ways or get dropped.

The more rigid interpretation of wides and no-balls, particularly relating ot the deliberate ball down the leg side and the very short bouncer, is to be commended and could well be considered in relation to first-class games in general.

Despite the advantage which a bowler can receive under the LBW law through bowling outside the off stump, it is quite obvious that the attack of far too many bowlers is still directed towards the leg stump. In fact I can't think of any current off-spin bowler who does not attack towards the leg stump with a strong on-side field. The predominant reason for this is to try and restrict the batsman's range of shots and thus the scoring rate.

But of course the same thing happens in first-class cricket where, to win matches, the team has to take wickets.

It would almost seem that bowlers are ignoring the possible benefits under the off-side LBW law.

During these developments in recent years the slow leg-spin bowler has virtually disappeared from the game. Whereas he used to be the cornerstone of an Australian XI, scarcely one is now on view. The whole English county scene is virtually devoid of a leg-spinner of any type.

When Pakistan recently unearthed one he was regarded as almost a miracle. Part of his success was undoubtedly due to the fact that batsmen had had very little practice against bowlers of this type.

It is obvious we are in an era of fast bowlers who, in the main, concentrate on bowling rather short of a length to restrict shots (and in my view most of them use a more liberal sprinkling of bouncers than is reasonable) and first-finger spinners who are mainly of the flatter kind, eschewing any real flight.

I think everyone would like to see something done to revive the cult of slow leg-spin.

Can it be done by a further LBW change?

A proposal was recently put forward from a West Indian source that a bowler could get an LBW decision to a ball pitched outside the leg stump providing the ball was delivered from the side opposite to that on which it pitched. Let me clarify this.

If you had a right-hand batsman, then a right-hand bowler would need to bowl over the wicket to get a leg-side LBW. But to the same batsman a left-hand bowler would need to bowl round the wicket.

It is a most intriguing suggestion and has a great deal of common sense behind the theory. It could very well be tried first as an experiment in one-day games.

I suggest the striker's pad would need to be struck 'between wicket and wicket' (as with the off side) when a shot was attempted, otherwise the law could well prove too severe and too difficult of judgment.

Frankly I doubt if there would be any noticeable effect on batting or scoring rates, but it would at least enable us to see whether the inducement would be of sufficient value to bring back bowlers of the leg-spin variety.

One unfortunate result might be that it would encourage more bowling at or around the leg stump whereas I am convinced that cricket is at its most attractive when the attack is drawn towards the off stump. For this latter reason I was always a strong advocate of the limitation of on-side fielders to five. With this restriction of five, the first-finger off-spinner, of necessity, needs to make more use of the off-side LBW.

Australia, in her domestic cricket, used the five on-side restriction for years but finally succumbed to the views of other countries, particularly England, that so long as not more than two men are behind square-leg, the bowler may deploy the rest as he pleases. I can't help thinking that England's attitude was coloured by the type of attack her players generally employ and that more regard should be had to the welfare of the game in general.

So, having canvassed the many facets of LBW, where should we go from here?

I firmly believe the most valuable alteration so far has been that the batsman can be given out to any off-side ball which would have hit his stumps and at which he has offered no shot.

In retrospect, this 'intent' law should perhaps have been brought in before the 1937 off-side change because it would undoubtedly have stopped the practice of shouldering arms and offering no shot, which was the prime cause of complaint from bowlers.

The demise of the leg-spin bowler worries me greatly.

Whether the off-side LBW has been a contributory factor is hard to tell. Some say yes, some say no. But inevitably I feel that types of bowlers, methods of play and batting styles are inextricably bound up with the LBW law.

The matter is of such paramount importance to the whole art of cricket that I would like to see a small world sub-committee of the International Cricket Conference elected to study and report on the various aspects referred to.

Is the current off-side LBW satisfactory or should it be made more severe? Should the LBW be extended to the leg side?

Would we get more attractive batting if we reverted to the 'pitched straight' LBW (whilst retaining the off-side 'intent' portion) in association with a substantial increase in the size of the wickets?

Is there anything more positive that can be done to bring back the slow leg-spinner?

I don't believe in complacency. People should always be prepared to search for improvement.

In the limited-over one-day cricket we now have a valuable tool which could be used for experimental purposes to try and assess any change thought worthwhile. An evaluation of any experiment could be made more quickly, and meanwhile there need be no interference with the traditional first-class games. No irreparable damage would be done to cricket or style if the experiment failed.

These thoughts may seem a bit revolutionary to some but the changes I have seen in cricket over the last sixty years make me feel we should not shrink from constantly applying our minds to improving what we already have.

Despite all the alterations which have been made in favour of the bowlers over the years – including the reduction in the size of the ball, increases in the size of the stumps and alterations to the LBW law – far too many games still remain unfinished. It is partially due to unskilled batsmen being able to occupy the crease too long by the defensive use of their legs.

Prior to the last LBW alteration a perusal of the English first-class batting averages shows that in every season since the end of World War I a certain number of batsmen had a batting average of more than 50. The highest number was 23 in 1928.

In 1935, the first year of the off-side LBW

experiment, NOT ONE batsman had an average over 50.

But as soon as the batsmen became accustomed to the law, averages started to rise again and in 1936, three men averaged more than 50, in 1937 there were 8 and in 1939 there were 7, whilst in 1947, just after the war, there were 11.

For the next thirty years the number fluctuated between 1 and 10 but we find 1980 produced 11 averages over 50, 1981 produced 13 and 1982 produced 14. What can we deduce from these figures?

Do they mean that batsmen are getting better, that bowlers are not so proficient, or that batsmen are getting more adept at circumventing the LBW rule? I can't answer the questions but the figures are significant.

Three of the four highest aggregates ever scored in an England season were made under the new off-side LBW law, namely

Compton, 1947, 3,816 runs at an average of 90.85

Edrich, 1947, 3,539 runs at an average of 80.43

Hutton, 1949, 3,429 runs at an average of 68.58.

With due modesty may I refer to my own figures. As mentioned earlier in this chapter I played two English seasons under the old LBW law, 1930 and 1934, when I averaged 98.6 and 84.1.

Then I played two more under the new and more severe off-side LBW law and averaged 115.6 and 89.9 respectively in 1938 and 1948.

Of the players who have had the highest batting averages in an English season and an average of 80 or more, at least half were recorded under the new off-side LBW law.

Those figures prove conclusively that the extended off-side LBW was no insurmountable hurdle to competent batsmanship.

Although I have not made a meticulous calculation as to the ratio of LBW victims in every season, spot checks indicate that it has remained fairly constant over the last fifty years.

Certain it is that we have not seen the last alteration in this controversial law.

Selectorship

It was my good fortune (or misfortune, whichever way you like to look at it) to serve on various selection committes, club, state and international, for well over thirty years.

This is a job which some people dodge because they know it brings much criticism and many heartaches but few rewards.

I was pleased to serve simply because I felt,

a] The authorities would not ask me to do so unless they felt I was fitted for the position, and

b] In which case I had a duty to cricket to do the best I could.

There was a great deal of fun associated with such posts and I worked with some grand fellows.

The criticism was an inevitable part of the job and naturally there is often merit in other people's arguments. There can be two legitimate points of view on many things.

Unfortunately for the selector he only has one choice – not like the armchair selector who picks his team and says, 'For the eleventh place I would have Smith or Jones.' Whatever the selectors' final choice they know it will be wrong in the eyes of some people.

Regrettably in Australia, but understandably, there is a predisposition for critics to support candidates from their own state. For instance if there is a match in Sydney where two batsmen make centuries on the same day, one of them a Victorian and the other a New South Welshman, the Sydney publicity is likely to draw attention to the local man's performance, whereas the Victorian headlines will feature their chap.

That is what they term 'local interest' in journalism. The same thing doubtless happens in England where the rivalry may be between North and South or Yorkshire and Lancashire.

A perfect example of narrow-mindedness is the following quotation from a letter to a newspaper:

'Selection of the Australian team to tour . . . is a very bad show for . . .', naming the state. The writer evidently hadn't the slightest interest in whether the team was a good selection for Australia. He was only concerned with the representation of his state.

If only we could get a broad national outlook in these matters it would make the selectors' job much easier.

Remember, too, that selection committees must work as a team. They must publish their collective choice on the majority vote.

I have known occasions when not one of the selectors had his own way. Every selector was outvoted two to one on some individual player. That is why it is so unfair and ridiculous for a player who is omitted to blame an individual selector or harbour a grudge.

Another point so often overlooked is that selectors must choose from the material available, be it good or bad.

If the team loses, what then?

A newspaper heading I recall ran something like this, 'Our team has taken a beating so throw out half the side.' The writer made no attempt to prove the losing side was not the best one available, but merely demanded a change.

What sort of recognition is that of the better players who are being asked to stand aside for inferior ones, solely because they didn't win?

Surely it is the selectors' duty to pick what they consider is the best team, except of course where they are specfically instructed to pick a Colts team, Second Eleven or suchlike.

When I was Australian XI captain and selector, I was castigated more than once for the omission of a certain man when in fact I fought for his inclusion. But such details couldn't be published at the time. I simply mention them in the hope that the difficulties of selection committes may be more fully understood.

Selectors invariably travel large distances and give up much valuable time to carry out their work. They don't expect thanks but they do appreciate tolerance. After all, they are usually far better informed and far better qualified to judge than their detractors.

And as their services are given in a voluntary capacity, it is scarcely to be wondered at when they take a little unkindly to biting criticism from people who never do any voluntary work for the game.

From my personal point of view I think my greatest worry about a selector's job was the necessity to be a party at times to the omission of a wonderful chap and friend because judgment and conscience said there was a better choice.

The worst experience I ever had in that regard was in helping to choose an Australian team for England prior to World War II. It came to a decision between two players from different states. There was very little between them in batting or bowling skill. One of them, in my opinion, had a better future as a batsman and he was the younger, but his opponent was a better field in a key position which needed filling. This latter point carried the day.

The boy omitted was a great personal friend of mine and a magnificent character and I was very grieved in casting my vote against him because my conscience so dictated. I scarcely slept a wink for two nights after that decision. However, I consoled myself with the thought that he was young and would go later. Alas, he never did. Instead he lost his life in the service of his country in World War II as a very gallant airman.

That is the kind of poignant memory one cannot avoid if one is conscientious in the job. The fact that your final choice does well is some compensation but then you never know how the other chap would have performed.

When I was first chosen to play for Australia the national selection committee consisted of four men. History records how I was made

twelfth man for the second Test but doesn't record how it happened.

My information is that on the night the selectors sat down to pick the team the voting was even – two wanted me in the eleven and two wanted me twelfth man. The impasse couldn't be resolved so they went to bed without announcing the team.

Next morning another meeting was held whereupon one of my supporters shifted his ground.

It was a pure coincidence that I was the meat in the sandwich but it highlighted the futility of having an even number of selectors and may have been responsible for the Board changing its stance and reverting to an odd number.

In all my years on the national committee we had three selectors.

There was then no policy of the captain *ipso facto* being a selector though in fact, whilst captain from 1938 to 1948, I remained a selector.

On my retirement from active playing I was asked to carry on and for a long time the future Australian XI captains were not selectors. Years later the Board completely reversed its stance and made it mandatory for the captain to be a selector.

This policy was put into operation for a few years but as I write has once more been changed and the captain is no longer a selector as of right.

A strong argument can be mounted for making the captain a selector. After all he is the man who must fashion his team and his tactics from the men at his disposal and it seems natural and right that he should have a say in choosing his compatriots.

Arguments against a captain being a selector centre around the distasteful possibility (not unknown) of his colleagues wishing to drop him, and of the captain having undue influence in support of his cronies.

Continuing a policy of vacillation the Board, at one stage, switched to having five selectors instead of three. What did this produce? For sure a very much heavier cost, because of travel and accommodation expenses.

But evidently the Board soon became convinced that five wise men instead of three did nothing towards getting better teams and again reverted to three.

Personally, I think three is the ideal number. If the captain does not happen to be one of the three, then, of course, the selectors should confer with him at great length to get the value of his opinion.

The question of choosing the captain and vice-captain has varied over the years. When I was first associated with Tests the selectors made a preliminary selection which was handed to the Board secretary who relayed it to the Board members.

The Board had the power to veto the selection of any player on grounds 'other than cricket ability', but as far as I can recollect the power was only used on one occasion.

The Board also chose the captain and the vice-captain.

This power was always retained for overseas tours though there have been periods when, for Australian matches, the Board referred the choice of captaincy to the selectors.

Certain legal and administrative problems can arise on overseas tours to make this question a grey area.

Assuming we have our selection committee, how do they set about their work? I should think most people would be intrigued to know what goes on behind the scenes.

From my experience they would be disappointed if they could sit in at a selectors' meeting, for it simply boils down to a question of cold hard logic.

Selectors see a lot of cricket throughout a season and have no difficulty in forming general impressions. They may be quite sure that Jones is a much sounder opening bat than Smith and that Watkins is the best man to open the bowling with the wind.

I have found surprisingly little disagreement on the top level as to the merits of individuals. There are times naturally when argument ensues. But not often.

The real issue is far more likely to arise over policy. Should Jones (an enterprising stroke player) be chosen to open the innings rather than Smith (a stolid defensive type)? Are four regular bowlers plus an all-rounder to be chosen or can we get away with three and so pick an extra batsman?

To decide such matters one has to consider the venue of the match, the standard and composition of the opposing team, likely weather conditions, etc.

I well remember a fast bowler, Tim Wall, being chosen for the Leeds Test in 1934 because the selectors thought he was more likely than anyone else to get rid of our opponents' best batsman, Wally Hammond, a dangerous player who was always likely to make a big score.

The fast bowler knocked Hammond's stumps over for 37 runs and did not obtain another wicket. The spinners took the rest. In the eyes of the public it may have escaped attention. The statisticians may have recorded his bowling effort a failure. The selectors regarded it as a minor triumph which they had to share in silence.

It is always a knotty problem to balance the attack so that reasonable insurance is taken out against changing circumstances. A match may start on a firm pitch but long before the end things may change enormously.

When an Australian team is chosen for England the selectors can't be expected to know in advance whether the summer will be wet or dry. Provision must be made for both contingencies if possible.

Selectors are sometimes faced with the problem of picking a team with only a win in mind. Let us assume the opposition is holding The Ashes, the score in the rubber is one all and there is one game to go. Not much use picking a team which has a good chance of making a draw but little hope of winning. Better to risk all for the win. Conversely, the side holding The Ashes might be tempted to go for length in batting to hold the advantage previously gained.

In most cases teams are built around key men. When there are two opening batsmen, one other batsman, a wicket-keeper, an opening fast bowler and a good spinner all outstanding and assured of selection, there is not much point in discussing them as individuals. The thing is to fit other parts around them.

It is in the final stages that fielding plays such an important part. A simple illustration is this.

You have your bowlers but there is one batting place to be filled. Two men have equal merit as batting candidates, one is a brilliant slip, the other a specialist in the covers. The question whether the team requires a slip or a cover fieldsman to balance it up assumes major importance.

For a touring side one cannot be oblivious of team spirit and personality, more so perhaps than for home matches. When seventeen men have to travel, eat and live together for weeks, it is not much fun to have a surly grouch in the party.

There are chaps who have the happy knack of lifting a team's morale in the dressing-room or in their daily lives by some witty remarks, or who can smooth over an argument before it develops too far. This sort of contribution doesn't figure in the averages.

One of the hardest problems of all is whether to select the best wicket-keeper pure and simple or a wicket-keeper batsman. There are some who dogmatically say, 'No doubt about it – always pick the best wicket-keeper'. But the older I get the more I am inclined to argue for a sane balanced outlook on such problems rather than dogmatically stick to a theory.

England once had a magnificent wicket-keeper in George Duckworth when along came Leslie Ames who was not quite so good but who was a fine batsman. Ames was very nearly good enough to be selected for England as a batsman only. The situation had to be weighed and the time came when Ames was chosen though I believe it was generally felt he was still a slightly inferior wicket-keeper.

What a thorn in Australia's side he was. In the 1934 Test series he had a batting average of 43.5 and made scores of 120 and 72. It is difficult for bowlers when they get through the recognised batsmen and then in comes such a splendid player just at the stage when they are tiring.

Ames fully justified his choice, and his wicket-keeping improved so materially with the experience of Test cricket that he was well worth his place as a wicket-keeper alone.

Another point to be considered is the type of bowling.

You may have a wicket-keeper who is a wizard at holding catches standing back to the fast bowlers but who is very shaky at the stumps against spinners. What does it matter if you have no spinners? But if spin was your trump card, the story would be quite different.

So I'm afraid I must sit on the fence with this one. I don't believe there is an inflexible answer to such a question. All factors must be weighed and the decision made accordingly.

And what a thin line sometimes stands between success and failure.

Take the 1956 Test series.

England's selectors took a courageous gamble in bringing back Cyril Washbrook, aged forty-one, because they had already decided to blood two new batsmen and wanted a third of experience.

On paper it looked questionable because Cyril had not played Test cricket for some years. The critics were, in the main, opposed to the idea. He came in to bat and had made one run when there was a confident LBW appeal against him. Washbrook was completely beaten and hit on the pad. In a flash thousands of eyes were riveted on the umpire who said 'not out', and I am sure the verdict went in Washbrook's favour by the narrowest of margins. How the selectors must have breathed sighs of relief. Cyril went on to play probably the finest innings of his career.

Fortified and encouraged by this success the selectors brought back Rev. David Sheppard, who duly made a brilliant century at Manchester, and then Denis Compton for The Oval. Denis played magnificently and the trio was complete.

But my point is that had Washbrook been out – had that ball been just perhaps one centimetre to left or right – there would have been such a blast at the selectors by the critics that it is doubtful whether they would have then risked Sheppard and maybe Compton as well. This is purely conjecture, but you see how one tiny thread may decide the destiny of several men.

Current form must always be considered. You can have a great batsman out of form and out of luck to such an extent that he has lost confidence in himself. The problem could be whether his confidence will be more quickly restored by some matches in a lower grade or boosted by giving him another chance. Temperament may then guide one's decisions.

Of one thing you may be sure – many discussions have taken place and most of the hard thinking has been done long before the selectors sit down at the conference-room tables or at the long-distance telephones.

Incidentally, this 'phone hook-up is quite an interesting and satisfactory method of getting together in countries like Australia where distances are so great. The telephone authorities arrange a fixed call on a closed circuit and several men can discuss problems just as though seated in one room.

Video conferencing via the phone and television screen is now possible so that distance is no bar to the conference table at all. You can see as well as hear.

Selectors should be good judges of cricket ability. They often need to be more than that. They need to understand psychology. It is bad judgment to select a young bowler too soon and watch him take a hiding which sets him back years; equally bad to leave one out if he has every quality, including temperament.

To balance youth and experience is a constant tug-of-war. So many chaps know the answers when they are too old and slow to get there in time, and so many youngsters have the speed of eye and muscle but haven't acquired the judgment.

A fascinating job really, despite its complexities. One is always conscious of looking out for a budding star, even in the parklands.

And it is a heart-warming experience to find a young protégé, see him develop and live up to your dreams.

It can't happen very often and no selector can make anyone a great player. He can merely do his best to see that the right ones get their opportunities.

Umpires

For those wonderful chaps who perform this thankless task, I have the most profound admiration.

Not for them any financial reward. Not for them the honour and glory, but what a storm breaks around their heads if they give wrong decisions.

They don't even need to give wrong decisions – it is only necessary for somebody to aver that they did.

I vividly remember one occasion when an umpire gave a certain batsman out LBW in a Test match. I was in a wonderful position to see because I was fielding practically straight at mid-on.

Below is a wonderful example to demonstrate the truth of what I have written here. The batsman has played at the ball, missed, and been struck on the pad. An appeal goes up for LBW and is answered in the affirmative. But by the time the photo was taken, the batsman had moved almost to the edge of the pitch. I should say he is more than a metre from where he was when struck by the ball. This is the sort of thing which happened in the incident I describe and shows how an umpire can be misjudged.
(The News, Adelaide)

In my opinion the batsman was plumb centre. The ball pitched on his stumps and would have hit the middle.

But immediately he was struck on the pads the batsman moved his legs away from the line and when a newspaper photograph of the incident appeared it showed the three stumps quite clearly, with the batsman's pads outside the line of the stumps.

A certain writer, who had viewed the incident from a position at right angles to the pitch, firmly declared that the batsman was 'not out'. He vilified the umpire unmercifully.

Yet the decision was correct without a doubt.

It goes to show how misleading a photograph can be when it is not taken at the precise moment, and it also shows how an umpire can be unfairly abused when in fact he has made no mistake at all.

I marvel at the good tempers which most umpires have.

Unwarranted appeals and all sorts of minor irritations come along but seldom does one show any feeling.

The job demands terrific concentration on every ball that is bowled. How would you like to sit down comfortably all day and do it? The umpire must never relax despite his backache or any other ailments.

To play cricket for hours is tiring but I am sure it is more so just to stand and watch.

Frank Chester, most widely known and respected of all umpires. Alas, his cheery countenance is seen no more. He died at the early age of sixty-one. He was without any doubt the greatest umpire under whom I had the privilege of playing.
(Hulton Picture Library)

Frank Chester lost his right arm below the elbow in World War I. Hence he always used his left for drawing stumps and giving decisions. Here we see him terminating the proceedings as the sun goes down on another day.
(Sport & General Press Agency Ltd)

Walk around a golf links to follow someone in action, and if you haven't a backache after two or three hours, it will be surprising. You will find it much more tiring than playing.

But these umpires have to stand for hours every day and very often five days a week. Physically it is a big strain and, particularly when important matches are being played, the mental strain must also be tremendous.

Every umpire must be on the *qui vive* for the most obscure possibilities and be prepared to give an answer immediately. There was a day at Adelaide when Geoff Noblet hit his wicket playing at a wide. An appeal ensued and he was given out, but I doubt whether anybody on the ground (except the umpire) knew the answer.

Hurried searches were made for rule books to check it. Who would ever dream that a batsman *could* hit his wicket playing at a wide? To be a wide the ball must be so far away from the stumps that it is not within the striker's reach.

But there you are. The incredible had happened and the umpire was right.

It is interesting to note the different attire worn by English and Australian umpires.

In the picture of that LBW decision on page 190 you will see an Australian umpire, short white coat, white hat, navy trousers and white boots.

The Englishmen used to wear a long white dust coat over their normal dress (far left). Nowadays they wear a shorter coat much like the Australians.

Having seen their wonderful work at close quarters, may I say that the topgrade umpire makes a tremendous contribution to batsmanship.

When one is in Test class and in form, you are prepared to back your judgment providing you feel you can trust the umpire.

Take a ball pitching on the leg stump but going across to that side. A batsman might have the choice of trying to score from a fine leg glance (in which case he would run some risk of missing the ball) or giving it the full face of the bat defensively towards mid-on.

The latter would certainly be the shot if there were any doubt about the umpire's keen judgment.

Understandably a goodly proportion of umpires (especially in England) are men who have passed beyond the playing age. They give excellent service and frequently their years of active cricket are a great advantage in providing them with an understanding of many points.

Nevertheless it is difficult to avoid the normal decline in eyesight and hearing.

For this reason I do earnestly appeal to any youngish man who feels inclined that way to take on umpiring whilst all his faculties are at their keenest.

His tangible rewards will be few but the service he may render to the game incalculable.

The two English umpires, Dai Davies (left) and T. J. Bartley, going out for the final Test at The Oval, 1956.
(Central Press Photos Ltd)

One of the rare pieces of humour connected with umpiring. A dog ran on to The Oval, 1948, and Sid Barnes caught it, but as he went to entrust the animal to umpire Skelding the latter refused to accept it as part of his function. He apparently didn't like dogs.

Television

The whole world of umpiring has taken on a new dimension since the advent of television and the instant replay.

Before television it could fairly be claimed that the umpire was in the best position to judge and good sportsmanship was to accept his verdict without question. But now things are inclined to be different. Only today, a few minutes before writing these lines, I was watching a match on the Sydney Cricket Ground on television.

There was an appeal for stumping on the leg side and the umpire ruled not out. The replay showed quite positively and graphically that the striker was out of his ground and was in the process of pushing his rear foot back over the crease when the appeal occurred. The bails were removed whilst the foot was still seven or eight centimetres out of the crease. It was an unfortunate error, proven by the camera.

For an LBW decision I would be opposed to allowing the camera to adjudicate because there are minute distortions of angles, a possible faint snick on the bat, and other factors which rightly must rest with the umpire's judgment. But I genuinely wonder now whether we might do the umpires and the game a great service by having a third umpire or referee sitting in the stand monitoring a TV set who could be appealed to by the field umpire if the latter felt in any doubt about the verdict. This could apply to run-outs in particular, and questionable catchings and stumpings.

It would be simple for the ground umpire to use a signal asking for a decision and in turn to arrange for a code by which the referee could indicate his verdict.

Decisions in cricket are probably more critical for a batsman than are decisions in any other sport because the batsman doesn't get a second chance – as a player does in tennis. I feel that point I have raised merits discussion between players, umpires and administrators at top level to find a mutually acceptable answer.

Methods of Signalling

Following a section on umpires seems an appropriate point to insert details of the approved method of signalling.

1. Boundaries shall be signalled by waving the hand from side to side.
2. A boundary six by raising both arms above the head.
3. Byes by raising the open hand above the head.
4. Leg byes by touching a raised knee with the hand.
5. Wides by extending both arms horizontally.
6. No-balls by extending one arm horizontally.
7. Dead ball, by crossing and re-crossing the wrists below the waist.
8. The decision 'Out' – by raising the index finger above the head.
9. One short by bending the arm upwards and by touching the top of the nearer shoulder with the tips of the fingers of one hand.

Umpires should wait until a signal has been answered by the scorer before allowing the game to proceed.

Besides signalling, the umpire should 'call' distinctly for the information of players.

Should an umpire desire to notify an alteration of a decision or call he shall do so by crossing his arms in front of his body with hands touching his shoulders.

BOUNDARY
FOUR

BOUNDARY
SIX

BYE

LEG BYE

WIDE

NO BALL

OUT

ONE SHORT

Temperament

There is probably a greater premium on temperament for a batsman than for any player in any branch of sport.

The tennis player may be so nervous he loses the first set but then pulls himself together and wins the match.

A golfer may duff his first drive but still win the championship.

Baseballers are not out if they miss the first pitch.

Footballers can make up later in the game for an early error.

Even the bowler at cricket can have time to recover from nerves and still perform well.

But what happens to the opening batsman who walks out to take strike to the first ball in a Test match. The air is electrical. He senses that everything is concentrated on him. There is no way of knowing how fast that first ball will be, whether it will be on the stumps or not, whether it will swing and if so which way. Will the wicket be fast or slow? Will the ball lift or come through normal height?

With all those possibilities the batsman is not allowed one error. A fatal snick and those fieldsmen are just dying to yell 'Howzat?'. It is a nerve-racking business.

Next time you see a batsman wending his

Is it any wonder temperament plays such a large part in batsmanship when everybody is waiting to pounce on you like this? The photo shows Peter May batting against Ray Lindwall and as he snicks one the Australians appeal en masse. This is rather an astonishing picture. Out of the nine fieldsmen who are visible, eight are appealing whilst the ninth seems to take the matter for granted, and five of the fieldsmen are completely off the ground.
(P.A. Reuter Photos Ltd)

way to the wickets, give a thought to these problems. He is human like you, and desperately anxious to do well.

Is it any wonder temperament plays such an enormous part in batting?

Strangely enough the player with the best temperament is seldom the phlegmatic, calm, unemotional person who gives you the impression that nothing could excite him.

Nor is it the nervy, excitable fellow who can't do his pads up, can't find his gloves or even think straight.

I always liked to see a player who was extremely conscious of his responsibility and all that went with it, who was really very thrilled and enthusiastic under the surface but who kept his emotions under control. The sort of chap who would find it difficult to sleep or eat as usual just before a Test match. That type usually possesses a high degree of nervous energy which comes into play at the critical hour.

He may be anxious on the morning of the match, but once he sets foot on the arena he is in full command of himself and his reflexes are quick. This man will play better in a Test than in a picnic match. He is the chap for the big occasion.

Sportsmanship

The margin between defeat and victory can be so small it may even depend upon the sportsmanship of an individual.

In the 1954/55 Test series, Australia won the first match and had a grand chance to win the second. England's last batsman came in to face the bowling of Lindwall and drove what looked like a catch back to him. Lindwall scooped it up and the batsman, thinking he was out, turned to walk to the pavilion. But Lindwall, as a great cricketer and sportsman should, signified that the ball had touched the ground before he caught it and so the batsman was not out.

The last partnership subsequently put on more runs than the final winning margin, so Lindwall's action probably saved the Test for England.

Had Australia been two up and three to go, I for one doubt if England could have then won the rubber. But with the score one all, a totally different psychology existed and she won the series.

That is cricket. Every fieldsman knows when he has made a fair catch and he should never appeal unless satisfied it is clean. On the contrary he should assist the umpire by immediately declaring himself.

Such acts of sportsmanship are the very essence of this great game.

A very happy portrait taken at Welbeck Abbey in 1948. The Duke of Portland (centre) is sharing a joke with Ray Lindwall (right) and myself. These Australian visits to Welbeck Abbey were indeed a privilege and the teams looked forward to them immensely.

Relaxation at Other Sports

A very high percentage of first-class batsmen play other sports for relaxation, and I should think golf is the most popular. This notable tendency is probably the reason why hundreds of people ask me, 'Does golf interfere with cricket?' My answer is, 'No – but cricket seriously interferes with golf. The games are opposites.'

In cricket you have a moving ball – in golf it is stationary. In cricket you are constantly pitting your wits against your opponents, and conditions often change from hour to hour. In golf it doesn't matter how well your opponent plays as long as you do a little better. You are really playing against yourself.

The grips bear no comparison. Most of all there is one basic difference which causes all the trouble. In cricket your arms are bent for practically every shot, but I've never found a golf professional who encouraged me to play with a bent left arm. The straighter you get it the better they seem pleased.

Cricketers are renowned for the way they slice a golf ball. When you are accustomed to playing cover drives and square cuts it is very difficult to suddenly prevent doing so altogether. The way a cricketer produces his cricket strokes has little connection whatever with a correct golf swing.

The great value of golf to a cricketer is the way it brings him mental relaxation. After a hard Test match I enjoyed nothing better than a

round of golf. It was equivalent to going from the heart of a great city, with trams, buses and cars, out on to a farm where life was leisurely.

Cricket is a big mental strain. It entails incessant concentration for long periods, and staleness can become a very real and tangible thing. Hence I like to see the Test match star having a breather on the golf links. I have no doubt he gains considerable benefit therefrom, both mentally and physically.

But if you are keen to become a plus-two golfer, believe me you'll find the task of achiev-

ing that ambition and Test match batting status at the same time a pretty difficult combination.

Kindred sports such as tennis and billiards are favourite pastimes, but for some reason which I cannot explain, no other sport seems to afford cricketers quite the same degree of relaxation as golf.

Clarrie Grimmett's favourite relaxation was tennis. Here we are together on a court in Adelaide in 1929.

By 1957 I was trying my hand at the 'old man's' game, bowls.

Actually more and more young men are playing it and undoubtedly bowls requires considerable skill. It also exercises more muscles than the onlooker would imagine. However, I would prefer to play a more strenuous sport whilst able.

The Ideal Eleven

What would be your Ideal Eleven if you were sole selector and given the job of naming the type of players whom you think would represent the perfect balance under normal playing conditions?

I can't find out your answer, but here is mine:

Two recognised opening batsmen of whom one shall be a left-hander;
three other batsmen of whom one at least should be a left-hander;
one all-rounder;
one wicket-keeper who is also a good bat;
one fast bowler to open with the wind;
one fast or medium-pace to open into the wind;
one right-hand off-spinner;
one left-hand orthodox first-finger spinner.

England's Test team at The Oval in 1956 went very close to it. She had a left- and right-hander to open, but there was neither a left-hand batsman nor an all-rounder in the next four. Otherwise the selection was very close in principle to the combination I have set out. This was her team:

Richardson	Sheppard	Tyson
Cowdrey	Washbrook	Lock
May	Evans	Laker
Compton	Statham	

The Australian team of 1921 also went very close. It was:

Collins	Taylor	Oldfield
Bardsley	Pellew	McDonald
Macartney	Armstrong	Mailey
Andrews	Gregory	

There were two recognised openers, one left-handed. Macartney was an all-rounder, right-hand bat and slow left-arm first-finger spin bowler.

There is not a left-hand batsman from two to six, but as Gregory was left-handed he partially made up for this.

Two fast bowlers opened, Gregory and McDonald. Then, instead of my theoretical right-hand off-spinner and my left-hand spinner, the team had Warwick Armstrong, a nagging, persistent type of slow leg-spinner (and a very fine batsman) with a genuine googly bowler, Arthur Mailey, to complete the side. It was by every standard a wonderful combination.

Another team which came very close to my ideal was Australia's fifth Test side at The Oval, 1948:

Barnes	Miller	Lindwall
Morris	Harvey	Ring
Bradman	Loxton	Johnston
Hassett	Tallon	

In this case Ring, a leg-spinner, took the place of my mythical right-hand off-spinner — otherwise all the qualifications were fulfilled.

Bill Johnston, being able to bowl fast left-hand swingers or slow spinners, according to the need, was really two bowlers in one.

A match between this side and Armstrong's 1921 team would have been worth seeing.

One can never be sure how weather conditions will turn out. On a hard dry pitch a leg-spinner such as Mailey may be better than an off-spinner like Laker, but on a sticky the positions would be reversed.

At least it is an interesting subject and one which can fill in many a pleasant hour.

An old friend of mine who was in hospital for several weeks amused himself by picking Test teams from players whose names began with a certain letter. Then he would try to beat it with players whose names contained seven letters and so on. Here are examples:

Seven letters in the name

Collins	Hassett	Saggers
Trumper	Darling	Trumble
Bradman	Gregory	O'Reilly
Jackson	Fairfax	

Names starting with the same letter

Hutton	Hardstaff	Hollies
Hobbs	Hearne, J. T.	Hearne, J. W.
Hammond	Hirst	Huish
Hendren	Hitch	

See if you can beat these random selections.

This whole question of 'best teams' could be expanded considerably. For instance it is great fun trying to pick the best eleven of all time out of those who played for England, for Australia, the West Indies, and so on.

One could be really parochial and get down to the best for a particular state, say NSW or Victoria.

I am reminded of a journalist (long since dead) who wrote his piece for a newspaper selecting what he considered should be the team to represent Australia in the next Test match. Late at night his sporting editor rang and said, 'You haven't included a wicket-keeper in your side.' There was a short silence as the stunned writer absorbed the comment. But he was a most humorous man and quickly came back with the retort, 'Oh well, with the side I have picked we won't need a wicket-keeper – the bowlers won't get a ball past the bat.'

Cricket Problem

Back in the 1930s, Sir Arthur Eddington produced a cricket problem. It sets out the scores in a mythical cricket match and gives certain basic information from which the student must work out the required facts. The puzzle is quoted below. It is absolutely genuine and soluble as it stands.

For a long time I worked thereon and failed to obtain the answer which, of course, must be as foolproof as one of Euclid's. Eventually, on the journey from England to Australia in 1956, I solved it.

To those who are not interested in mathematics and not prepared to spend many hours on the subject, my advice is don't try. For anyone with leisure and a love of cricket, it presents one of the most absorbing studies I have come across and I recommend it to you.

To illustrate the way one has to work, just let me say this.

Tosswell, who bowls seven overs of which five are maidens, for thirty-one runs, must have had seven fours and three singles hit off him because we are told the total score was made up of fours and singles. No other combination in twelve balls can possibly give you a total of thirty-one runs. That is the kind of hypothesis which must be applied throughout.

If you get as much fun as I did trying to find the answer, I'll be well rewarded, but don't blame me if you get mighty exasperated at times.

CRICKET SCORE

Atkins	6
Bodkins	8
Dawkins	6
Hawkins	6
Jenkins	5
Larkins	4
Meakins	7
Perkins	11
Simkins	6
Tomkins	0
Wilkins	1
Extras	0
Total	60

Bowling Analysis

	Overs	Mdns	Runs	Wickets
Pitchwell	12.1	2	14	8
Speedwell	6	0	15	1
Tosswell	7	5	31	1

The score was composed entirely of fours and singles.

There were no catches, no-balls or short runs.

Speedwell and Tosswell each had only one spell of bowling.

Pitchwell bowled the first ball to Atkins.

Speedwell was the other opening bowler.

Overs were of six balls each.

Whose wickets were taken by Speedwell and Tosswell?

Who was not out?

What was the score at the fall of each wicket?

Historical

In the course of my duties as a cricket administrator, I was once called upon to sit on a small committee which was to consider whether it favoured an alteration in the LBW law. One of the members was an ex-international player.

When asked for his views, this player stated his opposition to any alteration and when pressed for his reasons said, 'I am opposed to the alteration of any fundamental law of cricket.'

Imagine the astonishment of those present who knew the history of cricket.

However, our friend was even more astounded when informed that the original laws of cricket contained no LBW law at all, that since the game's inception there had been alterations in the size of the ball, the stumps, the shape of the bat, the method of bowling, the number of balls to the over, in fact almost every implement, measurement and law.

Obviously the value of this player's advice and experience on any technical matter was strictly limited because he just simply had no knowledge whatever regarding the development of the game.

That incident decided me to include in this book a brief survey of the origin and history of cricket and to tabulate the more important changes which have occurred over the years.

We who live in an age which readily and without difficulty chronicles modern history, sometimes find it hard to understand why there is no clear and concise record showing where and how the game of cricket had its genesis.

Had we been fated to live some hundreds of years ago, when so many of our modern devices would have been regarded as witchcraft, we would have appreciated the difficulties of leaving tangible material for historians.

There were certainly many games played in early times which bore some resemblance to cricket. Weight of evidence suggests that 'club-ball' may have been the parent of our modern game, though doubtless cricket's own character developed just as inventions are improved upon until they bear little resemblance to the original. Who would compare a modern aeroplane with the one which originally flew the Channel? Yet no one questions the genealogical descent.

Old works suggest that cricket is as old as the thirteenth century. A MS dated 1344 (no. 264 in the Bodleian Library at Oxford) represents a

Two old illustrations of Club Ball. (Taken from a MS in the Bodleian Library dated 1344.)

game called 'club and ball' or 'club ball'. It was apparently a single-wicket game in which the score was recorded as in cricket.

Research shows that 'creag' was the name of a game played in the year 1300. Now 'creag', it has been suggested, was a shortening of the word 'creaget'. Also 'creag' is very close to 'cricce' (or 'cric'), the Saxon term for a crooked stick (and in the game of cricket, bats were originally curved).

At one time it was thought cricket may have originated in France owing to the discovery in a fifteenth-century manuscript of a word 'cricquet', but no irrefutable evidence supports this theory.

The game of 'cat and dog' is described in the old literatures and bears comparison with double-wicket cricket, though earliest references to it would seem to appear in the seventeenth century.

There are writers who believe that the word 'cricket' appeared for the first time in 1685. Others claim to have traced it to nearer 1550.

Credence is given in some quarters to the game of 'handyn and handoute' being a kind of cricket. I trust the case fails if only because those who played it were liable to two years' imprisonment, whilst those who permitted it to be played on their premises were liable to three years. At that time it was not regarded as a game for gentlemen.

It is recorded that in 1654 the Church-wardens and Overseers of Eltham, Kent, fined some of their parishioners two shillings each for playing cricket on a Sunday. Perhaps the fine was attributable to the day of the offence as much as the nature.

There is no doubt betting was rife in the days of Mr Ward and Lord Frederick Beauclerk. Bookmakers attended Lord's no less regularly than Epsom. 'If gentlemen wanted to bet,' said Beldham, 'just under the pavilion sat men ready, with money down, to give and take the current odds.'

They had all sorts of tricks to make their betting safe. One artifice was to keep a player out of the way by a false report that his wife was dead. Without wireless or telephones, it was obviously a difficult matter to check such reports hastily.

That betting was an established fact is not surprising because matches were played for large sums of money. As much as one thousand guineas appears to have been common even as long ago as the eighteenth century.

Yes – times have changed since Lord George Kerr would provide bread, cheese and beer for as many as would come out and practise on a summer's evening.

Irrespective of the precise origin of cricket (if in fact there was one), the game evidently developed rapidly in the seventeenth century with underarm bowling, curved bats and a

---

Illustrations taken from a genealogical roll of the Kings of England, written in the reign of Henry III.
(Strutt's Sports & Pastimes of the English People*)*

'Cricket in the Wealds' circa 1700. From an old print.

The Evolution of Cricket Dress:

1. The era of Club Ball.   2. Circa 1700.   3. Circa 1760.   4. A Hambledon man.

5. Top hat and braces,   6 and 7. Billy-cock hat and cap of 1865.   8. Circa 1900.
circa 1827.
(Annals of Cricket W. W. Read)

'The Royal Academy Club in Marylebone Field.' From a picture by F. Hayman, RA, belonging to the Marylebone Club. What a remarkable contrast between cricket then and now.

Note particularly the stumps, square-leg umpire, long-stop and the wicket-keeper who has no gloves. Bowling is underarm.

wicket two feet wide and one foot high with a hole dug in the ground between the stumps into which the ball had to be 'popped' for a run-out.

In the year 1700 the first newspaper advertisement appeared and in 1719 'the Londoners v. the Kentish men' results were published, whilst the first code of laws is dated 1744, even though evidence suggests their existence some fifty years earlier.

Only one umpire seems to have been utilised until double-wicket cricket demanded a second.

There were no prepared pitches. At first the winner of the toss selected the stretch of turf on which he chose to play and naturally did so to suit his own team.

Primitive though the game was it is claimed that 20,000 people saw Hampshire play Kent in 1772.

That is not to be wondered at, for we are told Lord Tankerville's Surrey Eleven won a match for £2,000 in 1773.

The first LBW law did not appear until 1774 and no decisions under it can be found prior to 1794, though this may have been due to inadequate records.

Evidently the game produced its hazards, even then, for according to Wraxall's memoirs, Frederick, Prince of Wales, father of George III, died in 1751, as a result of an abscess caused by a blow from a cricket ball.

There was a match in which five legs were broken. Fortunately, they were only wooden legs. The match was between the one-armed and one-legged pensioners of Greenwich and Chelsea.

The dress of the players gradually changed. Back in 1740 it consisted of a jacket, silk stockings and shoes, and answered to the description:

'Cricket, nimble boy and light
In slippers red and drawers white.'

A tremendous change in the method of bowling was evolved towards the end of the eighteenth century. Much argument and bitterness ensued until 1835 when legislation by MCC permitted the hand to be as high as the shoulder.

A further twenty-nine years ensued before the bowler was free to bowl overarm as we know it today and that is possibly the greatest single change in the development of the game, for

---

'Lord's Cricket Ground, St John's Wood, 1818.'
From an old print.

modern cricket without overarm bowling cannot be imagined.

How far have we progressed from the days of 1851 when the Rev. James Pycroft, who was regarded as possibly cricket's greatest author, wrote his treatise on the game and expounded that 'every hit excepting the cut is made by no other change of attitude, than results from the movement of the left foot alone'. I wonder how that reads to the modern batsman?

It might be good for cricket if we could revert to Pycroft's advice, but then he didn't have to contend with the problems of the twentieth century.

At least we have progressed in some respects. A score sheet of the match Notts v Sheffield in 1772 says Notts 1st Innings 14, Sheffield 1st Innings 70. Notts gave in. It would cause a sensation if Yorkshire played Lancashire today and forfeited if 56 behind on the first innings.

There may, of course, have been other reasons. Notts players might have had to harness up their horses for a long journey home. No petrol-driven limousines waited at the door for them.

At a later date, in a match between Surrey and the MCC, Southerton is recorded as out, 'Retired – thinking he was caught'.

There was a time when the bowler could only change ends once in the same innings. In 1870 that was altered to 'twice', but as a concession the bowler was allowed to bowl two overs consecutively.

Despite the efforts of some enthusiasts in foreign lands, cricket remains predominantly British.

The members of the I Zingari Club, formed in 1845, may have had hopes of extending its ramifications because one of their rules provided that 'all directions connected with the game may be conveyed in the French or Italian languages'.

They had some other peculiar rules which makes one wonder whether the language rule was serious. For instance, Rule V provided 'that the entrance be nothing and that the annual subscription do not exceed the entrance'.

Also they laid it down that batsmen and fieldsmen being hit were not entitled to 'scratch or rub'.

An obviously sincere admonition was, 'Keep your promise, keep your temper, keep your wicket up'.

A view of the new Mound Stand at Lord's Cricket Ground, taken during the MCC Bicentenary match in August 1987. (Patrick Eagar)

So the march goes on. There are no fundamental laws of cricket. They are still being developed and any player who has ambitions to become proficient in its arts would do well to study its history. Without that knowledge he will ever be so much the poorer.

And every player should make himself thoroughly conversant with the laws.

Why? Since I commenced writing this book, a player who had recently retired, but who had played first-class cricket for very many years, argued with me that the striker could not be given out 'handled the ball' unless in the umpire's opinion the ball would have hit the stumps.

He probably broke the law many times during his career without knowing it and survived simply because nobody appealed.

It is not only essential to understand the laws, it is an education to read them.

The Pitch

The length has never been altered from 22 yards (20.12 m). Originally the popping crease was 46 inches from the wicket but this was increased in 1818 to 48 inches.

The bowling crease was originally three feet each side of the stumps but in 1902 this was increased to four feet.

When the width of the stumps was increased to nine inches in 1931, the length of the bowling crease remained unchanged at eight feet eight inches, with the stumps in the centre, so that today the bowling crease is actually 120.65 cm (3 feet 11½ inches) each side of the stumps.

Lay-out of wicket (above), and crease area.

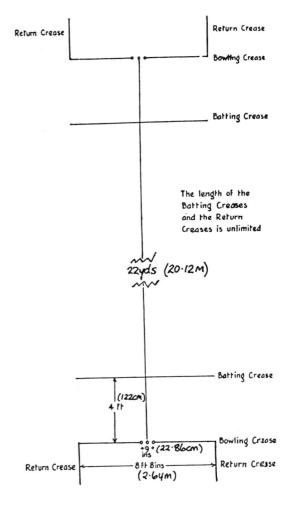

Lay-out of wicket and crease area.

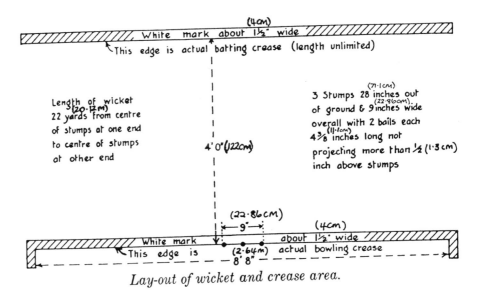

The Wicket

Wisden Cricketer's Almanack, usually referred to as 'The Cricketer's Bible', and regarded as the ultimate authority on matters pertaining to cricket, in its section relating to dates in cricket history, lists the changes in the size of the wicket as under:

Year	Stumps	Height	Bails	Breadth
c.1700	2	22 inches	1	6 inches
c.1776	3	22 inches	1	6 inches
1785	3	22 inches	2 or 1	6 inches
1798	3	24 inches	2 or 1	7 inches
c.1819	3	26 inches	2	7 inches
c.1823	3	27 inches	2	8 inches
1931	3	28 inches	2	9 inches*

*Optional till 1947

This is, understandably, a simple and concise tabulation and does not make reference to certain happenings, particularly in the early evolutionary years when records were not meticulously kept. For instance, in his authoritative *A History of Cricket*, H. S. Altham says that in a small manuscript known to Ward and Nyren, embodying the recollections of an old player of the game as he knew it about the beginning of the eighteenth century, the wicket is described as 1 foot high and 2 feet wide.

It is not clear when the size was fixed as 22 inches high and 6 inches wide, though it must have been early in the eighteenth century, and that size was certainly prescribed in the original laws of 1744.

Originally there was a hole in the ground between the stumps into which the ball had to be 'popped' for a batsman to be run out, but I cannot find when this practice was changed.

A single bail was introduced about 1700 but by 1785 it became optional to have 1 or 2 bails and this apparently remained the case until about 1819.

The early wickets were of two stumps only but the third or middle stump came into use about 1776.

As the width of the wicket increased, so did the size of the individual stumps in order that a ball could not pass between them. It is quite

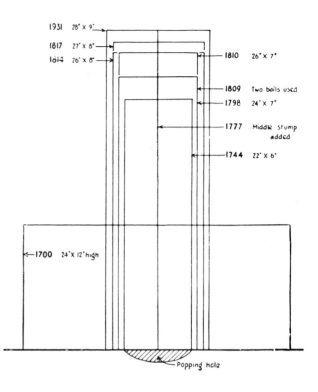

surprising how much larger the modern stump is than the ones in use when I first started to play. I have a small table top mounted on stumps illustrating the contrast.

The last change came in 1931 when it became optional (for manufacturing and economic reasons) to play with a wicket 27 inches by 8 inches, or 28 inches by 9 inches, but the larger size became mandatory in 1947.

A small graph has been drawn (see illustration above) showing the variations in size to scale.

Also I have included as a matter of interest a drawing of 'The evolution of the wicket'. This is reproduced from *Annals of Cricket* by W. W. Read. (See overleaf.)

It would appear to differ in some respects from the table in *Wisden* but is of great interest in depicting how the changes have occurred over some three hundred years.

Below 1, 2, and 3. Rural wickets, any date.
4. One foot by two feet prior 1700.
5. and 6. 1½ feet by 6 inches, with or without cross-piece, just before 1777.
7. Raised to 22 inches by 6 inches, with a middle stump. Circa 1777.

8. Raised to 26 inches by 8 inches, with bail, in 1814.
9 and 10. Raised to 27 inches by 8 inches, with bail, in 1817.
11. Stumps 28 inches by 9 inches, with bails, 1931.

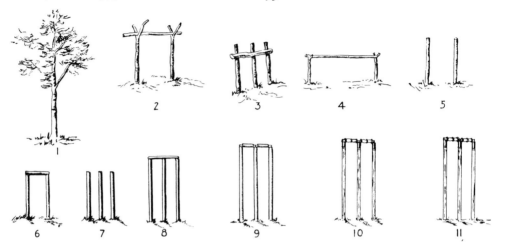

The Ball

It is remarkable how uniform the ball has remained over the years.

The original laws provided only that the weight should be between five and six ounces.

In 1774 the weight was determined as being not less than 5½ nor more than 5¾ ounces (155.9 to 163 g), whilst the circumference was allowed to be within the limits of 9 inches minimum, 9½ inches maximum.

A further change designed to assist bowlers was decided upon in 1927 when the tolerance of size was reduced to $8^{13}/_{16}$ inches (22.4 cm) minimum, 9 inches (22.9 cm) maximum.

Experiments were conducted in England in 1955 with a smaller ball. Its circumference was $8^{11}/_{16}$ inches to $8^{13}/_{16}$ inches but it did not produce any favourable results and the Advisory County Cricket Committee decided to shelve the idea.

I have played with both the pre-1927 and the post-1927 balls. It is quite remarkable how much smaller and more compact the latter feels.

Undoubtedly, it assists one with a smaller hand to grip the ball, but I am doubtful whether the same weight in a smaller sphere is so conducive to a deceptive flight by spin bowlers. Clarrie Grimmett always expressed a preference for the larger ball.

Balls to an Over

The 1744 laws provided that four balls would constitute an over. The number was increased to five in 1889 and in 1900 to six.

Australia decided in 1918 to use the eight-ball over and endeavoured to persuade England to fall into line. England duly experimented but finally settled upon the six-ball over.

England's preference for the six-ball over and her persistent argument that rules and regulations should, as far as possible, be uniform throughout the world, finally persuaded Australia to fall into line. The six-ball over is now universally used.

It is more popular with fast bowlers, some of whom claim difficulty in going flat out for eight consecutive deliveries.

I make no secret of my personal belief that eight balls to the over are the ideal, but this is not the only regulation with which I disagree

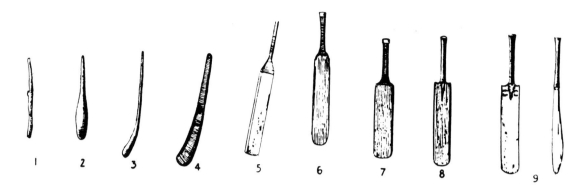

'The Evolution of the Bat.'
(Annals of Cricket, W. W. Read)

and upon which my views have not gained majority support.

In keeping with the spirit of cricket I must bow to the democratic vote but I will continue to argue, whenever I get the chance, for what I believe is best for the game – not just for one section of it.

The Bat

The original bats resembled hockey sticks. They were curved, had a long handle and there was no arbitrary size.

In 1744 the width was limited to 4¼ inches (10.8 cm) and in 1840 the length to 38 inches (96.5 cm).

There has never been any rule regarding the relative sizes of the handle and the blade.

At Lord's one can see a bat of 1771 vintage weighing 2.3 kg compared with today's average of perhaps half that weight.

Declarations

There was no original provision for declarations. If a team wished to terminate its innings, the batsmen had to get out. The development of the game forced a change. In 1889 a declaration was allowed but only on the third day.

In 1900 a declaration was permitted after lunch on the second day, whilst in 1910 declarations at any time on the second or third days became permissible.

Experiments in later years resulted in a new law enabling a declaration to be made at any time.

Understandably, however, it may always be necessary to have special provisions governing a local competition where points are awarded to decide the winning team.

Abbreviated Dates in Cricket History

1300 First probable reference to cricket in the wardrobe accounts of King Edward I, locality, Newenden, Kent.

1344 (*c.*) Club ball, early form of single wicket, played, and believed to have been started in, 13th century.

1622 At Boxgrove in Sussex six parishioners prosecuted for playing cricket in the churchyard on Sunday.

1646 First recorded cricket match, at Coxheath, Kent.

1676 First reference to cricket abroad, played by English residents at Aleppo.

1709 First 'county match' – Kent v. London.

1729 Date of earliest surviving bat, inscribed 'J.C.' (John Chitty, 1729). This bat is in the pavilion at The Oval.

1744 The first great match of which the full score is preserved – Kent v. All England, on the Artillery Ground, Finsbury. Laws of Cricket, a revision of an earlier code, were drawn up by the London Club.

1767 (*c.*) Foundation of the Hambledon Club, which often defeated England.

1769 First recorded century. Minshull, 107 for Duke of Dorset's XI versus Wrotham.

1780 Dukes of Penshurst (est. 1760) manufacture the first 6-seamed ball.

1787 First match (Middlesex v. Essex) on Thomas Lord's first ground on the site of Dorset Square.
Formation of MCC by members of the White Conduit Club.

1788 MCC played their first match at Lord's.
First revision of the laws by MCC.

1800 Publication of first book on technique by Thomas Boxall.

1806 First Gentlemen v Players match at Lord's.

1809 Lord's second ground opened at 'North Bank'.

1814 Lord's third ground opened on its present site. The original turf of the first ground was transplanted at each move.

1817 First two separate centuries, 107 and 157, by William Lambert for Sussex v Epsom at Lord's.

1820 First recorded score over 200, 278 by William Ward for MCC versus Norfolk at Lord's.

1828 MCC authorised the bowler to raise his hand level with the elbow.

1835 MCC adopt a revised code of the laws.

1838 Melbourne Cricket Club formed.

1841 The Duke of Wellington issues an order that a cricket ground is to be made as an adjunct to every military barracks.

1844 First match between Canada and USA.

1849 First Yorkshire v. Lancashire match.

1850 J. Wisden bowled all ten batsmen in an innings, North v. South at Lord's.

1851 First Inter-Colonial match. Tasmania v Victoria at Launceston.

1856 First match between New South Wales and Victoria at Melbourne.

1859 First touring team to leave England visits USA and Canada.

1861 First visit of an English team to Australia.

1862 Edgar Willsher of Kent no-balled for having his hand higher than his shoulder.

1864 'Overhand bowling' authorised.

1868 Visit to England by a team of Australian Aborigines.

1870 The heavy roller first used at Lord's.

1877 First Test match. Australia beat England by 45 runs at Melbourne.

1878 Visit of first Australian team to England. Australians played in America on their way home from England.

1880 First Test match in England. England beat Australia at The Oval.

1882 First Australian victory in a Test match in England at The Oval.

	Creation of the tradition of 'The Ashes'.		1975	First World Cup tournament in England.

Creation of the tradition of 'The Ashes'.

1884 Completely revised code of laws adopted by MCC.

1890 South African Cricket Association established.

1892 Inauguration of the Sheffield Shield competition.

1894 New Zealand Cricket Council established.

1899 Record individual score, 628* by A. E. J. Collins. Made for Clarks v. North Town in a junior house match at Clifton College.

1900 First West Indian team to visit England.

1905 Australian Board of Control set up.

1909 Imperial Cricket Conference (ICC) constituted with MCC, Australia and South Africa the original members.

1910 First visit to Australia of South African team.

1926 India, New Zealand and West Indies admitted to the ICC.

1930 First West Indian team to visit Australia.

1937 Sir Pelham Warner first cricketer to receive a knighthood.

1938 Test matches at Lord's televised for the first time.

1947 First visit to Australia of an Indian team.

1949 First Australian, Sir Donald Bradman, knighted for his services to cricket.

1952 Pakistan admitted to ICC.

1953 Imperial Cricket Memorial Gallery at Lord's opened.

1954 First Australian team visited West Indies.

1961 South Africa ceased to be a member of ICC.

1963 Distinction between amateurs and professionals abolished in English first-class cricket.

1964 First visit to Australia by Pakistan.

1965 Imperial Cricket Conference changes its name to International Cricket Conference.

1975 First World Cup tournament in England.

1977 Kerry Packer forms World Series Cricket (WSC) in opposition to the official game.

1980 WSC disbanded. Laws of cricket revised.

THE BAT

No dimensions specified in original laws when the bat was curved and much longer in the handle.

1771 Width of bat limited to 4¼ inches.

1835 Length of the bat limited to 38 inches.

THE BALL

1744 Between 5 and 6 ounces.

1774 Between 5½ and 5¾ ounces.

1838 Circumference to be between 9 and 9¼ inches.

1927 Circumference to be between 8$\frac{13}{16}$ and 9 inches.

THE OVER

1744 4 balls.

1844 5 or 6 balls legalised in one-day cricket.
6 balls first used in Australian first-class cricket.

1889 5 balls introduced for 2- and 3-day matches.

1900 6 balls introduced for 2- and 3-day matches.

1918 8-ball overs used in all domestic cricket in Australia, except MCC matches in 1920/21, all Tests 1928/29 to 1932/33 inclusive and Victoria v. MCC, March 1929.

1939 8 balls used experimentally in England in first-class matches. Not reintroduced after the war when England reverted to 6 balls.
Other countries experimented from time to time with the 8-ball over but reverted to 6. Eventually, for the sake of uniformity, Australia also reverted to 6 which, since 1980/81, is universal.

THE PITCH

The 22 yards, laid down in the laws of 1744, have never been varied.

THE POPPING CREASE

In 1744 the distance between the bowling crease and the popping crease was laid down as 46 inches. In 1819 it was increased to 48 inches.

THE BOWLING CREASE

In 1744 the length of the bowling crease was set at 3 feet either side of the wicket. This was increased in 1902 to 4 feet. Since 1939, when the width of the wicket was increased from 8 to 9 inches, the bowling crease has been reduced to 3' 11½" either side of the stumps.

THE WICKET

Year	Stumps	Height	Bails	Breadth
c.1700	2	22 inches	1	6 inches
c.1776	3	22 inches	1	6 inches
1785	3	22 inches	2 or 1	6 inches
1798	3	24 inches	2 or 1	7 inches
c.1819	3	26 inches	2	7 inches
c.1823	3	27 inches	2	8 inches
1931	3	28 inches	2	9 inches*

*Optional till 1947

The Virtues of Cricket

As I commenced the task of writing this book about the wonderful game of cricket, my mind reflected upon the extraordinary change in world events since the game first started.

Quite recently I left home one morning about seven o'clock and by 11 am was watching a Sheffield Shield match in another state, nearly 1,500 kilometres away. I wonder what Fuller Pilch and W. G. Grace (men who walked miles just to practise) would have thought about that?

Does this tremendous change in the tempo of life have any bearing on cricket?

I think perhaps it influences spectators and writers to demand more action, and such a mood is not an unhealthy sign. Our sports and entertainments can scarcely escape the need for adaptability which permeates other forms of activity.

Nevertheless in the mad rush for speed and yet more speed, I can't help thinking man would be wise to stop and ponder over certain essentials in life which he can only ignore at his own peril, be it this century or next, whether we walk or go by aeroplane and so on. Many a business tycoon has received his doctor's warning, relax or die.

I suggest the world, whether realising it or not, needs sports such as cricket more than ever before to help it keep other matters in proper perspective.

Every claim by a trade union for a shorter working week, longer holidays, etc., inevitably has as its corollary more leisure for the workman. Every move by the employer to install more up-to-date machinery, implement automation and so on, must bring in its train a similar possibility.

That additional leisure must have a healthy occupation.

If the recipient sits down and does precisely nothing or if he reverts to drinking and gambling, the hard-won freedom will merely bring decadence. The proper types of sport and recreation can play a valuable part in combating any such unfortunate trend.

This is not a completely modern thought. That writer of yesteryear, Nyren, has penned the following magnificent lines for those who are interested in playing the game.

As he puts it, 'The brain must glow with nature's fire and not depend upon a spirit lamp. You, sir, with pallid face and shaky hand, rise with the lark and scent the morning air. And when your veins are no longer fevered with alcohol nor puffed with tobacco smoke, come again and devour up my discourse.

'Our noble game has no sympathy with gluttony, still less with the habitual "diner out", on whom outraged nature has taken a vengeance by emblazoning what was his face, encasing each limb in fat, and condemning him to be his own porter to the end of his days.'

What are the virtues of cricket? Why do some people implicitly believe that it typifies all that is good and spend their lives rendering the game invaluable service because they have faith in it, almost as a religion?

I have no doubt that it moulds in an individual the right type of character better than any other sport.

If that can be substantiated no other recommendation is required because character must surely be one of the greatest assets any nation, through its citizens, can possess.

A healthy recreation such as cricket encourages clean thinking and clean living. Cricket, above all games, teaches unselfishness.

There are, let us admit, some cricketers who are too selfish – players who try to hog the strike, dodge the difficult bowling, play for their own averages and so on. But they are few and usually lead a short and unhappy existence in the game.

217

Many a good player has been left out of a team – no reason given – and the lesson has been learnt. The scorn of teammates for a selfish act does not need to be expressed in words. In fact, no cricketer can be selfish without having a conscience.

I don't think any other game promotes self-control to the same extent.

We are all familiar with sports wherein a display of 'temperament' is rather expected. There are games in which teams are encouraged to needle their opponents, goad them into losing their tempers because of the adverse effect it will have on their play.

During my regime in cricket the 'needling' of opponents, or 'sledging' (which I believe to be the modern term for the same thing) was virtually unknown.

Regrettably in the 1960s and the 1970s a few misguided people began to indulge in the practice and caused the time-honoured phrase 'it isn't cricket' to lose some of its authenticity.

But the character of cricket cannot be offended for long.

The weight of opinion from the players themselves, most of whom resented this departure from custom, and the legislative attempt to control it, with obvious approval from the broad mass of supporters, quickly had a salutary effect.

It is my belief that this temporary defection from acceptable standards of conduct by a minority of participants has now waned to the point where even some of its protagonists have changed their spots.

Having said that, I do see a more belligerent competitiveness in modern cricket due no doubt to the greater financial rewards which are at stake.

I don't frown on that, providing it comes within the framework of decency and fair play.

Cricket discipline should be strict without being boisterous.

A sergeant-major may order the private to do a job in a manner which leaves the poor recruit in fear and trembling. The same obedience is taught on the cricket field by the captain changing his bowling, taking a man off who thinks he should be left on, altering his field placing, changing his batting order and so on. The game is constantly one of unquestioning obedience.

Sportsmanship prevails. Players must acknowledge defeat, the umpire's adverse decision and a hundred other things with a smile.

When I first started to play cricket I thought of it only as a lovely recreation, and the idea that it called for courage never really occurred to me.

Later in my career I was speaking to a world-famous dirt-track speedway rider who astonished me by saying that nothing would induce him to stand up against a fast bowler. That amused me. I thought he was quite mad as well as fearless to risk his neck on a motorbike.

Jem Mace, the great boxer, once said he would rather stand in the ring for an hour than 'keep wickets' for five minutes. Every man to his own game.

But actually I suppose it does take courage to face a cricket ball coming at you at over 100 kilometres an hour.

I think that is partly because you have plenty of time beforehand to contemplate the possibilities. You don't just do it on the spur of the moment like a man who dives into shark-infested waters to save a person from drowning. You may even have an hour or two to meditate upon your fate before you bat.

Then there is the moral as well as physical courage of facing up to hard training, to bowl fast for hours under a hot sun on a flint-hard pitch, to feel the agony of seeing dropped catches nullify your best work and so on.

When every muscle is crying out for a rest and the pleadings of your feet are indescribable, but the captain says 'bowl on'; when you are itching to have a go, but must hold up your end for someone else; those are the moments when cricket teaches you perseverance and patience, too.

How many great cricketers have held the stage long who were not modest about their own ability. None of this 'I'm the greatest in the world and will lick anybody' stuff. No – that doesn't go with cricket.

And the minute a player shows signs of getting a swollen head he is well on the way towards getting a duck, no wickets or dropping a catch.

I met a country cricketer one day who boasted during the luncheon interval that he had never dropped a catch. He was quite upset when someone suggested that perhaps no opportunities had come his way, or at least no hard ones. Anyway, he dropped four that afternoon, to his great discomfort and our pleasure.

And, believe me, it is impossible for the greatest bombast in the world not to feel humble when he gets bowled for a duck before a large audience and he has to walk back to the pavilion from the scene of disaster.

Mentally, cricket develops the ability to think, to reason out a problem, and to act quickly. A batsman has perhaps less than a second in which to see the ball, decide what to do, and then put his plan into action, so there is little time for reflection.

The run-out, whereby in a flash the fieldsman must decide the right end to throw. There are dozens of other ways in which decision and action are virtually simultaneous and if that isn't good mental training, I don't know what is.

When one gets into the higher realms, the question of overseas travel and education can be mentioned, though I realise they are for the chosen few. And there is no game – indeed, is there any substitute at all? – which is better able to bring together on a common level and unite tens of thousands of people. Just think of the myriad adoring small boys in India who will flock to see their Australian cricket idols play when they visit that country.

Different in colour, differing in religious beliefs and in other respects but still human beings, flesh and blood, who have a common heritage in their desire to work and play without devastating the earth for selfish, greedy ends.

I once spent an evening talking nothing but cricket to a team of West Indian players. The goodwill which they so obviously exuded because we all played and loved the same game was a thrill and lives in my memory. I did not know their families, their homes, their country, their mode of living, or really very much about them at all, but we were friends in the truest sense.

It was a great Indian, Prince Ranjitsinhji, who wrote, 'No institution is perfect – it will always tend to excess or defect. But how nearly perfect is cricket. It is a game which keeps boys out of mischief. It is a training of youth for a manly life. It lays up a store of strength and health against old age. It makes individual men life-long friends.

'Learning itself has gradually learnt to take up a different attitude towards cricket. It has discovered that cricket is consistent with study and that the cricketer makes a good schoolmaster.

'The truth is that athletics are an integral part and a powerful support of all education.'

Written in the nineteenth century. How true still.

When I read of the millions which are constantly poured out on defence preparation, overseas trade missions, and so on, I sometimes wonder whether politicians give sufficient thought to the reward which might accrue from a little more expenditure on the development and encouragement of cricket in schools and elsewhere. Character, health and suchlike virtues, and particularly international goodwill, cannot be seen on a balance sheet like freehold property. They are none the less real.

There can be no saner national insurance than building up young citizens imbued with the spirit of decency, fair play and all those qualities which combine to make a great people.

I'm not sure that we shouldn't include loyalty. Anyone who has been to a Yorkshire v Lancashire match will know what that means.

Is there anything wrong with a man rabidly supporting his own kith and kin?

The northerners take their sport very seriously, according to the time-honoured stories which are recounted. There was the occasion when a spectator asked his neighbour a question about the game they were watching. But when he admitted on cross-examination that he was neither a Yorkshireman nor a Lancastrian was told it was none of his business.

But don't tell me there is no humour in Yorkshiremen. What about the one who was implored by an American to observe the wonderful sight of 'all that water pouring over Niagara Falls' and who drily remarked, 'I see now't to stop it'?

But for the unconscious humour I still like the one about the Lancastrian who finally persuaded his totally uninterested wife to go and see a typical Battle of the Roses, Yorkshire v. Lancashire. After the match had been in progress some time, she sweetly asked, 'Tell me, dear, which one is Denis Compton?' What the husband said to her for daring to even bring a Middlesex thought into that atmosphere is not recorded.

However, I am straying from my path.

I know there are many shortcomings in the way certain individuals play the game of cricket. And because of the actions of a miserable minority, some people condemn the game itself. They may just as well say a poison is an evil thing because, taken contrary to the doctor's prescription, it will destroy life.

There must be no confusion between the game of cricket and those who may wrongly interpret it. Played in the right spirit there is no sport which is capable of developing man's finest qualities to anything like the same extent.

Common clay must go through the heat and fire of the furnace to become porcelain. But once through the furnace it can never be clay again. In the same way a man's character must remain permanently enriched by his experiences at cricket.

That grand Englishman and cricketer, Lord Harris, one-time Governor of Bombay and an Under-Secretary for India under Lord Randolph Churchill, once wrote, 'You do well to love cricket, for it is more free from anything sordid, anything dishonourable, than any game in the world. To play it keenly, honourably, generously, self-sacrificingly, is a moral lesson in itself and the classroom is God's air and sunshine. Foster it, my brother, so that it may attract all who can find the time to play it; protect it from anything that would sully it, so that it may grow in favour with all men.'

But surprisingly we are indebted to an American author for the following splendid utterance:

'Our constitution is dedicated to liberty and has of necessity to assume a moral code of honourable conduct without which there can be no liberty – only licence. Our youth cannot be properly trained for that heritage unless games and sports are infused with the inner compulsion towards honourable and generous conduct.

'If cricket is alien to our ideal of democracy, so much the worse for our democracy; because in the end it is the decent respect lodged in the breast of each citizen for the feelings and opinions of others that alone can preserve it.'

What a great thing it would be if America could capture the interest and enthusiasm which can be found for cricket in England, Australia, New Zealand, South Africa, India, West Indies and Pakistan.

May cricket continue to flourish and spread its wings. The world can only be richer for it.